Nursing Research Using Grounded Theory

Mary de Chesnay, PhD, RN, PMHCNS-BC, FAAN, is professor and immediate past-director of WellStar School of Nursing, Kennesaw State University, Georgia, as well as a licensed psychotherapist and a nurse–anthropologist researcher. In her private psychotherapy practice (active practice since 1973), Dr. de Chesnay has specialized in treating sexually abused and trafficked children, has developed culturally based interventions, and has taught content about vulnerable populations for many years. The third edition of Dr. de Chesnay's book, *Caring for the Vulnerable,* was published in 2012. She has also authored six book chapters and 19 journal articles. She is principal investigator (PI) or co-PI on numerous grants and has served as a consultant on research, academic, continuing education, and law enforcement projects. Recently, Dr. de Chesnay was invited to serve on the Georgia State Governor's Task Force called CSEC (Commercial Sexual Exploitation of Children). She has presented nationally and internationally in nursing and anthropology, and has published on incest and sex tourism and about applying various qualitative approaches to clinical research. She has been invited as a keynote speaker at numerous conferences including Sigma Theta Tau and the International Society of Psychiatric Nurses.

NURSING RESEARCH USING GROUNDED THEORY

QUALITATIVE DESIGNS AND METHODS IN NURSING

Mary de Chesnay, PhD, RN, PMHCNS-BC, FAAN

EDITOR

SPRINGER PUBLISHING COMPANY

NEW YORK

KH

Springer Publishing Company, LLC
11 West 42nd Street
New York, NY 10036
www.springerpub.com

Acquisitions Editor: Joseph Morita
Production Editor: Brian Black
Composition: Exeter Premedia Services Private Ltd.

ISBN: 978-0-8261-3467-7
e-book ISBN: 978-0-8261-3468-4

14 15 16 17 / 5 4 3 2 1

The author and the publisher of this Work have made every effort to use sources believed to be reliable to provide information that is accurate and compatible with the standards generally accepted at the time of publication. The author and publisher shall not be liable for any special, consequential, or exemplary damages resulting, in whole or in part, from the readers' use of, or reliance on, the information contained in this book. The publisher has no responsibility for the persistence or accuracy of URLs for external or third-party Internet websites referred to in this publication and does not guarantee that any content on such websites is, or will remain, accurate or appropriate.

Library of Congress Cataloging-in-Publication Data
Nursing research using grounded theory : qualitative designs and methods in nursing / Mary de Chesnay, editor.
    p. ; cm.
    Includes bibliographical references.
    ISBN 978-0-8261-3467-7—ISBN 978-0-8261-3468-4 (e-book)
    I. De Chesnay, Mary, editor.
    [DNLM: 1. Nursing Research—methods. 2. Nursing Theory. 3. Qualitative Research. 4. Research Design. WY 20.5]
    RT81.5
    610.73072—dc23

                                                                                      2014007675

Printed in the United States of America by Gasch Printing.

2/23/16

QUALITATIVE DESIGNS AND METHODS IN NURSING

Mary de Chesnay, PhD, RN, PMHCNS-BC, FAAN, Series Editor

For my cousin, Lisa Surtees, a fellow dog lover and woman of humor, integrity, and many skills.

—MdC

CONTENTS

Contributors

Davina Banner, PhD, RN, is an assistant professor in the School of Nursing at the University of Northern British Columbia. Davina has a passion for research, and her interests are in cardiovascular health and rural health service delivery. Davina has been involved in a wide range of research studies through her clinical and academic work to date, including grounded theory studies in the UK and Canada. Davina teaches research at the undergraduate and graduate levels and is the chair of the research committee for the Canadian Council of Cardiovascular Nurses of British Columbia and Yukon.

Anne W. Batson, RN, FNP-BC, is a nurse practitioner with 16 years of clinical experience in family medicine and, more recently, sleep medicine. She has been a clinical advisor and preceptor to nursing students from several nursing programs in Georgia and Alabama. She is currently working toward her doctorate in nursing at Kennesaw State University. This is her first publication.

Joan L. Bottorff, PhD, RN, FCAHS, FAAN, is professor of nursing at the University of British Columbia, Okanagan campus, faculty of Health and Social Development. She is the director of the Institute for Healthy Living and Chronic Disease Prevention at the University of British Columbia.

Shirley S.-Y. Ching, PhD, RN, FHKAN (Education), is an assistant professor at the School of Nursing of The Hong Kong Polytechnic University. She has conducted studies adopting the grounded theory method among Chinese people. She has supervised postgraduate research students and taught the grounded theory method in master's programs.

Mary de Chesnay, PhD, RN, PMHCNS-BC, FAAN, is professor of nursing at Kennesaw State University and secretary of the Council on Nursing and Anthropology (CONAA) of the Society for Applied Anthropology (SFAA). She has conducted ethnographic fieldwork and participatory action research in Latin America and the Caribbean. She has taught qualitative research at all levels in the United States and abroad in the roles of faculty, head of a department of research, dean, and endowed chair.

Yvonne D. Eaves, PhD, RN, is associate professor of nursing at Kennesaw State University, WellStar School of Nursing. Her program of research is focused on caregiving, caregiving transitions, and long-term care decision making in rural African American families caring for older adult relatives with chronic illnesses, stroke, dementia, and Alzheimer's disease. Dr. Eaves has methodological expertise in several qualitative research methods, mixed-methods research, health disparities research, and diverse ethnic aging research. She has been funded by the National Institute on Aging/ National Institutes of Health, and the National Alzheimer's Association.

Lorraine F. Holtslander, PhD, RN, CHPCN(c), is an associate professor of nursing at the University of Saskatchewan, in Saskatoon, Canada. She has completed three published grounded theory studies as primary researcher and supervised graduate students in their own qualitative research projects. She teaches family nursing to undergraduate nursing students and qualitative research methods at the graduate level. Lorraine maintains a clinical practice in the community as a palliative home care nurse.

Jennifer S. Laurent, PhD, FNP-BC, is an assistant professor at the University of Vermont in the Department of Nursing. Her research interests are in the field of obesity and eating behaviors in preadolescents. She continues clinical practice part time as a nurse practitioner in Burlington, Vermont.

Ida M. Martinson, PhD, RN, FAAN, is emerita professor of nursing at the University of California, San Francisco. Dr. Martinson has taught and conducted qualitative research and advised doctoral students in the United States, Hong Kong, and other countries in Asia.

Antoinette M. McCallin, PhD, MA (Hons), BA, RN, is an associate professor of nursing, working in the Faculty of Health and Environmental Sciences at the Auckland University of Technology, Auckland, New Zealand. She has supervised many grounded theory health science research projects at the master's and doctoral levels and taught qualitative research for master's and doctoral students for many years.

Alvita Nathaniel, PhD, APRN-BC, FNP, FAANP, is associate professor of nursing and interim associate dean of graduate practice programs at West Virginia University. She is an ethicist and author of a nursing ethics textbook and has conducted classic grounded theory research into nurses' moral decision making. She is a fellow of the Grounded Theory Institute. She has taught grounded theory research for many years in the PhD program at West Virginia University.

Tommie Nelms, PhD, RN, is professor of nursing at Kennesaw State University. She is director of the WellStar School of Nursing and coordinator of the Doctor of Nursing Science program. She has a long history of conducting and directing phenomenological research and has been a student of Heideggerian philosophy and research for many years. Her research is mainly focused on practices of mothering, caring, and family.

Ellen F. Olshansky, PhD, RN, WHNP-BC, FAAN, is professor and founding director of the Program in Nursing Science at the University of California, Irvine. She has taught qualitative research methods at the University of Washington, Duquesne University, the University of Pittsburgh, and currently at the University of California, Irvine.

Denise Saint Arnault, PhD, RN, is an associate professor of nursing at the University of Michigan. She is a past president of the CONAA. Her research on East Asian mental health and help-seeking has received federal funding. She has also carried out ethnographic research, mixed-methods research, and clinical ethnography research on Native American populations and women who have experienced domestic violence trauma.

Brian Sengstock, PhD, BA, LLM, MLitt, MEmergMgt, JD, BBus (HRM), is a paramedic and legal academic in the paramedic science discipline at the University of the Sunshine Coast, Queensland, Australia. He has led grounded theory research studies in both nursing and paramedicine, having completed a doctorate using grounded theory approaches. He has taught qualitative and quantitative research at the undergraduate and postgraduate level in business and health faculties across a number of Australian universities.

FOREWORD

When I was a doctoral student, I wondered whether Adler's concept of early recollections could provide insight into how nurses respond to patients with physical pain, handicap, or imminent death. Previously, to help nurses understand their tendencies to react to such patients, exercises included the query, "How would you want to be treated if you were dying?" Yet, not a lot of research existed that would shed light on this phenomenon. Indeed, the preferred treatment assumed that the nurse would want what the patient would want.

In my research methods classes, information about Glaser and Strauss's grounded theory approach intrigued me. Here was a method that seemed perfect for building nursing theory where none existed. I had done a quantitative study for my master's thesis, so rounding out my research skills with a qualitative study seemed very attractive. I also liked the interpretive aspect of the approach. I brought in trained analysts to check my own interpretations. Indeed, I needed an expert in rehabilitation counseling to point out differences in the responses to the handicapped section that I had overlooked.

I combined some quantitative techniques to run checks on the theory, reflecting sustenance, which emerged from the data. This combination of quantitative and qualitative techniques was controversial at the time, but it was geared not toward theory testing, but rather, was part of validity and reliability checks. More recently, such checks include trustworthiness in different ways.

Nurses' earliest recollections of death, handicap, and physical pain illuminate their responses to patients in these situations better than how they prefer to be treated. Nurses' earliest recollections were differentiated by being alone or being supported in their experiences. Nurses who recalled being supported were better able to provide a wider array of responses to patients and support more autonomy for them.

The personal nature of gathering data for a study using grounded theory requires special attention to the privacy and confidentiality of the participants. The analysts in my study were not associated with the medical center from which the nurses were recruited. Each nurse was given a number that corresponded with each answer in the subsections of the study relating to directed earliest recollections, preferred treatment for self, and responses to patients in the situations of death, physical pain, and handicap. Even the words used in the study were carefully selected. For example, "handicap" was used instead of "disability" or "challenged" to provoke feelings and to use a word commonly used in the nurses' childhoods.

I wish I had the advantage of having Dr. de Chesnay's book while I was working on my dissertation. The book provides new pioneers in developing nursing theory a wonderful road map to an important form of qualitative analysis. In addition, it provides information about what it can do for nursing research. The book also shows the reader how to use the technique to generate theory grounded in reality. Dr. de Chesnay's book also gives concrete examples of grounded theory's utility in critical life situations.

Research utilizing grounded theory methodology can change how nurses manage and change care. It can enable nurses to find out just what the client has used or needs to cope with life changes. Out of grounded theory comes new information that can change practice. Using this knowledge, we can design care to improve the lives of patients and caregivers alike.

Susan Y. Stevens, PhD, APRN, PMHCNS-BC
President, Perimeter Adult Learning and Services
Dunwoody, Georgia

SERIES FOREWORD

In this section, which is published in all volumes of the series, we discuss some key aspects of any qualitative design. This is basic information that might be helpful to novice researchers or those new to the designs and methods described in each chapter. The material is not meant to be rigid and prescribed because qualitative research by its nature is fluid and flexible; the reader should use any ideas that are relevant and discard any ideas that are not relevant to the specific project in mind.

Before beginning a project, it is helpful to commit to publishing it. Of course, it will be publishable because you will use every resource at hand to make sure it is of high quality and contributes to knowledge. Theses and dissertations are meaningless exercises if only the student and committee know what was learned. It is rather heart-breaking to think of all the effort that senior faculty have exerted to complete a degree and yet not to have anyone else benefit by the work. Therefore, some additional resources are included here. Appendix A for each book is a list of journals that publish qualitative research. References to the current nursing qualitative research textbooks are included so that readers may find additional material from sources cited in those chapters.

FOCUS

In qualitative research the focus is emic—what we commonly think of as "from the participant's point of view." The researcher's point of view, called "the etic view," is secondary and does not take precedence over what the participant wants to convey, because in qualitative research, the focus is on the person and his or her story. In contrast, quantitative researchers take pains to learn as much as they can about a topic and focus the research data collection on what they want to know. Cases or subjects that do not provide information about the researcher's agenda are considered outliers and are discarded or treated as aberrant data. Qualitative researchers embrace outliers and actively seek diverse points of view from participants to enrich the data. They sample for diversity within groups and welcome different perceptions even if they seek fairly homogenous samples. For example, in Leenerts and Magilvy's (2000) grounded theory study to examine self-care practices among women, they narrowed the study to low-income, White, HIV-positive women but included both lesbian and heterosexual women.

PROPOSALS

There are many excellent sources in the literature on how to write a research proposal. A couple are cited here (Annersten, 2006; Mareno, 2012; Martin, 2010; Schmelzer, 2006), and examples are found in Appendices B, C, and D. Proposals for any type of research should include basic elements about the purpose, significance, theoretical support, and methods. What is often lacking is a thorough discussion about the rationale. The rationale is needed for the overall design as well as each step in the process. Why qualitative research? Why ethnography and not phenomenology? Why go to a certain setting? Why select the participants through word of mouth? Why use one particular type of software over another to analyze data?

Other common mistakes are not doing justice to significance and failure to provide sufficient theoretical support for the approach. In qualitative research, which tends to be theory generating instead of theory testing, the author still needs to explain why the study is conducted from a particular frame of reference. For example, in some ethnographic work, there are hypotheses that are tested based on the work of prior ethnographers who studied that culture, but there is still a need to generate new theory about current phenomena within that culture from the point of view of the specific informants for the subsequent study.

Significance is underappreciated as an important component of research. Without justifying the importance of the study or the potential impact of the study, there is no case for why the study should be conducted. If a study cannot be justified, why should sponsors fund it? Why should participants agree to participate? Why should the principal investigator bother to conduct it?

COMMONALITIES IN METHODS

Interviewing Basics

One of the best resources for learning how to interview for qualitative research is by Patton (2002), and readers are referred to his book for a detailed guide to interviewing. He describes the process, issues, and challenges in a way that readers can focus their interview in a wide variety of directions that are flexible, yet rigorous. For example, in ethnography, a mix of interview methods is appropriate, ranging from unstructured interviews or informal conversation to highly structured interviews. Unless nurses are conducting mixed-design studies, most of their interviews will be semi-structured. Semi-structured interviews include a few general questions, but the interviewer is free to allow the interviewee to digress along any lines he or she wishes. It is up to the interviewer to bring the interview back to the focus of the research. This requires skill and sensitivity.

Some general guidelines apply to semi-structured interviews:

- Establish rapport.
- Ask open-ended questions. For example, the second question is much more likely to generate a meaningful response than the first in a grounded theory study of coping with cervical cancer.

> Interviewer: Were you afraid when you first heard your diagnosis of cervical cancer?
>
> Participant: Yes.

Contrast the above with the following:

> Interviewer: What was your first thought when you heard your diagnosis of cervical cancer?
>
> Participant: I thought of my young children and how they were going to lose their mother and that they would grow up not knowing how much I loved them.

- Continuously "read" the person's reactions and adapt the approach based on response to questions. For example, in the interview about coping with the diagnosis, the participant began tearing so the interviewer appropriately gave her some time to collect herself. Maintaining silence is one of the most difficult things to learn for researchers who have been classically trained in quantitative methods. In structured interviewing, we are trained to continue despite distractions and to eliminate bias, which may involve eliminating emotion and emotional reactions to what we hear in the interview. Yet the quality of outcomes in qualitative designs may depend on the researcher–participant relationship. It is critical to be authentic and to allow the participant to be authentic.

Ethical Issues

The principles of the Belmont Commission apply to all types of research: respect, justice, beneficence. Perhaps, these are even more important when interviewing people about their culture or life experiences. These are highly personal and may be painful for the person to relate, though I have found that there is a cathartic effect to participating in naturalistic research with an empathic interviewer (de Chesnay, 1991, 1993).

Rigor

Readers are referred to the classic paper on rigor in qualitative research (Sandelowski, 1986). Rather than speak of validity and reliability, we use other terms, such as accuracy (Do the data represent truth as the participant sees it?) and replicability (Can the reader follow the decision trail to see why the researcher concluded as he or she did?).

DATA ANALYSIS

Analyzing data requires many decisions about how to collect data and whether to use high-tech measures such as qualitative software or old-school measures such as colored index cards. The contributors to this series provide examples of both.

Mixed designs require a balance between the assumptions of quantitative research while conducting that part and qualitative research during that phase. It can be difficult for novice researchers to keep things straight. Researchers are encouraged to learn each paradigm well and to be clear about why they use certain methods for their purposes. Each type of design can stand alone, and one should never think that qualitative research is *less than* quantitative; it is just different.

Mary de Chesnay

REFERENCES

Annersten, M. (2006). How to write a research proposal. *European Diabetes Nursing,* 3(2), 102–105.

de Chesnay, M. (1991, March 13–17). *Catharsis: Outcome of naturalistic research.* Presented to Society for Applied Anthropology, Charleston, SC.

de Chesnay, M. (1993). Workshop with Dr. Patricia Marshall of Symposium on Research Ethics in Fieldwork. Sponsored by Society for Applied Anthropology, Committee on Ethics. Memphis, March 25–29, 1992; San Antonio, Texas, March 11–14, 1993.

Leenerts, M. H., & Magilvy, K. (2000). Investing in self-care: A midrange theory of self-care grounded in the lived experience of low-income HIV-positive white women. *Advances in Nursing Science,* 22(3), 58–75.

Mareno, N. (2012). Sample qualitative research proposal: Childhood obesity in Latino families. In M. de Chesnay & B. Anderson (Eds.), *Caring for the vulnerable* (pp. 203–218). Sudbury, MA: Jones and Bartlett.

Martin, C. H. (2010). A 15-step model for writing a research proposal. *British Journal of Midwifery,* 18(12), 791–798.

Patton, M. Q. (2002). *Qualitative research and evaluation methods* (3rd ed.). Thousand Oaks, CA: Sage.

Sandelowski, M. (1986). The problem of rigor in qualitative research. *Advances in Nursing Science,* 4(3), 27–37.

Schmelzer, M. (2006). How to start a research proposal. *Gastroenterology Nursing,* 29(2), 186–188.

PREFACE

Qualitative research has evolved from a slightly disreputable beginning to wide acceptance in nursing research. Approaches that focus on the stories and perceptions of people, instead of what scientists think the world is about, have been a tradition in anthropology for a long time, and have created a body of knowledge that cannot be replicated in the lab. The richness of human experience is what qualitative research is all about. Respect for this tradition was long in coming within the scientific community. Nurses seem to have been in the forefront, though, and though many of my generation (children of the 1950s and 1960s) were classically trained in quantitative techniques, we found something lacking. Perhaps because I am a psychiatric nurse, I have been trained to listen to people tell me their stories, whether the stories are problems that nearly destroy the spirit, or uplifting accounts of how they live within their cultures, or how they cope with terrible traumas and chronic diseases. It seems logical to me that a critical part of developing new knowledge that nurses can use to help patients is to find out first what the patients themselves have to say.

In the first volume of this series, the focus is on ethnography, in many ways the grandparent of qualitative research. Subsequent volumes address grounded theory, life history, phenomenology, historical research, participatory action research, and data analysis. The volume on data analysis also includes material on focus groups and case studies, two types of research that can be used with a variety of designs, including quantitative research and mixed designs. Efforts have been made to recruit contributors from several countries to demonstrate the global applicability of qualitative research.

In this volume, grounded theory is the focus. Drawn from sociology, the design can be seen as the parent of all qualitative research in that all qualitative data are grounded in reality—whether the focus is culture, history, or the experience of a phenomenon. Widely used in nursing, grounded theory enables us to apply what we learn from those interviewed to a wider client population and to understand what it is like to endure those life conditions.

There are many fine textbooks in nursing research that provide an overview of all the methods, but our aim here is to provide specific information to guide graduate students and experienced nurses who are novices in the designs represented in the series in conducting studies from the point of view of our constituents/patients and their families. The studies conducted by the book's contributors provide much practical advice for beginners as well as new ideas for experienced researchers. Some authors take a formal approach, but others speak quite personally from the first person. We hope you catch their enthusiasm and have fun conducting your own studies.

Mary de Chesnay

ACKNOWLEDGMENTS

In any publishing venture, there are many people who work together to produce the final draft. The contributors kindly shared their expertise to offer advice and counsel to novices, and the reviewers ensured the quality of submissions. All of them have come up through the ranks as qualitative researchers and their participation is critical to helping novices learn the process.

No publication is successful without great people who not only know how to do their own jobs but also how to guide authors. At Springer Publishing Company, we are indebted to Margaret Zuccarini for the idea for the series, her ongoing support and her excellent problem-solving skills. The person who guided the editorial process and was available for numerous questions, which he patiently answered as if he had not heard them a hundred times, was Joseph Morita. Also critical to the project were the people who proofed the work, marketed the series, and transformed it into hard copies, among them Chris Teja.

At Kennesaw State University, Dr. Tommie Nelms, director of the WellStar School of Nursing, was a constant source of emotional and practical support in addition to her chapter contribution to the phenomenology volume. Her administrative assistant, Mrs. Cynthia Elery, kindly assigned student assistants to complete several chores, which enabled the author to focus on the scholarship. Bradley Garner, Chadwick Brown, and Chino Duke are our student assistants and unsung heroes of the university.

Finally, I am grateful to my cousin, Amy Dagit, whose expertise in proofreading saved many hours for some of the chapters. Any mistakes left are mine alone.

I have learned that success is to be measured not so much by the position that one has reached in life, as by the obstacles which he has overcome while trying to succeed.

—Booker T. Washington, educator and author, in
Up From Slavery: An Autobiography

CHAPTER ONE

OVERVIEW OF GROUNDED THEORY

Ellen F. Olshansky

Grounded theory is a commonly used methodological approach to conducting qualitative research. It is, in fact, arguably the most widely used qualitative design among researchers. Developed by sociologists, it is used frequently by nurse scientists, many having had the privilege of studying with these sociologists at the University of California, Department of Social and Behavioral Sciences, San Francisco School of Nursing. This qualitative research method is also used by researchers and scientists in other health fields as well as fields in humanities and social sciences. Grounded theory is also, in many ways, one of the most widely misunderstood methods. This chapter presents an overview of the method of grounded theory, including its history and theoretical underpinnings, ongoing development, and clarification of many of the misconceptions.

As a starting point, it is important to clarify one major misconception of grounded theory. It is not a theory at all, but a method that strives to generate theory that is grounded in the data; hence the name "grounded theory." Through the method of grounded theory, the researcher engages in a specific approach to qualitative data collection and analysis, ultimately generating a theoretical explanation for the phenomenon being studied. This theoretical explanation must be based on, founded on, or "grounded" in the data generated. Thus, grounded theory is a methodological approach to qualitative research as well as an outcome of such research—the development of a "grounded theory" that explains the phenomenon of interest. The actual process of conducting such a study and generating a theory that is grounded in the data is described in Chapter 3. The important message here is that there is not a theory called "grounded theory"; there are theories that are generated through the qualitative research method referred to as grounded theory. Chapter 2 describes a variety of studies that have used grounded theory as the method, and then Chapter 3 describes one study in depth that was guided by grounded theory.

HISTORY OF THE DEVELOPMENT OF GROUNDED THEORY

Grounded theory was developed by sociologists Anselm Strauss and Barney Glaser in the 1960s. The philosophical foundation of this method is symbolic interaction, a term coined by Herbert Blumer (1969), based on the work of George Herbert Mead in the 1930s. Blumer, a sociologist, studied with Mead at the University of Chicago. Mead was described as being from the "oral tradition" because the publication of his work was the result of the notes his students took in his lectures. It was his students, in fact, who compiled these notes that became his classic book, *Mind, Self, and Society* (Mead, 1934). The basic premise of Mead's book was that a person (self) creates meaning (mind) based on interactions with others and with oneself within a social context (society). Blumer then wrote his now classic book, following on Mead's work, describing symbolic interaction as the subjective process in which individuals construct meaning for their reality as a result of their interactions with others, as well as with themselves, within a social context. Blumer's work was referred to as the "Chicago school of symbolic interaction," as differentiated from the "Iowa school." (Of note is that the Chicago school eventually became the Berkeley school of symbolic interaction, after Blumer took a faculty position at UC Berkeley.)

The Chicago School and the Iowa School of Symbolic Interactionism

The theoretical underpinnings for the method of grounded theory are derived from a social psychological theoretical framework that is referred to as symbolic interactionism (Blumer, 1969). Blumer coined the term symbolic interactionism, and he was part of what is known as the "Chicago school of thought" in regard to symbolic interactionism. However, it is important to note that there is also another school of thought that is known as the "Iowa school of thought." This chapter takes the perspective of the Chicago school because the grounded theory method was developed out of the Chicago school. For purposes of clarity and for better understanding of the theoretical underpinnings of grounded theory, the following section distinguishes between the two schools of thought in order to provide a more comprehensive understanding of the theoretical underpinnings of the method of grounded theory.

The Chicago School

Several prominent thinkers from the University of Chicago in the 1920s and 1930s were influential in developing the beginnings of a theoretical framework that would eventually be termed "symbolic interactionism" (Musolf, 2003; Reynolds, 2003). These thought leaders included William James, John Dewey, George Herbert Mead, Charles Cooley, and W. I. Thomas, among others (Musolf, 2003). William James wrote about truth as something that is not static, but is dependent on what works, which was the beginning of a pragmatist view of truth and meaning. John Dewey built on James's work and contributed his view of pragmatism that became a primary tenet of symbolic interactionism (Reynolds, 2003). W. I. Thomas emphasized the concept of the "definition of the situation," in which the social context is critical in one's construction of one's self. Cooley referred to the "looking glass" self, in which a person has a perspective of himself or herself based on how he or she sees himself or herself as another might, which is similar to Mead's notion of "taking the role of other." Mead described the "I" and the "me" as parts of one's self, emphasizing the notion that an individual actually interacts with himself or herself and that the self is socially constructed. All of these concepts contributed to the development of symbolic interactionism, which purported that persons construct a sense of themselves as well as meanings through interaction with others within a social context. In other words, according to symbolic interactionism, reality is socially constructed (Blumer, 1969).

The Iowa School

Two key thought leaders in symbolic interactionism at the University of Iowa, among others, were Manford Kuhn and Carl Couch (Iowa school of symbolic interactionism; Katovich, Miller, & Stewart, 2003). Kuhn believed in Mead's more subjective approach to understanding reality (as differentiated from the positivist approach that predominated scientific thought), but differed from Mead in that Kuhn believed there were some "core" meanings that were constants in a person's view of reality. Kuhn and McPartland (as cited in Katovich et al., 2003), developed the 20 Statements Test, which measured a person's core attitudes and definitions of self. Thus, the Iowa school of thought consisted of a pragmatic and subjective view of reality, consistent with important tenets of symbolic interactionism, but differed from the more fluid and constantly changing view of reality that comprised the Chicago school of thought. The Iowa school believed there was more consistency and more stability in each person with less fluidity.

The Chicago School Transformed to the Berkeley School With
San Francisco as the Center for Grounded Theory

At the University of Chicago, Anselm Strauss studied under the tutelage of Herbert Blumer. Taking seriously Blumer's recommendation that the next step in symbolic interaction was to develop a research method, Strauss began to work on that very issue. Fortuitously, Strauss, along with Leonard Schatzman, was recruited to University of California San Francisco (UCSF) by Dean Helen Nahm, to teach in the newly formed Department of Social and Behavioral Sciences. At around the same time, Herbert Blumer relocated to the University of California, Berkeley, and the Chicago school of symbolic interactionism became known as the Berkeley school of symbolic interactionism. In California, Strauss began a partnership with Barney Glaser, writing their now classic book, *The Discovery of Grounded Theory*. A few years later, Schatzman and Strauss (1973) wrote *Field Research: Strategies for a Natural Sociology*. Glaser (1978) also wrote *Theoretical Sensitivity*. Many doctoral students in sociology and then in nursing, after the creation of the Doctor of Nursing Science program (eventually changed to the PhD in nursing program) at UCSF, studied with Strauss, Glaser, and/ or Schatzman. UCSF became known as an institution in which qualitative methods, particularly grounded theory, were embraced.

ONGOING DEVELOPMENT OF GROUNDED THEORY

Over the years, Strauss and Glaser began to develop approaches to grounded theory that differed from one another. Glaser wrote a book titled *Theoretical Sensitivity*. Together with Strauss, Glaser wrote *The Discovery of Grounded Theory* (Glaser & Strauss, 1967). Strauss, in collaboration with Juliet Corbin, wrote *Basics of Qualitative Research*. The philosophical differences between them are complicated, but seem to be distilled into the question of the degree to which data that are generated are "forced" into a preconceived framework or trajectory rather than the framework or trajectory "emerging" from the data. It is beyond the scope of this chapter, however, to explain the differences, as each of these now evolving schools of thought related to grounded theory has its own views and perceptions. What is interesting is that Schatzman began to develop an even newer qualitative research method, described by some as an offshoot of grounded theory. Schatzman created "dimensional analysis," which embraces the notion that all of us, as humans, naturally analyze things and events and ideas continually. His view was that, for research purposes, we were simply formalizing a process that each of us does naturally every day. A few scholars have addressed dimensional analysis as a qualitative research method (Bowers & Schatzman, 2009; Kools, McCarthy, Durham, & Robrecht, 1996).

Morse, Stern, Corbin, Bowers, Charmaz, and Clarke (2009) addressed the evolution of grounded theory over the past several years. The major movements in grounded theory include the split between Glaser and Strauss's original grounded theory method into two schools of thought, consisting of the Glaserian and the Straussian schools; Schatzman's development of dimensional analysis as an alternative way of grounding data; Charmaz's (2000, 2005) constructivist grounded theory; and Clarke's (2003, 2004) situational analysis. It is beyond the scope of this chapter to describe all of these approaches in adequate detail. All of these scholars have worked with either Strauss or Glaser and are thus considered the "second generation" of scholars.

The concern as grounded theory has evolved to the "third generation" is that this new generation is removed from the original scholars and some of the basic principles of pragmatism and social construction have been diminished and the method has become too "prescribed" or has taken too much of a "positivist" perspective. Charmaz articulates well this concern and she aptly wrote about seeking to reconfirm the constructivist roots of the Chicago school of thought.

DESCRIPTION OF THE GROUNDED THEORY METHOD

Grounded theory consists of processes of defining a research area that involves developing a research question that seeks to understand a phenomenon of interest. Such a research question will naturally lead to an initial inductive mode of inquiry that becomes more deductive as the research process continues. Data are collected (or "generated") through various modes, most commonly individual interviews, but could also include focus group interviews, observation, and documents (e.g., text from historical papers or journaling done by research participants).

Corbin and Strauss (2008) have outlined a guide for conducting grounded theory research. They presented a process that is described in detail in Chapter 3, again, with the caveat that their description is a guide rather than a set of rules to follow absolutely. For purposes of explanation in this chapter, the process of analysis includes open coding, selective coding, axial coding, and theoretical integration. Data analysis, however, is not a completely separate step from data collection. The processes of data collection and analysis are simultaneous, iterative, and ongoing. This means that data analysis begins with initial data collection and initial data analysis, leading to ongoing data collection and analysis, with analysis influencing the ongoing data collection and, in turn, the ongoing data collection leading to an ongoing process of analysis. Analytic questions are generated from the beginning data analysis, which influences further data collection. Questions become more focused and deductive, based on the ongoing analysis, which leads to provisional hypotheses. Eventually, the research team generates enough data to be able to make the case for having arrived as theoretical saturation and concepts are integrated into a conceptual or theoretical scheme that reflects the phenomenon of interest.

MISCONCEPTIONS OF GROUNDED THEORY

As noted earlier, grounded theory is one of the most misunderstood of the various qualitative research methods. One reason for this could be that it is so widely used by so many people that many of the processes involved in grounded theory have been poorly communicated or understood.

One misconception is the notion, as described earlier, that grounded theory is a specific theory. As explained, grounded theory is a method for generating a theory or theoretical explanation of a phenomenon of interest. This resulting theory is grounded in or supported by the data.

Another misconception is that there is one prescribed way of doing grounded theory research. Although Glaser has noted the importance of generating a basic social process and Strauss has noted the importance of generating a trajectory, these concepts need not be "reified" such that a researcher believes this is the outcome that must be achieved. Similarly, although Corbin and Strauss have outlined a succession of steps involved in grounded theory analysis, this is really a guide to analysis. The most important point is that the researcher is actively interacting with the data, using an iterative and ongoing process of collecting and analyzing data. That is, as data are collected, analysis begins; as analysis continues, further data collection ensues, which leads to further data analysis.

A third misconception is that a researcher approaches a grounded theory study as a "tabula rasa," or blank slate. This could not be farther from the truth. The researcher certainly has many ideas and preconceived notions; the challenge is to recognize those ideas and to separate what the participants tell the researcher from what the researcher already believes to be "true."

SUMMARY

This chapter has presented an overview of the qualitative research method referred to as grounded theory. Grounded theory is a systematic qualitative research method of data collection and analysis, ultimately leading to a theoretical explanation (a "grounded theory") that is grounded in those data and that explains a phenomenon of interest. The grounded theory method was developed by Glaser and Strauss, in response to Blumer's call for a method founded on concepts of symbolic interactionism, the social psychological theoretical framework that provides the guiding tenets of grounded theory methodology. Over the years, grounded theory has undergone an evolution of sorts. An alternate method of grounding data in qualitative research is dimensional analysis. Other scholars have developed variants of grounded theory, such as constructivist grounded theory and situational analysis.

REFERENCES

Blumer, H. (1969). *Symbolic interactionism: Perspective and method*. Berkeley, CA: University of California Press.

Bowers, B., & Schatzman, L. (2009). Dimensional analysis. In J. Morse, P. Stern, J. Corbin, B. Bowers, K. Charmaz, & A. Clarke (Eds.), *Developing grounded theory: The second generation*. Developing qualitative inquiry series. Walnut Creek, CA: Left Coast Press.

Charmaz, K. (2000). Constructivist and objectivist grounded theory. In N. K. Denzin & Y. S. Lincoln (Eds.), *Handbook of qualitative research* (2nd ed.). Thousand Oaks, CA: Sage.

Charmaz, K. (2005). Grounded theory in the 21st century: Applications for advancing social justice studies. In N. K. Denzin & Y. S. Lincoln (Eds.), *Handbook of qualitative research* (3rd ed.). Thousand Oaks, CA: Sage.

Clarke, A. E. (2003). Situational analyses: Grounded theory mapping after the postmodern turn. *Symbolic Interaction, 26*, 553–576.

Clarke, A. E. (2004). *Situational analysis: Grounded theory after the postmodern turn*. Thousand Oaks, CA: Sage.

Corbin, J., & Strauss, A. L. (2008). *Basics of qualitative research* (3rd ed.). Thousand Oaks, CA: Sage.

Glaser, B. G. (1978). *Theoretical sensitivity*. Mill Valley, CA: Mill Valley Press.

Glaser, B. G., & Strauss, A. L. (1967). *The discovery of grounded theory*. Chicago, IL: Aldine.

Iowa School of Symbolic Interactionism. Retrieved June 15, 2013, from http://www.uiowa.edu/~grpproc/iowasymbolicInteraction.htm

Katovich, M. A., Miller, D. E., & Stewart, R. L. (2003). The Iowa School. In L. T. Reynolds & N. J. Herman-Kinney (Eds.), *Handbook of symbolic interactionism*. Walnut Creek, CA: Alta Mira Press (a subsidiary of Roman & Littlefield).

Kools, S., McCarthy, M., Durham, R., & Robrecht, L. (1996). Dimensional analysis: Broadening the conception of grounded theory. *Qualitative Health Research, 6*(3), 312–330.

Mead, G. H. (1934). *Mind, self and society*. Chicago, IL: University of Chicago Press.

Morse, J. M., Stern, P. S., Corbin, J., Bowers, B., Charmaz, K., & Clarke, A. E. (2009). *Developing grounded theory: The second generation*. Walnut Creek, CA: Left Coast Press.

Musolf, G. R. (2003). The Chicago School. In L. T. Reynolds & N. J. Herman-Kinney (Eds.), *Handbook of symbolic interactionism*. Walnut Creek, CA: Alta Mira Press (a subsidiary of Roman & Littlefield).

Reynolds, L. T. (2003). Intellectual precursors. In L. T. Reynolds & N. J. Herman-Kinney (Eds.), *Handbook of symbolic interactionism*. Walnut Creek, CA: Alta Mira Press (a subsidiary of Roman & Littlefield).

Schatzman, L., & Strauss, A. L. (1973). *Field research: Strategies for a natural sociology*. Englewood Cliffs, NJ: Prentice-Hall.

CHAPTER TWO

LITERATURE REVIEW OF GROUNDED THEORY NURSING RESEARCH

Anne W. Batson and Mary de Chesnay

This chapter on the grounded theory literature in nursing describes the extent to which nurse researchers have published grounded theory studies. A 10-year search of the journal and dissertation literature was conducted in order to capture the widest array of studies published to date. The first section describes selected dissertations, excluding the ones that are presented in subsequent chapters by the authors themselves (Laurent, 2010; Sengstock, 2008). Following is a state-of-the-art literature review of journal articles using the grounded theory design.

SEARCH METHOD

To identify the state of the art of nursing research in grounded theory, we carried out a thorough search of studies published from 2000 until the present. We searched broadly for nursing studies that used the grounded theory method, as well as articles related to the application of grounded theory, and methodological review. Search terms and keywords were nursing, grounded theory, research, qualitative design, and study. The search was restricted to peer-reviewed, journal articles that were available in English. Articles from Finland, China, New Zealand, Australia, Brazil, and the United Kingdom were found and had been translated prior to publication.

AREAS OF EMPHASIS

There is much in the literature relevant to the state of the art in grounded theory, much more so in more recent years. Researchers utilized grounded theory to achieve different goals demonstrating a variety of applications. Several researchers aimed to thoroughly explore a phenomenon while others described and prescribed strategies to better manage a specific nursing interest. Some researchers sought to develop concepts or constructs for future theory development. Some were successful in creating a new theory from the constructs identified in their grounded theory work. This literature review serves to organize and present the recent, existing published works that included the grounded theory method. The literature will be presented categorically based on the purpose of the researcher. It is in this manner that the variety of applications of grounded theory can be best appreciated.

There are several articles that introduce grounded theory as a research method. For example, Hall, Griffiths, and McKenna (2013), produced an article exploring the evolution of grounded theory, key contributors to this methodology, and their diverse conceptual positioning that influences its application to this day. The information included in this work includes theoretical paradigms and philosophical foundations and provides an excellent overview of grounded theory and its many uses.

Hunter, Murphy, Grealish, and Casey (2011a) published an academic guide to illustrate and employ grounded theory. They diagram the application of grounded theory in four main areas: theory development, methodological rigor, emergence of core category, and inclusion and self-engagement with study participants. Hunter and colleagues (2011b) refer to Glaserian style of grounded theory. Another academic tutorial on grounded theory (Hoare, Mills, & Francis, 2012a, 2012b) guides the reader to view the data in different ways for the purpose of acquiring theoretical sensitivity. This is a working example of a study of nurses' use of evidence-based medicine using constructivist grounded theory as described by Charmaz (2006). Puolakka, Haapasalo-Pesu, Kiikkala, Astedt-Kurki, and Paavilainen (2013) also use a working study to illustrate the use of grounded theory. Their example study on the mental health of schoolchildren results in the creation of substantive theory using the approach recommended by Glaser, Corbin, and Strauss.

Another author who has used a working example of grounded theory is Cooney (2012), who developed a theory of "finding home." This theory is applicable to older people and their perceptions of "being at home" in long-term care facilities and influencing factors. She published an informative article using her work on "finding home" theory to explain rigor in a qualitative study using grounded theory. Similarly, Chen and Boore (2009) provide a methodological review of the theory with additional explanation on synthesizing the different and sometimes opposing methods of grounded theory. They employ Glaser's classical grounded theory model as well as

Strauss and Corbin's more contemporary approach. They illustrate the use of Charmaz's contributions to grounded theory. They review the methodologies and compare the analytic processes of the three differing approaches.

One particularly interesting study is the self-analysis study by Cassidy (2013) that examined the awareness of personal hubris during the interpretive data analysis process of qualitative research. Cassidy used the grounded theory method in a study in which he was the participant. The study is another working example that describes the methodology of grounded theory.

Other authors have contributed meaningful instructional papers for grounded theory use. Skeat and Perry (2008) produced a profession-specific discussion of the use of grounded theory in speech and language therapy. Their paper critiques different qualitative methodologies and emphasizes the benefits of a grounded theory approach for nurses, sociologists, and therapists within the realm of language research.

There are some well-written papers on the use of grounded theory and its evolution over time. Different interpretations and uses of the theory exist, and nurse researchers need to be aware and savvy to these to select the approach that best suits their area of interest and one that is a good fit for their study. Chen and Boore (2009) authored a guide to using a synthesized technique for grounded theory researchers. This paper provides a deep understanding of the different versions of the theory and supports the use of blended versions and a multistep approach using the work of Glaser, Charmaz, and Strauss and Corbin. The above articles as well as information included in text and reference books are enough to provide the researcher with a basis for using grounded theory, and the working examples are an effective way to understand its application.

Grounded theory is commonly used for descriptive studies even when theory development is not the ultimate goal of the study. One such paper by Mirzaei, Fatemeh, and Forough (2012) investigated Iranian nursing students' time management skills in the context of their satisfaction with their academic stressors. Wilson and Baker (2012) described the experience of indigenous Māori mental health nurses in New Zealand. Another international paper (Wu, Liu, & He, 2013) analyzed the stress levels of dual-qualification nursing teachers in the Chengdu–Chongqing economic zone of China. Researchers (Van Brummen & Griffiths, 2013) from the United Kingdom authored a paper describing the experiences of palliative care nurse specialists and midwives. Authors from Australia have contributed to the descriptive research of the nursing profession. Bonner and Greenwood (2006) investigated the acquisition of nephrology nursing expertise, and Deegan (2013) explored nurses' clinical decision making using grounded theory.

There are many clinically relevant studies in the body of literature of grounded theory. Andersson, Eriksson, and Nordgren (2013) explored the differences between heart failure clinics and primary health care. Their work illuminated themes and areas of need among the heart failure patients as they shifted their care away from a primary care setting to a specialty clinic. Some studies are diagnostic specific and serve to describe patients' experiences. Feinberg, Law, Singh, and Wright (2013) evaluated patients with neuroendocrine tumors; Khair, Collier, Meerabeau, and Gibson (2013) researched the day-to-day experiences among males with hemophilia, and Fenwick, Chaboyer, and St. John (2012) published an extensive report on self-management of chronic pain.

There are studies to aid clinical practice by describing phenomena associated with patients' perceptions toward health care issues. Hill and Cox (2013) investigated factors influencing decisions to get a measles–mumps–rubella (MMR) vaccine. Other studies (Stoddart, 2012; Ryan & McKenna, 2013) relate to the community health nurse–patient relationship in countries such as the United Kingdom and Australia, where the setting is very rural and the community health nurse may have a different role than in the United States. Many descriptive studies (Elliott & Umeh, 2013; Perrett & Biley, 2013; Yeboah, Bowers, & Rolls, 2013) all seek to make transparent observations pertaining to patient care. These studies help gain insight into a person's experience and provide explanations for such behavior or decision making. Yeboah and colleagues (2013) explored relocation experiences of the elderly who were born overseas and might have cultural and language differences. The studies, though specific to one particular group, serve to further characterize and clarify an important issue that is meaningful to the individuals in that circumstance.

There are studies that explore ethical dilemmas that impact nurses and patients. Using grounded theory, Moe, Kvig, Brinchmann, and Brinchmann (2013) reflected on the invisible work that nurses perform and argued that "behind the scenes" care by a mental health care nurse is a paternalistic approach to patient care. They make an argument to restructure the care approach to mentally ill patients. Another study of nursing ethics pertaining to psychiatric nursing is from Graor and Knapik (2013). They consider the ethical challenges of doing qualitative research on patients with schizophrenia and bipolar disorder.

Grounded theory studies are commonly found in the literature review of mental health studies. McCann and Clark (2003) applied grounded theory in a paper that reported influential factors in adults with schizophrenia and their caregivers to seek mental health care early in their symptoms.

An Australian study by Gibb (2003) applied this methodology to better explore rural community mental health nursing characterized as solo practice. This inquiry sought to determine how rural lifestyles are accommodated within a solo nurse role.

One other area where grounded theory has been used to support descriptive research is in nursing education. Melrose and Wishart (2013) investigated the transition from a licensed practical nurse (LPN) to a bachelor of science in nursing (BSN). This study led to the development of a theory of developing independence. There are studies (Kerr, 2013) that investigate nurses' decision making using charting by exception. This study led to the development of a theory of creating a protective picture. Giske and Cone (2012) explored nursing students' beginnings with spiritual care of their patients. Ashcroft and Lutfiyya (2013) used grounded theory in their study of nurse educators' perspectives of disabled students.

Moving beyond the descriptive studies that are structured using grounded theory are the studies that serve not only to describe but to prescribe. Practice issues can be addressed and an action plan can result from a study whereby grounded theory was used to analyze data. Elliott (2010) developed strategies to improve clinical judgment of advance practice nurses by identifying a core element of "mutual intacting," which highlights the cognitive practices that practitioners rely on when making clinical decisions. This study resulted in thought-provoking actions rather than constructs for theory development. A study that led to an action plan for staff in nursing homes (Shaw, 2004) used grounded theory to explore the staff responses to aggressive behavior from residents. Shaw described what was learned about the problem, identified core elements and commonalities, and then produced seven strategies for managing aggression. The recommendations include calming and fear-reducing, time and pace-altering, distancing, time-out, and other tools for staff to resolve the situation. Leach and Mayo (2013) used grounded theory to evaluate the effectiveness of rapid response teams in the emergency department of a large teaching hospital. They evaluated the aspects of effective teamwork and generated data to improve areas in which communication and care were deficient.

Grounded theory has proven to be a malleable methodology that adapts well for a variety of applications. The largest body of grounded theory literature, however, relates to theory development. Many nursing theories have evolved after a descriptive study identified concepts and constructs clearly and transparently enough for their creation. Some studies serve to develop a theoretical model that potentially will be a usable theory at some point. The study might need to be modified or reproduced before it has enough explanatory power to generate a theory. Examples of studies that elucidate the constructs necessary to create a theoretical model include a study by Ching, Martinson, and Wong (2012), who created the term "meaning making" after the completion of a grounded theory study of Chinese women with breast cancer. They identified two core concepts of reframing and identifiable meaning throughout the participants' cancer experience and these constructs can, perhaps, result in a future theory of meaning making. Other studies (Lee, Long, & Boore, 2009; Siedlecki et al., 2013) have resulted in concept development.

Actual theory development is a domain in which grounded theory thrives. Several middle range theories are found in recent nursing literature including the theory of postpartum fatigue (Runquist, 2007) and the theory of "doing the best I can" (Musto & Schreiber, 2012) in which the authors explored moral distress in adolescents. The theory of moderated guiding (McCallin, 2011) addresses aspects of providing end-of-life care. The theory of investing in self-care (Leenerts & Magilvy, 2000) can apply to low-income women who have HIV. The results of this grounded theory study identified four core categories: focusing self: imaging/reimaging self; fitting resources: switching things around; feeling emotions; and finding meaning that when integrated with investing in self-care, proved to provide satisfactory data for theory creation. Atkinson and Peden-McAlpine (2013) authored the theory of advancing adolescent maternal development. The theory identifies the social and psychological problems of at-risk adolescent–maternal development and calls for public health nursing interventions throughout the pregnancy to achieve better patient outcomes for mother and baby. Taverner, Closs, and Briggs (2012) created the theory of the journey to chronic pain. This theory suggests that patients follow a series of phases as they move from acute pain to chronic pain syndromes.

Though patient care seems to be the focus of the bulk of the grounded theory work in the current literature, there are theories that pertain to clinic operations and the experiences of nurses. Cranley, Doran, Tourangeau, Kushniruk, and Nagle (2012) created the theory of recognizing and responding to uncertainty. Their work helps explain how staff nurses respond to work-related uncertainties. This study is relevant to bedside nurses and their nurse managers as they consider the complexities of patient care and the multitude of decisions nurses make every day. This study encompasses the experience of the nurse, the patient, the nurse manager, and implications for nursing education and research. This theory, created using grounded theory, is an excellent example of a theory that applies to every nurse. It has clinical relevance, educational relevance, administrative relevance, and research relevance. Studies such as this are necessary for the profession because they simultaneously address issues global to nurses.

SUMMARY

This literature review, though extensive, is not exhaustive as new theories are constantly being generated. Certainly, there are other theories not mentioned in this chapter. Grounded theory is proving to be a reliable foundation for qualitative research and a good fit for many nurse scientists as they analyze meaningful data that contribute to the ever growing knowledge base that supports contemporary nursing.

Nurse researchers have to understand the differences in grounded theory application. The paradigm model of Strauss and Corbin is unique compared with the wider approach suggested by Glaser. Nurses can use a synthesized method of application as suggested by Chen and Boore (2009).

Grounded theory, because it is inductive and the ideas and theories are created from realities constructed in the interactions of people, is what makes it so beneficial to nursing. Individuals are active in the creation of meaning and in turn they are participants in the creation of theory. Nursing theories search for language that can apply to social processes. The theories generated from grounded theory characterize how individuals define and act on their social circumstances. By generating properties and categories about a human interaction, hypotheses about phenomena are discovered and validated.

There is a need in nursing for the creation of theory related to nursing practice. Grounded theory can help close the ever present practice–theory gap by facilitating theories that are "grounded" in data and "grounded" in the exposed and raw experiences of individuals. This is the opposite of deductive research, which imposes ideas from objective observations and prior assumptions. If one wants to fully understand an occurrence, grounded theorists agree that the subjective data is where the answers exist and as exemplified for the list of very recent research in this chapter, nurse researchers are well aware of the appropriateness of this methodology of investigation.

REFERENCES

Andersson, L., Eriksson, H., & Nordgren, L. (2013). Differences between heart failure clinics and primary health care. *British Journal of Community Nursing, 18*(6), 288–301.

Ashcroft, T., & Lutfiyya, Z. (2013). Nursing educators' perspectives of students with disabilities: Grounded theory study. *Nursing Education Today, 33*, 1316–1321. doi:10.1016/j.nedt.2013.018

Atkinson, L., & Peden-McAlpine, C. (2013). Advancing adolescent maternal development: A grounded theory. *Journal of Pediatric Nursing, 13,* 00254–00256. doi:10.1016/j.pedn.2013.08.005

Bonner, A., & Greenwood, J. (2006). The acquisition and exercise of nephrology nursing expertise: A grounded theory study. *Journal of Clinical Nursing, 15*(4), 480–489.

Cassidy, S. (2013). Acknowledging hubris in interpretive data analysis. *Nurse Researcher, 20*(6), 27–31. http://www.ncbi.nlm.nih.gov/pubmed/23909109

Charmaz, K. (2006). *Constructing grounded theory: A practical guide.* London, UK: Sage.

Chen, H., & Boore, J. (2009). Using a synthesized technique for grounded theory in nursing research. *Journal of Clinical Nursing, 18,* 2251–2260. doi:10.1111/j.1365 -2702.2008.02684.x

Ching, S., Martinson, I., & Wong, T. (2012). Meaning making: Psychological adjustment to breast cancer by Chinese women. *Qualitative Health Research, 22*(2), 250–262.

Cooney, A. (2012). "Finding home": A grounded theory on how older people "find home" in long term care settings. *International Journal of Older People Nursing, 7,* 188–199. doi:10.1111/j.1748-3743.2011.00278.x

Cranley, L., Doran, D., Tourangeau, A., Kushniruk, A., & Nagle, L. (2012). Recognizing and responding to uncertainty: A grounded theory of nurses' uncertainty. *Worldviews on Evidence-Based Nursing, 9*(3), 149–158. doi:10.1111/j.1741 -6787.2011.00237.x

Deegan, J. (2013). A view from the outside: Nurses' clinical decision making in the twenty first century. *Australian Journal of Advanced Nursing, 30*(4), 12–18.

Elliott, G., & Umeh, K. (2013). Psychological issues in voluntary hospice care. *British Journal of Nursing, 22*(7), 377–383.

Elliott, N. (2010). 'Mutual intacting': A grounded theory study of clinical judgement practice issues. *Journal of Advanced Nursing, 66*(12), 2711–2721. doi:10.1111 /j.1365-2648.2010.05412.x

Feinberg, Y., Law, C., Singh, S., & Wright, F. (2013). Patient experiences of having a neuroendocrine tumour: A qualitative study. *European Journal of Oncology Nursing, 17*(5), 541–545.

Fenwick, C., Chaboyer, W., & St. John, W. (2012). Decision-making processes for the self-management of persistent pain: A grounded theory study. *Contemporary Nurse, 42*(1), 53–66.

Gibb, H. (2003). Rural community mental health nursing: A grounded theory account of sole practice. *International Journal of Mental Health Nursing, 12*(4), 243–250.

Giske, T., & Cone, P. (2012). Opening up to learning spiritual care of patients: A grounded theory study of nursing students. *Journal of Clinical Nursing, 21,* 2006–2015. doi:10.1111/j.1365-2702.2011.04054.x

Graor, C., & Knapik, G. (2013). Addressing methodological and ethical challenges of qualitative health research on persons with schizophrenia and bipolar disorder. *Archives of Psychiatric Nursing, 27*(2), 65–71.

Hall, H., Griffiths, D., & McKenna, L. (2013). From Darwin to constructivism: The evolution of grounded theory. *Nurse Researcher, 20*(3), 17–21.

Hill, M., & Cox, C. (2013). Influencing factors in MMR immunization decision making. *British Journal of Nursing, 22*(15), 893–898.

Hoare, K., Mills, J., & Francis, K. (2012a). Dancing with data: An example of acquiring theoretical sensitivity in a grounded theory study. *International Journal of Nursing Practice, 18*, 240–245. doi:10.1111/j.1440-172x.2012.02038.x

Hoare, K., Mills, J., & Francis, K. (2012b). Sifting, sorting and saturating data in a grounded theory study of information use by practice nurses: A worked example. *International Journal of Nursing Practice, 18*(6), 582–588. doi:10.1111/ijn.12007

Hunter, A., Murphy, K., Grealish, A., & Casey, D. (2011a). Navigating the grounded theory terrain. Part 1. *Nurse Researcher, 18*(4), 6–10.

Hunter, A., Murphy, K., Grealish, A., & Casey, D. (2011b). Navigating the grounded theory terrain. Part 2. *Nurse Researcher, 19*(1), 6–11.

Kerr, N. (2013). 'Creating a protective picture:' A grounded theory of RN decision making when using a charting-by-exception documentation system. *Medsurg Nursing, 22*(2), 110–118.

Khair, K., Collier, C., Meerabeau, L., & Gibson, F. (2013). Multimethodology research with boys with severe haemophilia. *Nurse Researcher, 20*(6), 40–44.

Leach, L., & Mayo, A. (2013). Rapid response teams: Qualitative analysis of their effectiveness. *American Journal of Critical-Care Nurses, 22*(3), 198–210.

Lee, S., Long, A., & Boore, J. (2009). Taiwanese women's experiences of becoming a mother to a very-low-birth-weight preterm infant: A grounded theory study. *International Journal of Nursing Studies, 46*(3), 326–336. doi:10.1016/j.ijnurstu.2008.10.004

Leenerts, M., & Magilvy, J. (2000). Investing in self-care: A midrange theory of self-care grounded in the lived experience of low-income HIV-positive White women. *Advances in Nursing Science, 22*(3), 58–75.

McCallin, A. (2011). Moderated guiding: A grounded theory of nursing practice in end-of-life care. *Journal of Clinical Nursing, 20*(15–16), 2325–2333. doi:10.1111/j.1365-2702.2010.035543.x

McCann, T., & Clark, E. (2003). A grounded theory study of the role that nurses play in increasing clients' willingness to access community mental health services. *International Journal of Mental Health Nursing, 12*(4), 279–287.

Melrose, S., & Wishart, P. (2013). Resisting, reaching out and re-imagining to independence: LPNs' transitioning towards BNs and beyond. *International Journal of Nursing Education Scholarship, 10*(1), 1–7. doi:10.1515/ijnes-2012-0033

Mirzaei, T., Fatemeh, O., & Forough, R. (2012). Nursing students' time management, reducing stress and gaining satisfaction: A grounded theory study. *Nursing and Health Sciences, 14*(1), 46–51.

Moe, C., Kvig, E. L., Brinchmann, B., & Brinchmann, B. S. (2013). 'Working behind the scenes'. An ethical view of mental health nursing and first-episode psychosis. *Nursing Ethics, 20*(5), 517–527.

Musto, L., & Schreiber, R. (2012). Doing the best I can do: Moral distress in adolescent mental health nursing. *Issues in Mental Health Nursing, 33*(3), 137–144. doi:10.3109/01612840.2011.641069

Perrett, S., & Biley, F. (2013). Negotiating uncertainty: The transitional process of adapting to life with HIV. *Journal of the Association of Nurses in AIDS Care, 24*(3), 207–218. doi:10.1016/j.jana.2012.06.007

Puolakka, K., Haapasalo-Pesu, K., Kiikkala, I., Astedt-Kurki, P., & Paavilainen, E. (2013). Using grounded theory to create a substantive theory of promoting schoolchildren's mental health. *Nurse Researcher, 20*(3), 22–27.

Runquist, J. (2007). Persevering through postpartum fatigue. *Journal of Gynecologic & Neonatal Nursing, 36*(1), 28–37. doi:10.1111/j.152-6909.2006.00116.x

Ryan, A., & McKenna, H. (2013). 'Familiarity as a key factor influencing rural family carers' experience of the nursing home placement of an older relative: A qualitative study. *BMC Health Services Research, 13*, 252–262.

Shaw, M. (2004). Aggression toward staff by nursing home residents. *Journal of Gerontological Nursing, 30*(10), 43–54.

Siedlecki, S., Modic, M., Bernhofer, E., Sorrell, J., Strumble, P., & Kato, I. (2013). Exploring how bedside nurses care for patients with chronic pain: A grounded theory study. *Pain Management Nursing, 30*(10), 43–54. doi:10.1016/j.pmn.2012.12.007

Skeat, J., & Perry, A. (2008). Grounded theory as a method for research in speech and language therapy. *International Journal of Language and Communication, 43*(2), 95–109.

Stoddart, K. (2012). Social meanings and understandings in patient-nurse interaction in the community practice setting: A grounded theory study. *BMC Nursing, 11*(14), 1–10.

Taverner, T., Closs, A., & Briggs, M. (2012). The journey to chronic pain: A grounded theory of older adults' experiences of pain associated with leg ulceration. *Pain Management Nursing, 15*(1), 186–198. doi:10.1016/j.pmn.2012.08.002

Van Brummen, B., & Griffiths, L., (2013). Working in a medicalised world: The experiences of palliative care nurse specialists and midwives. *International Journal of Palliative Nursing, 19*(2), 85–91.

Wilson, D., & Baker, M. (2012). Bridging two worlds: Māori mental health nursing. *Qualitative Health Research, 22*(8), 1073–1082. doi:10.1177/1049732312450213

Wu, Y., Liu, H., & He, H. (2013). Stressors of dual-qualification nursing teachers in the ChengDu–ChongQing economic zone of China—A qualitative study. *Nurse Education Today, 33*(12), 1496–1500.

Yeboah, C., Bowers, B., & Rolls, C. (2013). Culturally and linguistically diverse older adults relocating to residential aged care. *Contemporary Nurse, 44*(1), 50–61.

CHAPTER THREE

GENERATING THEORY USING GROUNDED THEORY METHODOLOGY

Ellen F. Olshansky

*A*s discussed in an earlier chapter, the term *grounded theory* (Glaser & Strauss, 1967) refers to a qualitative research method that has as its goal the generation of theory (or beginning theory) that is "grounded" in the data. Data are collected from research participants in their naturalistic settings, capturing their everyday life experiences. Data analysis focuses on discovering, explaining, and understanding these everyday life experiences as related to the phenomenon of interest in the research study. In grounded theory, data collection and analysis consist of a systematic series of steps that are iterative. In other words, they are not linear or conducted in two separate phases, but rather they occur in a simultaneous and ongoing fashion. As data are collected, they are analyzed; analysis influences further data collection; this process is ongoing until saturation of data is achieved. This chapter describes the method of conducting a grounded theory study, using examples of several grounded theory studies on experiences of infertility as well as a grounded theory study on how people manage diabetes in their everyday lives. Because grounded theory methodology was developed in the 1960s and 1970s and further clarified in later decades, many of the references in this chapter are "classics" and thus several decades old.

DESCRIPTION OF THE PROCESS OF CONDUCTING A GROUNDED THEORY STUDY

This section presents a description of how data are collected and analyzed. Although organized according to generation of data and then analysis of data, as noted, these are not mutually exclusive phases, as the process involves simultaneous and ongoing steps, which will become more obvious through this description.

Collection/Generation of Data

Data in grounded theory consist of qualitative information, most commonly in the form of transcripts from interviews with research participants. Data can also include field notes of observations, journal entries by the researcher or by the research participant, historical documents, texts, electronic communication, or other sources. Ultimately, the researcher collects words (hence, the term "qualitative" rather than "quantitative," which refers to numbers) that must be interpreted.

In the case of interviews, the researcher develops an interview guide. The term "guide" is used purposely here because it is a guide rather than a specifically constructed script that cannot change. The construction of the interview guide begins with creating several open-ended questions, such as "tell me about your experience with infertility." Each open-ended question is followed by several probes, which are ways of restating the question in case the participant does not seem to understand what the researcher is getting at. Probes facilitate a focus on more specifics, such as "Tell me about what it was like when you first learned you were infertile." Probes also are used to restate a question in case the research participant does not understand what is being asked. Questions should be open-ended rather than "yes" or "no" type of questions. The researcher is actively involved in the interview (rather than simply reading a list of questions from a script), which means that the researcher actively responds to the answers from the participant, by asking for clarification if needed or asking the person to expand. This type of interview is referred to as a semi-structured interview because, while structured to some extent with predetermined questions, there is room for variation in wording and for clarifying questions. Also, as the study progresses, the interview questions will change and become more focused, based on ongoing data analysis. Through the data analysis, provisional hypotheses are generated and data continue to be collected in a more focused way, guided by these provisional hypotheses. The researcher, in this more focused mode, is looking for support for these provisional hypotheses in order to confidently present these "findings" or descriptions and explanatory observations. Of course, if support is not generated in the data, or only weak support is evident, data analysis will continue, and eventually other provisional hypotheses will be generated, guiding further data collection. Eventually, with enough data, the researcher should arrive at "theoretical saturation" (Glaser, 1978), a term described below under the section on analysis of data. Thus, as described, it is clear why this process of research is iterative—simultaneous and ongoing.

It is important to note that in this type of research the interviewer is, in fact, considered to be the "instrument" for the research. The researcher (interviewer) is not passive, but, as described earlier, takes an active role in conducting the interview. The interviewer is really an "active listener" responding to the participant, constantly probing and "digging deeper" in order to understand the participant's experiences.

Interviews are recorded and transcribed verbatim for data analysis. Another important part of data generation is also field notes and personal reflections on the part of the researcher.

ANALYSIS OF DATA

Data analysis consists of series of steps, again not linear, that eventually lead to the construction of a beginning theory or theoretical explanation for the phenomenon of interest. Strauss and Corbin (1998) referred to open coding, axial coding, selective coding, and theoretical integration. In the third edition, written by Corbin with Strauss as a posthumous author (2008), emphasis is placed on the process of interaction between the researcher and the data. It is this process that is core to conducting grounded theory research. Terms such as open coding, comparative analysis, conceptual saturation, and theoretical sampling, with reference to axial coding (but this term is not used as frequently) are used. While these terms are useful, the more important point to emphasize in data analysis is that it is an active and systematic process in which the researcher is in constant and ongoing interaction with the data. This chapter uses these terms, as they are useful to describe the process of data collection and analysis. The caveat, however, is that while grounded theory is a systematic process of data collection and analysis, it is not as prescriptive as many quantitative studies. In other words, not all grounded theory studies lead to a "trajectory" or a "basic social process." Ultimately, the goal of a grounded theory study is to generate a beginning theoretical explanation that reflects human experiences of everyday life conditions.

This data analytic process begins with "open coding," wherein the researcher looks at the data (transcript) and generates initial codes that reflect the meaning in the data. At this point in the analysis, the researcher must work hard to keep an open mind, writing codes that may or may not "hold up" in the data as the study progresses. This is the period in which the researcher is "open" to any and all interpretations. In fact, I tell my students to "not be embarrassed" about bringing up ideas that may, with further data, prove to be unfounded. The open coding process is the opportunity to brainstorm and to look at the data from all angles and perspectives. And, a key point to remember is that we are not seeking "right" or "wrong" answers; instead, we are seeking to understand the data as best as we can from the perspectives of the participants who were interviewed. Thus, it is helpful to imagine the researcher/data analyst interacting with the data, which is proxy for the research participant, in order to understand the participant's point of view. To do this, any and all questions must be raised in interaction with the data; hence, open coding is a way of embracing these questions by posing them as potential codes that reflect the meaning in the data. With further data collection through the iterative process that is central to grounded theory methodology, many of these questions will be answered and the codes will be narrowed to those that continue to receive "support" from the ongoing data collection.

Along with open coding is a process that Strauss and Corbin have, in the past, referred to as "axial coding," although this term is used less frequently now. The idea of axial coding is to look at the codes from various perspectives (or "turning the codes on their axes") and to combine codes to see how they compare and how they overlap, because they are likely not mutually exclusive. Through this process of axial coding, the researcher achieves a much richer and deeper understanding of the initial codes being generated and is able to, eventually, narrow the codes by selectively focusing on those codes with greater support from the data.

As the data analytic process continues, the researcher begins to engage in "selective coding," in which those codes with enough support in the data are focused on and further refined. At some point in the grounded theory process, the researcher achieves "theoretical saturation," a condition in which fewer and fewer new codes or categories are being generated while data continue to support certain codes or categories. Determining when theoretical saturation is reached is a judgment call in many ways, but it is incumbent on the researcher to demonstrate the evidence for theoretical saturation.

As the codes are further analyzed, examining them from multiple perspectives, often a paradigm of looking at conditions and consequences as well as strategies for dealing with consequences (Corbin & Strauss, 2008) is used as a way of organizing the codes/categories. Strauss also spoke of "trajectories," and Glaser spoke of "basic social processes." Schatzman, in his work on dimensional analysis, a variant of grounded theory (Bowers & Schatzman, 2009; Kools, McCarthy, Durham, & Robrecht, 1996), spoke of a matrix or a "calculator of consideration" of various risks, benefits, conditions, and consequences, which all influence how a person perceives his or her situation (Schatzman, 1991, p. 309).

The important point is that the researcher is able to synthesize the codes and concepts into a useful theoretical integration that reflects, as close as possible, the meaning in the data from the perspectives of the research participants. As noted earlier, grounded theory is not so prescriptive, but embraces several variant approaches.

A process that is core to the entire data analytic process is "constant comparative analysis." This process consists of comparing data to other data within a transcript, comparing transcripts to other transcripts within the study, and comparing data and transcripts to other situations beyond the immediate research study, including everyday life experiences. The researcher's own life experiences can be compared to the data with the caveat that the researcher must be very clear on the separation of the data from his or her life experiences. However, everyday life experiences help to provide an understanding of the possibilities of the varied meanings in the data. Constant comparative analysis is done throughout the analytic work. Schatzman actually referred to this as "natural analysis," emphasizing that as human beings we are constantly involved in analyzing data from a perspective that is useful, highlighting the fact that grounded theory is rooted in the philosophical views of pragmatism.

Eventually, codes are collapsed into categories that subsume several codes; and categories are raised to more abstract levels. Often a "core category" is generated, around which other categories are integrated, arriving at a theoretical explanation ("theoretical integration") for the phenomenon of interest.

There are many computer software packages to assist in qualitative data analysis. Regardless of the specific method used, it is important to note that these software packages provide ways of storing and organizing data for easy retrieval, but the actual analysis/interpretation of data is done by the researcher(s).

EXAMPLE OF A GROUNDED THEORY STUDY: EXPERIENCES OF INFERTILITY

In this section, I present my own program of research on women's and men's (mostly women's) experiences of infertility in an effort to demonstrate how grounded theory is used to generate a beginning theory and how subsequent grounded theory studies can build on the initial study to further refine and expand on the "grounded theory" generated (Olshansky, 2005). I also present a subsequent grounded theory study on a different topic (living with diabetes) to demonstrate an example of developing "formal" theory from initial "substantive" theory.

To begin this discussion, it is helpful to present the research process and findings of my initial grounded theory study in infertility (Olshansky, 1987a). In that study, I explored how women and men experienced unwanted infertility. Through individual and dyadic interviews (with couples), I underwent an iterative process of first generating numerous codes through brainstorming (open coding). Such notions include feeling as though infertility is present all the time, difficulty focusing on other aspects of life, feeling different, feeling sad, distressed, angry, and many others. As the data collection and analytic process continued, I began to focus on the "all-encompassing" experience of infertility. Through selective coding, I was able to generate more and more data that supported this idea, with less and less new information being generated. I coded words from the participants that described infertility being present, being with them all the time, infertility preventing them from focusing on other things, eventually collapsing these words into a more abstract category that I referred to as "all-encompassing." In fact, as data analysis continues, the coding becomes more abstract, albeit always with the challenge to the researcher/analyst to be sure that the more abstract words are "grounded" in words of the research participants.

Eventually, through the use of constant comparative analysis, a process of comparing data to other data within each transcript, comparing transcript to transcript, comparing participants' words with my everyday life experiences, and comparing words/codes with existing theoretical constructs, I focused on an even more abstract concept. I collapsed the notion of "all-encompassing" and its attendant descriptors into the core category of "identity."

"Identity as infertile" became the core category around which I integrated and synthesized other categories, eventually developing a trajectory that reflected the experiences of the research participants interviewed. This trajectory was referred to as "the work of taking on and managing an identity of self as infertile." The trajectory consisted of phases that, although seemingly linear, were circular, reflecting the complexities of human experiences. Women and men began with "symbolic rehearsal" of being parents. They then became engaged in "informal fertility work," followed by "formal fertility work." Through all of this "fertility work," one's identity as infertile changed, often becoming larger within the context of their views of self. Conceptually, they were engaged in taking on managing an identity of self as infertile. Based on the consequences of the formal fertility work, they experienced various consequences: (a) overcoming infertility as a result of, or despite, treatment, (b) resolving infertility through adoption, or (c) deciding to not become parents. Over time, as they were able to move on from infertility, their identity as infertile ebbed, though this experience was very different for different people, even for individuals within dyads. In a sense, they were undergoing a process of "normalizing" their identities.

After conducting this initial study of persons' experiences of infertility, I continued a series of grounded theory studies of infertility. My goal was to add complexity to and a deeper understanding of this beginning substantive theory of "identity of self as infertile." I did this by studying married women and men (Olshansky, 1988a), and then I focused only on women (in this case, I did refocus my program to women exclusively, recognizing that more research is needed on men's experiences as well as families' experiences) in various contexts, including women with careers (Olshansky, 1987b), women undergoing assisted reproductive technology treatment (Olshansky, 1988b), and women who became pregnant after infertility (Olshansky, 1990). This series of studies demonstrated how an initial grounded theory study can lead to further studies, in order to attain the concept of "theoretical elaboration" (Vaughn, 1992), resulting in a more robust theoretical explanation of the phenomenon of interest (Olshansky, 1996). Even after publishing this theoretical integration of several studies of infertility, I continued to explore the experience of infertility in various contexts. In 2005, I published a study on the experiences of menopausal women with a history of infertility, focusing on how women construct an identity of themselves as "normal" despite feeling different from other women while they were going through infertility (Olshansky, 2005).

The above example demonstrates how a "substantive theory" (identity of self as infertile) was generated through the process of grounded theory research. Next, I present an example of another research study that exemplifies the beginning construction of "formal theory." Olshansky and colleagues (2008) explored the experiences of persons living with diabetes, using a grounded theory approach. The core category generated in this study was "normalizing the process of managing diabetes." The research participants described feeling different from others in society because of their specific lifestyle modifications that they had to make to control their diabetes. As they engaged in trying to "normalize" these experiences, they found that they were able to view their own lifestyle modifications as ways of maintaining their health. These research participants were, in effect, normalizing their identities as people with diabetes. This is similar to the research participants in my previous study in which they took on an identity as infertile.

The above section describes the process of developing substantive theory based on a series of grounded theory studies on experiences of infertility, followed by a study of experiences of managing diabetes, leading to the generation of formal theory. This beginning formal theory (and I emphasize beginning because more research that tests these ideas is necessary in order to refer to this as a true theory) provides a conceptual understanding of how people "normalize" their everyday lives in the face of having health conditions that may make them feel "other than" rather than "normal."

From a grounded theory perspective, the series of studies on infertility, followed by the study on diabetes, the process of generating formal theory has been explicated. When Glaser and Strauss (1967) developed the method of grounded theory, as sociologists they were interested in creating a systematic method to generate theory to explain experiences and situations. For nurses and other health care providers who employ the grounded theory method to generate theory, another purpose is to be able to apply this theory to the development of clinical interventions.

SUMMARY

This chapter presents an overview of the process of conducting a qualitative study using grounded theory as the method. The method is explained by using a series of studies on infertility as an example, followed by a study of diabetes. Thus, the operations of the grounded theory method are described as well as how a substantive theory generated through grounded theory can eventually lead to a beginning formal theory.

REFERENCES

Bowers, B., & Schatzman, L. (2009). Dimensional analysis. In J. M. Morse, P. N. Stern, J. Corbin, B. Bowers, K. Charmaz, & A. E. Clarke (Eds.), *Developing grounded theory: The second generation*. Walnut Creek, CA: Left Coast Press.

Corbin, J., & Strauss, A. (2008). *Basics of qualitative research: Techniques and procedures for developing grounded theory* (3rd ed.). Thousand Oaks, CA: Sage.

Glaser, B. G. (1978). *Theoretical sensitivity*. Mill Valley, CA: Sociological Press.

Glaser, B. G., & Strauss, A. L. (1967). *The discovery of grounded theory: Strategies for qualitative research*. New York, NY: Aldine.

Kools, S., McCarthy, M., Durham, R., & Robrecht, L. (1996). Dimensional analysis: Broadening the conception of grounded theory. *Qualitative Health Research, 6*(3), 312–330.

Olshansky, E. F. (1987a). Identity of self as infertile: An example of theory-generating research. *Advances in Nursing Science, 9*(2), 54–63.

Olshansky, E. F. (1987b). Infertility and its influence on women's career identities. *Health Care for Women International, 8*(3), 185–196.

Olshansky, E. F. (1988a). Married couples' experiences of infertility. *Communicating Nursing Research, 21,* 47.

Olshansky, E. F. (1988b). Responses to high technology infertility treatment. *Image: The Journal of Nursing Scholarship, 20*(3), 128–131.

Olshansky, E. F. (1990). Psychosocial implications of pregnancy after infertility. *NAACOG's Clinical Issues in Women's Health and Perinatal Nursing, 1*(3), 342–347.

Olshansky, E. F. (1996). Theoretical issues in building a grounded theory: Applications of an example of a program of research on infertility. *Qualitative Health Research, 6*(3), 394–405.

Olshansky, E. (2005). Feeling normal: Women's experiences of menopause after infertility. *MCN: The American Journal of Maternal Child Nursing, 30*(3), 195–200.

Olshansky, E., Sacco, D., Fitzgerald, K., Zickmund, S., Hess, R., Bryce, C. . . . Fischer, G. (2008). Living with diabetes: Normalizing the process of managing diabetes. *The Diabetes Educator, 34*(6), 1004–1012.

Schatzman, L. (1991). Dimensional analysis: Notes on an alternative approach to the grounding of theory in qualitative research. In D. R. Maines (Ed.), *Social organization and social process: Essays in honor of Anselm Strauss* (pp. 303–314). New York, NY: Aldine de Gruyter.

Strauss, A. L., & Corbin, J. (1998). *Basics of qualitative research: Techniques and procedures for developing grounded theory* (2nd ed.). Thousand Oaks, CA: Sage.

Vaughan, D. (1992). Theory elaboration: The heuristics of case analysis. In H. Becker and C. Ragin (eds.), *What is a case?* (pp. 173–202). New York: Cambridge University Press.

CHAPTER FOUR

THE PATHWAY TO MAKING CHANGE: HOW PARENTS PROMOTE HEALTH FOR THEIR OVERWEIGHT OR OBESE CHILD

Jennifer S. Laurent

Childhood overweight and obesity are a global epidemic with the United States experiencing the highest levels in the world of children who are overweight and obese. As of 2004, 35% of schoolchildren are above the International Obesity Task Force (IOTF) criteria of being overweight (greater than 85th percentile for age and gender) and 13% are obese (greater than 95th percentile for age and gender) by this definition (Lobstein & Jackson-Leach, 2007). Current statistics estimate that one of every three children and adolescents is overweight, a threefold increase from 1970 (Ogden, Carroll, & Flegal, 2008). The rates of being overweight and obesity vary across the nation from 23% in Utah to 44% in Mississippi (Trust for America's Health, 2009). Minority children and those at lower socioeconomic levels are at greater risk for being overweight and obese (Gortmaker, Must, Perrin, Sobol, & Dietz, 1993; Hedley et al., 2004).

PURPOSE OF THE STUDY

The purpose of this study is to explore, discover, and explicate the experiential process of parents as they promote health for their overweight or obese child. Implicit within this goal is to discover the worldview of parents during this process and to understand the complex matrix influencing their knowledge, choices, actions, and reactions.

BACKGROUND AND SIGNIFICANCE

Despite the 2009 ranking as the healthiest state (United Health Foundation, 2009), Vermont falls at the national average of percentage of overweight and obese children (Vermont Department of Health [VDH], 2006b). Vermont has the ninth lowest percentage of overweight and obese children in the nation. Approximately 27% of Vermont youths aged 10 to 17 are overweight or obese (Trust for America's Health, 2009). Trends reported by the Vermont Department of Health's 2008 Health Status Report demonstrate an increasing prevalence of overweight and obesity in children and adults (VDH, 2008). Targeted efforts addressing childhood overweight and obesity once absent from Healthy Vermonters 2010 (VDH, 2000) have now claimed priority (VDH, 2006a). Wang, Beydoun, Liang, Caballero, and Kumanyika (2008) project that, by 2030, the prevalence of overweight status in children residing in the United States will double. The incidence and prevalence of obesity do not appear to be slowing down at the national level, and Vermont will not be an exception to the crisis.

Given what we know, why is overweight and obesity continuing to escalate? Theoretically, the treatment of overweight and obesity should be straightforward. Consume less and expend more. However, the examination of hierarchical factors such as economics and politics interwoven with the child's environment, social interaction, and physiology reveals a quagmire of complexity.

Feeding practices and attitudes are grounded in the environmental context of the culture in which one is reared (Gable & Lutz, 2000; Gardiner & Kosmitzki, 2005). Throughout development, food choices and feeding practices are balanced and transformed by the social interaction between parent and child (Broughton, 1987; Chiva, 1997). Coupled with subjective preferences are objective realities such as financial resources and availability and access to nutritious foods (Gortmaker et al., 1993; Stunkard & Sorensen, 1993). The increased availability of calorie-dense, poorly nutritious foods has placed children at risk. Globalization of such foods has contributed to the worldwide obesity epidemic (Zimmet, 2000). Food practices, behaviors, and attitudes are rooted in one's culture and stem from the socialization process from childhood to adulthood (Chiva, 1997; Gardiner & Kosmitzki, 2005). These elements define one's particular taste, behaviors, and food choices, aid in the cognitive and physical identity construction of the child, and are reliant on the parent or caregiver to a large extent until mid to late adolescence (Newman & Newman, 2006).

The disadvantaged family faces further hardship. Food insufficiency has been found to play an independent role in its contribution to overweight and obesity. These households are of low socioeconomic status and defined as families who lacked enough food to eat over the previous 12 months. Alaimo, Olson, and Frongillo (2001) demonstrated greater overweight status in food-insufficient households than households with food sufficiency. Calorie-dense, nutrient-deficient foods are economically feasible, highly palatable, and easily accessible (Zimmet, 2000). Academy Award nominee for best documentary, *Super Size Me*, found 83 McDonalds food chains in Manhattan, New York, an estimated four restaurants per square mile (Spurlock, 2004). Globally, Spurlock cites over 30,000 McDonalds in 100 countries on 6 continents, representing 46% of the fast food market share. Houston, voted the 2003 fattest city, boasts 253 locations of the fast food chain (CNN.com, 2003). The power of commerce, its culture and lifestyle, is clearly a fundamental driver underpinning the rise in obesity.

Humans, by necessity, must consume food to live. They do not need to exercise. With advancing technologies and reliance on other sources of transit, humans are increasingly sedentary (Zimmet, 2000). Increasing physical activity may be prohibitive for some children. Booth and colleagues (2001) report the United States as the least walkable nation. Increased residential traffic (Sturm, 2004), fewer sidewalks (Kerr et al., 2006), and crime (Richmond, Field, & Rich, 2007) may place children at risk for harm. Child-safe areas for play and physical activity are of increasing concern for parents and public health officials (Baur & O'Connor, 2004).

Competing with physical activity and playtime is the ever-increasing draw and array of sedentary activities. Screen time, comprising television, movies, computer use, and video games, has replaced physical games for many children creating an overwhelming imbalance of energy consumed versus energy expended (Myers, Strikmiller, Webber, & Berenson, 1996). Adachi-Mejia and colleagues (2006) demonstrated a 30% increased risk of overweight status for those children with a television in their bedroom. Of the overweight children, 50% had a television in their bedroom.

Obesity and obesity development are more than societal factors promoting both inactivity and food consumption. Parental weight has demonstrated a direct relationship to childhood adiposity (Whitaker, Deeks, Baughcum, & Specker, 2000) and is predictive of future obesity (Whitaker, Wright, Pepe, Seidel, & Dietz, 1997). Christakis and Fowler (2007) have hypothesized that in one's social network, obesity and being overweight play an important role for initiating and "spreading" obesity through social ties. For the child, his or her social network, to a large extent, is the parent. This places the burden of a child's healthy weight on the shoulders of the parent within the obesogenic world in which we live.

This study provides nursing knowledge for future studies specific to the needs of parents and their children during their search for guidance, intervention, and support. Identified relationships will provide further opportunities for investigators to explore avenues of initiating, encouraging, and enhancing health-promoting strategies. Nursing knowledge generated from this study will contribute to practice through theory and provide for the health and well-being of families and their future. Additionally, study findings will guide health promotion strategies that may address the escalating and burdensome health care costs associated with obesity and obesity-related disease.

RESEARCH QUESTION AND DEFINITIONS

To fulfill a vital knowledge deficit in the pediatric and obesity literature, the following overarching question is posed. How do parents promote the health of their overweight or obese child? Subquestions are as follows:

- What processes do parents use to promote their child's health within the context of overweight or obesity?
- What is it like for parents as they promote the health of their overweight or obese child and how does it affect the choices they make for their child?

Child. Child is defined as a youth between the ages of 9 and 14 years (DeHart, Sroufe, & Cooper, 2004).

Overweight status. Overweight, as defined by the IOTF, is greater than the 85th but less than the 95th body mass index (BMI) percentile for age and gender, calculated as weight in kilograms divided by height in squared meters (Lobstein & Jackson-Leach, 2007).

Obese status. Obese, as defined by the IOTF, is greater than the 95th BMI percentile for age and gender, calculated as weight in kilograms divided by height in squared meters (Lobstein & Jackson-Leach, 2007).

Parent. Parent is defined as an adult, over the age of 18 years, who partakes in the active role of parent or guardian and is responsible for the primary needs of the child who is biological, adopted, or under guardianship for greater than 1 year.

ASSUMPTIONS

The following assumptions underlie this study.

- Parents acknowledged their child is overweight or obese.
- Parents, by the nature of being a parent, desired to promote the health of their child.
- The concept of promoting health may not be congruent among parents and health professionals.

LIMITATIONS

The findings of the study relied on the premise that parents were aware of their child's overweight or obese weight status and were active in promoting the health of their child. Many parents are not cognizant of their child's overweight or obese status or may not perceive such status as concerning or warranting attention. The problem of raising parental awareness was only partially addressed through study findings. Lastly, fathers were underrepresented in this study making the findings less transferable to this population. Participants were recruited from within the state of Vermont and suburban Upstate New York. Due to the predominantly Caucasian population characteristics of these regions, the study sample does not represent the general population as a whole. This limitation will decrease the transferability of the study findings to more heterogeneous populations. Further long-term studies to include diverse populations are warranted to support and lend credibility to the findings of this study and address the difficult problem of raising parental awareness.

REVIEW OF LITERATURE

It is important to address the methodological framework prior to reviewing the state of the literature. Historically, leading experts in grounded theory have advised against a priori literature review citing fear of future analytic contamination and constraint by the investigator. The concern is that approaching the inductive process of grounded theory with such preconceived ideas prior to one's investigation will hamper the investigator's ability to discover new emerging concepts, themes, and theory contrary to the state of the extant literature (Glaser, 1992, 1998; Glaser & Strauss, 1967).

This tabula rasa approach is rejected by many scholars who believe research begins with relevant preconceived ideas that assist in formulating the nature of further investigation (Hutchinson & Skodol-Wilson, 2001). Without some conception of the phenomenon of interest, contrary ideas and novel concepts would not be apparent to the investigator (Bryant & Charmez, 2007; Charmez, 2006; Dey, 1999). Congruent with this latter perspective, the objective of this chapter is not to stifle the creative skillfulness of the investigator who uses the grounded theory process but to present data that support and lay a foundation for the nature of this inquiry.

There is an abundance of literature exploring the many facets of childhood overweight and obesity. Due to the shortening of the dissertation into a chapter, this section is abbreviated to include brief mention of the major categories:

- Child determinants of being overweight and obesity (Dietz, 1994, 1998; Freedman et al., 1987; Jarvie, Lahey, & Graziano, 1983; Must, 2005; Nader et al., 2006; Puhl & Latner, 2007)
- Parent, home, and family determinants of childhood overweight and obesity (Baumrind, 1971; Borra, Kelly, Shirreffs, Neville, & Geiger, 2003; Darling & Steinberg, 1993; DeHart et al., 2004; Gardiner & Kosmitzki, 2005; Klesges, Stein, Eck, Isbell, & Klesges, 1991; Laurent, 2007; Lissau & Sorensen, 1994; Lumeng & Burke, 2006; Rhee, Lumeng, Appugliese, Kaciroti, & Bradley, 2006; Stein, Epstein, Raynor, Kilanowski, & Paluch, 2005)
- Family- and parent-based treatment programs (Dietz & Robinson, 2005; Epstein, Klein, & Wisniewski, 1994; Golan, Kaufman, & Shahar, 2006; Golan & Weizman, 2001; Golan, Weizman, & Fainaru, 1998; Golley, Magarey, Baur, Steinbeck, & Daniels, 2007; Jiang, Xia, Greiner, Lian, & Rosenqvist, 2005; Nemet et al., 2005; Nowicka & Flodmark, 2008; Paineau et al., 2008; Snethen, Broome, & Cashin, 2006; White et al., 2004)
- Role of the health care provider (HCP; Laurent, 2007; Lutfiyya, Lipsky, Wisdom-Behounek, & Inpanbutr-Martinkus, 2007)

DESIGN

A grounded theory approach provided the methodology for understanding the complex, dynamic process specific to health promotion by parents within the context of their world. Implicit within this approach and considered foundational to grounded theory is symbolic interactionism (Hutchinson & Skodol-Wilson, 2001; Manis & Meltzer, 1967). Within the paradigm of the social constructionist philosophy, symbolic interactionism lends itself as a theoretical orientation underpinning the grounded theory approach. The weaving of symbolic interactionism as a philosophical foundation for grounded theory allows for fuller discovery and explication of not only the process of parents promoting health of their overweight or obese child but the meaning, experience, and interpretation, which are bound within that interaction as described by parents.

Setting

The majority of this study was conducted in the state of Vermont and to a lesser degree in Upstate New York. In Vermont, approximately 11% of children, grades 8 through 12 are overweight and an additional 15% are at risk for being overweight (VDH, 2006b). The prevalence of overweight children aged 6 to 11 years is 18% in New York (DiNapoli, 2008). Healthy Vermonters' 2010 goals are to reduce the percentage of youth who are overweight to 5% from the reported 11% in 2003 by encouraging health-promoting behaviors (VDH, 2006a).

Ethical Considerations

Permission to conduct this study was obtained from the institutional review board (IRB) of the author's degree program. Customary procedures were followed to enable participants to ask questions, be assured of confidentiality, and select a pseudonym. With the exception of identifiers, all data, field notes, and personal notes were transcribed verbatim and entered into password-encrypted qualitative software data manager program, NVivo 8 (QSR International, 2008). The importance of confidentiality and securing the audiotapes and transcribed notes was reviewed with each transcriptionist. Both transcriptionists read and signed a confidentiality agreement to ensure the confidentiality of all informants and the data accessed through transcribing audiotapes.

Participants

Inclusion Criteria

The inclusion criteria for study participation consisted of English-speaking adults older than the age of 18, of either gender, who assumed the active role of parent or guardian and was responsible for the primary needs of the child, 9 to 14 years old, who was biological, adopted, or under guardianship for greater than 1 year. Eligible participants self-reported child height and weight measurements. Calculated BMI was used to classify weight status according to the IOTF cut points for overweight or obese (Lobstein & Jackson-Leach, 2007).

Recruitment

Participants were recruited initially through advertisements in the public domain and purposeful sampling from colleague referrals and known contacts of the principal investigator. Study fliers were posted in common areas such as primary care and specialty care health clinics, banks, grocery stores, and in other areas freely accessible to the public. Colleague referrals were initiated by means of individual distribution of study fliers to interested individuals. Participant recruitment occurred over a 9-month time period and proved more difficult than anticipated. Consequently, after 6 months the investigator sought approval from the IRB to enhance recruitment by advertising in regional newspapers and similar publications, which provided the remainder of participants necessary for the completion of the study. During this time, subsequent sampling methods included word of mouth.

Consistent with grounded theory methods, theoretical sampling was implemented as data analysis revealed avenues of inquiry requiring further exploration and investigation (Corbin & Strauss, 2008; Strauss & Corbin, 1998). Fathers were particularly difficult to enroll. Access to this population occurred primarily through snowball sampling of mother participants. Interested fathers contacted the investigator directly. At no time during data collection was third-party contact information obtained or sought. Self-identified willing participants contacted the investigator by phone or e-mail.

Individual interviews were scheduled at a comfortable location agreeable to both the investigator and the participant. Two interviews were conducted by phone. Three participants preferred to be interviewed in their homes. The remaining participants were interviewed in public areas such as a coffee shop or library.

Interviews lasted approximately 20 to 90 minutes and occurred on only one session. Only one couple was interviewed together; the remaining participants were interviewed on separate occasions. A $20 honorarium was given at the conclusion of the interview as a token of appreciation for participant time, travel, and assistance with the study. The honorarium was mailed to phone participants following the completion of the phone interview the following day. A follow-up e-mail 1 week later was sent to confirm receipt.

Data Collection

The interview began with the collection of demographic information about the participant, the child, and the child's father. To capture the richness and complexity of the parenting experience, several open-ended, semi-structured questions were posed to guide individual interviews. Each interview began with the question, "How did you come to realize your child was overweight?" and continued from there. This was a flexible interview guide, and questions varied in relation to the participant's responses. During the process of interviewing, data generation, and data analysis, supplementary interview questions were required for further exploration or to support or explain evolving concepts, themes, and linkages (Corbin & Strauss, 2008; Strauss & Corbin, 1998). As data collection continued and gaps in data emerged or concepts reached proper density, theoretical analysis determined further inquiry.

Additional data included memoing, journaling, field notes, and other personal or theoretical notes by the principal investigator throughout the course of the study. These observations, ideas, and thoughts served to enhance the self-awareness of the principal investigator and her potential biases and identify nonverbal behavior in which meaning was transmitted. Two of the study participants who voluntarily came forth received their health care from the investigator. On these occasions, the investigator gave additional assurances to the participants that their thoughts, recollections, beliefs, and ideas would not impinge on the HCP–patient relationship. All attempts were made by the investigator to remove any perceived power imbalance by the participant. Care was taken to "bracket" personal feelings and reflection to ensure the investigator could objectively search out and understand their world without judgment and preconceptions (Hutchinson & Skodol-Wilson, 2001).

Data Analysis

Consistent with grounded theory methodology, data were continually coded and analyzed beginning with the onset of data collection. Ongoing exploration through comparative analysis provided direction and guidance until saturation was achieved. Strauss and Corbin's (Corbin & Strauss, 2008; Strauss & Corbin, 1998) paradigm model of data analysis allowed for coding categories and properties, which allow substantive and theoretical codes to emerge, causal conditions to be revealed, and context to be described. The investigator continually searched the data for meaningful "dimensions, phrases, properties, strategies, consequences, and contexts of behavior"

(Hutchinson & Skodol-Wilson, 2001, p. 217). With increasingly higher levels of abstraction, the core basic social process (BSP) was revealed within the participant's words (Glaser, 1978, 1992, 1998; Strauss & Corbin, 1998). For this study, saturation was reached by interview 13. The data collection process continued for an additional four interviews to ensure broad, dense, core concepts, tightly linked relationships, and theoretical parsimony. With assistance from the dissertation committee, the criteria for judging conceptual description and theory were based on Strauss and Corbin's (Corbin & Strauss, 2008; Strauss & Corbin, 1998) scholarly view of reproducibility, generalizability, and the adequacy of the research process.

Rigor

Qualitative methods are no less rigorous than those employed in quantitative research. The positivistic concept of reliability and validity requires reconceptualization in qualitative methodologies. Lincoln and Guba (1985) redefine the means of judging rigor to be more congruent with the naturalistic paradigm. Reliability or "consistency" is rather inherent in qualitative methods and more specifically in grounded theory. Through constant comparative methods of data analysis, the data were consistently and systematically reviewed for themes and patterns (Creswell, 2003). Contrary cases and unusual conditions or occurrences were investigated, explored, and described enhancing the reliability throughout the research process (Hutchinson & Skodol-Wilson, 2001).

Trustworthiness of the study was based on two methods outlined by Lincoln and Guba (1985), member checking and audit trails. Member checking was both formal and informal. During data collection, participants were asked to correct errors of fact or interpretation during the interview process. This form of informal member checking allowed the principal investigator immediate validity of categories, interpretations, and constructions as the data evolved. As further information was obtained, data were confirmed, and clarifications were made. At the completion of data collection, participants were sent a copy of the theoretical model and requested to freely comment on its explanatory power and truthfulness. Participants were asked whether the theoretical model explained the how, what, and why of promoting health for their overweight or obese child and what were the relevant contextual factors in doing so. This served as the method of formal member checking in addition to expert checking by the dissertation committee (Green, Creswell, Shope, & Clark, 2007). Each provided complementary avenues of establishing trustworthiness for this study.

Confirmability or credibility was achieved through audit trails as defined by Lincoln and Guba (1985). This procedure allowed a systematic and, at times, a reiterative review of the research process from infancy to completion. Research events, personal writings in the form of memos and journaling, interviews, and field notes were logged chronologically whereby the analytic decision-making processes were externally verified by the dissertation committee (Green et al., 2007).

Although Strauss and Corbin (1998) do not outline criteria for evaluating theory genesis in grounded theory, they do provide a criterion for judging the empirical grounding of a research study. During the research process and theory development, the following questions were utilized to ensure such findings were from the voice of the informant and grounded within the data. They were:

- Are the concepts generated from the study itself?
- Have linkages been made between concepts and are they systematically related?
- Are there tight linkages between concepts and significant density within the categories?
- Is variation inherent within the theory?
- Can this variation be explained, given the conditions set forth?
- Has the process been accounted for?
- Are the theoretical foundations significant?
- Will the theory be parsimonious and withstand ardent and scholarly critique while directing further avenues of inquiry?

FINDINGS

Study Participants

Interviews with 17 parents provided extensive data from which the investigator was able to construct a substantive theoretical process grounded in the participant's words, thoughts, and beliefs. Three participants from a previous unpublished mini-study conducted from July to November of 2008 were enrolled into the larger study conducted from March to December of 2009. Of the 17 participants, all were self-identified as Caucasian, three women were single parents, and the remaining 14 parents were married or identified a significant partner. All male participants ($n = 4$) were married to women who participated in the study. Three of four married couples were interviewed individually by choice. Only one married couple preferred to be interviewed together. One participant was a grandparent but met inclusion study criteria fulfilling the parenting role of the child. Nine participants were obese, three were overweight, and five were of normal weight as defined by the Centers for Disease Control and Prevention (Lobstein & Jackson-Leach, 2007).

Study participant children's ages ranged from 9 to 14 years old. All but two children (n = 13) were classified as obese according to IOTF definitions. However, the remaining two children met the criteria for overweight status and were just below the 95 BMI percentile cut point for clinical obesity (Lobstein & Jackson-Leach, 2007).

There was wide variation among participant-reported child at-risk behaviors such as consumption of sugar-sweetened beverages such as soda, sports drinks, and other sugar-laden beverages and screen time (computer, television, and video games). Only three children were taking medications. Of these three children, one girl was taking cholesterol and thyroid medication related to her obesity. The other two children were taking inhaled steroids and stimulants as treatment for their asthma and attention deficit hyperactivity disorder, respectively. Reported partner weight was that of the child's parent regardless of biology. Certain demographic data and characteristics from participants in the mini-study (n = 3) were not collected altering the total number of data collected for specific characteristics.

Framework for Coding, Analysis, and Theory Development

Open Coding

The analytic process began with the first interview using the method of open coding. Open coding is a technique for breaking open the data to identify, define, and develop categories through their properties and dimensions representing the phenomena under study. This type of microanalysis breaks down the data into discrete fragments, which allows the investigator to "uncover, name, and develop concepts" (Strauss & Corbin, 1998, p. 102) and provides for closer inspection. Data are analyzed for similarities and differences. Key events, terms, concepts, and themes are identified from deep within the data. For example, the concept of comfort was identified early and frequently in data collection by participants to describe comfort eating, a process of eating either by themselves or by their child to feel better emotionally. Through continual open coding and comparative analysis, the concept of comfort expanded to include multiple properties and dimensions such as eating for comfort, taking comfort in friends, finding comfort in oversized clothing, comfortable habits, comfort by proxy, and comfort in their surroundings. Worry was identified in the first interview and in each subsequent interview during data collection. Through open coding, several properties, such as the worry for current health, future health, self-esteem, and public perception were identified. There was broad dimensional variation ranging from "I worry all the time" and "I worry about what people will think" to "I worry about 4 to 5 years from now" and "we are just dodging a bullet" or "it can't be good for her heart." Open coding allowed the investigator full exploration into the theme of worry and how it varied among participants and within subcategories.

The process of open coding revealed numerous codes that represented key elements, concepts, or data fragments the investigator discovered during data analysis. To ensure grounding of data in the words of the participants, in vivo codes were maximized. In vivo coding involves using the words of the participant to identify fragments of data to "preserve participants' meanings of their views and actions" (Weiner, 2007, p. 303). For example, the code identified as the turtle effect was used by a father to describe the physical act of shrinking back into the self that his daughter does when he tells her to stop eating because of her weight.

Co-occurrent with the onset of open coding, the investigator initiated memo writing. Early memo construction allowed the investigator to capture novel thoughts, emerging ideas and relationships, and future areas of exploration as data collection continued. The process of coding through line-by-line analysis continued until no new categories emerged and rich density of their properties and dimensions was achieved.

Axial Coding

Axial coding is "the process of relating categories to their subcategories" (Strauss & Corbin, 1998, p. 123). During axial coding, the data are analyzed for structure and process. Linkages between concepts at the level of properties and dimensions are made by examining, comparing, and contrasting data for their preconditions, context, action strategies, and consequences in which a category or phenomenon is situated. This is a crucial step in theory development as it allows the investigator to discover how concepts and categories relate to one another (Corbin & Strauss, 2008; Strauss & Corbin, 1998) and reassembles the fractured data during earlier analysis adding richness, depth, and structure to emerging concepts and categories (Charmez, 2006).

An example of axial coding can be seen using the in vivo code of "food police" that became apparent early in data collection. Several participants acted like the food police, to describe their negative feelings associated with strict or "police-like" moderating, monitoring, and/or saying no to their children's choice or quantity of food and/or their eating patterns. Food police was closely linked with several other identified categories and/or concepts. Categories such as worry, overweight awareness, health status, and the child's relationship with food directly impacted the dimensional range of the food police. Parents who demonstrated more worry, greater awareness of their child's weight status and dysfunctional eating patterns, and/or concerns for their child's current health were more likely to engage in food police such as "moderating everything," "taking stuff away," considering a "lock box," "[getting] rid of candy and chips," and "avoid[ing] crap in the house." Consequences of these actions resulted in altering the availability and access of enticing foods and thereby changing the diet to healthier foods or minimizing consumption of nonnutritious foods. Food police served as an action strategy for making change. Refinement and revision of concepts and categories and their linkages continued throughout analysis by means of ongoing investigator reflective journaling and memo writing until theoretical saturation was achieved.

Selective Coding

Selective coding represented the final stage of analysis whereby categories have achieved maximum density and the investigator turns to the process of "integrating and refining" categories, thereby achieving increased levels of abstraction in the form of core process concepts. It is these core process concepts that serve as the foundation for theory construction and development (Strauss & Corbin, 1998). In the final analysis, five core process concepts were identified and used as the basis for theory construction. They were discovery, taking the lead, making change, engagement, and teamwork. Each core process concept was dense in the data, parsimonious, and grounded in the words of the participant. Parental buy-in, parental worry, finding the hook, and creating the gel were the core process linking concepts that moved the parent toward the basic social process of making change. These processes were dynamic, fluid, and clearly dependent on the contextual elements. In sum, the core process concepts, core process linking concepts, and contextual elements formed the substantive theory, the pathway to making change.

THE SUBSTANTIAL THEORY: PATHWAY TO MAKING CHANGE

The remainder of this chapter presents an abbreviated discussion of the theoretical model, the pathway to making change, its concepts, processes, relationships, and contextual conditions. Because this chapter is derived from a full dissertation and it is not possible to include all the findings and discussion, readers who wish to read the entire study are referred to the dissertation (Laurent & Zoucha, 2014). The theory is presented as a model with quotes that illustrate the concepts. Table 4.1 presents the model.

Methodological Position of Symbolic Interactionism on Data Analysis and Theory Development

The philosophical premise of symbolic interactionism places the symbol as the heart of social interaction. The symbol constitutes a social object used to represent what individuals, groups, and society agree it shall represent. The symbol conveys held meanings. It is our guide to what we see, what we notice, how we interpret, how we define, and, finally, how we act. Symbolic interactionism contends that humans are active participants in their world and by nature are influenced by the environment around them. Humans think, define, are influenced by past experiences, and make decisions based on perceptions within the immediate situation. This process is in a continual state of unfolding and accounts for the uniquen, dynamic, and unpredictability of human nature and interaction (Blumer, 1969; Charon, 2004). It highlights the complexity of human behavior when examining, describing, and interpreting interactions between persons and symbols.

During the research process, attention was given to the parent-held meaning of body shape as fatness and health. These two symbols of body shape and health influenced current and future decisions, actions, interactions, and ultimately the worldview of the parent. The overarching contextual conditions provided the investigator with an understanding of the variability of actions revealed during data analysis and the complexity that situations posed for parents as they promoted the health for their overweight or obese child.

Through this lens, symbolic interactionism guided the investigator in finding meaning in the life processes of participants involved within the context of their lived world (Blumer, 1969). These processes will be described in terms of its parts; yet they describe the wholeness of how parents make changes in relationship to their child's overweight or obesity.

Table 4.1 The Pathway to Making Change: The Relationship of Core Social Process Concepts and Their Linkages to Attributes and Data

Core Process Concept	Attributes of Core Process Concept	Linking Process Concept	Participants' Quotes
Discovery	Predisposition		*Some people have a genetic makeup where they can eat anything they want and their metabolism is just different.*
	Turning point		*I think that his weight really started coming on probably 4 to 5 years ago. And I think there was stress within our household and shortly after that we had to sell the house and move into an apartment…big factor in amount of weight he gained.*
	Husky build		*He's husky looking.* *A girl with curves.*
	Compared to others		*I'm heavy—she's insane—out of control.*
	Health care provider		*He pretty much only said, you know—he can't gain any more weight so that he can grow taller and grow out of it.* *I think he was like 110 or something—that is not okay—not even funny—just not safe—not healthy.*
Taking the lead	Mom's the boss		*My wife wears the pants around here.*
	Parental angst		*She's very self-conscious of her appearance. And it just breaks my heart. I do what I can to encourage her and reinforce all the positive aspects and how athletic and healthy and strong she is. But she sees in the mirror what she sees in the mirror.*
		Parental worry	*So I know in my mind that oh gosh, and you hear on TV you know how obese these kids are now. I'd much rather not have to deal with that. Life's hard enough…without the complications from that are so big.*

Making change	Strategies:	
	Food police	There was one day I caught her on her third bottle [of soda] and I… dumped it down the drain. You just wasted that—but you didn't need it and now it's gone.
	Active bodies	You've got to move your body. The more you move the healthier your body is.
	Role modeling	I try not to eat sweets later in the day and she knows that. She sees that.
	Hitting the media	It's still a big issue—a big issue. I've got a bias against TV anyways. I'd rather read a book. Although I do watch some TV. But my son is very much into watching TV.
	Barriers:	
	Competing demands	Sometimes…I can just say no…and then sometimes I'm just, you know the cat needs food, there's 9,000 other things going on and it's just like fine. Go. Whatever you want. Go get it. Eat. Fine.
	Come to me	I want him to be able to come to me when he decides that enough is enough and he wants to do more to lose the weight.
	Food intimacy	He is very much into the tactile. And I think food is another piece of that… you figure you're tasting it and you're smelling it—very stimulating.
	Shuts me down	Leave him alone. He's a kid.
	Finding the hook	Get the kid to buy into it.

(continued)

Table 4.1 *The Pathway to Making Change: The Relationship of Core Social Process Concepts and Their Linkages to Attributes and Data (continued)*

Core Process Concept	Attributes of Core Process Concept	Linking Process Concept	Participants' Quotes
Engagement	Motivating force		*She loves the library—she loves the horses. So I'm holding it out as, you can have those things but here's what you have to do—and she's open to that.*
	Influential peers		*She gave up [on boxing] and her friend was with her and she said, oh, I'm not going in there so she let her friend influence her.*
	Social and fun		*So my mom was trying to find something that was geared to kids. So she found a program for overweight kids. My daughter was gung ho for it—she had a ball at every meeting.*
		Creating the gel	*I'll say, are you going to play sports this year? And you know, if he says yes, then we'll make sure he has the tools to do it and the time.*

Teamwork	Balance and consistency	That's what I try to say to the kids—it's all about balance. It's all out there and I want it all but tomorrow's a new day. And if I didn't have apple pie today I had M&Ms and well, tomorrow I'll have apple pie.
	United front	So that way it's a little bit easier and they can't wear me down because I can say no, your mother and I have made an agreement. We've already decided.
	Supportive others	My mother and my mother-in-law support what I say about food. When I'll say to the kids, you're done—no matter whose table I'm sitting at, well, Mom says you're done...so I feel our extended families have been good.
	The anti-team	My husband's is not an approach that I think works...cause he just comes out and says things.
	Speed bump	I think it's made us step back and go, okay, we can do this better which will in turn help us and help her...another speed bump to get over.
	The whole package	I want her to feel comfortable in her body and who she is. I don't want her to be obsessive about her weight but I want her to be healthy and...not embarrassed...making sure she is happy deep down inside.

Overarching Contextual Conditions

To fully understand the phenomena of interest, one must describe the context and conditions under which the phenomena exist. Through use of the conditional/consequential matrix described by Strauss and Corbin (1998), this investigator was able to identify the micro- and macroconditions that affected and gave shape and meaning to the theoretical process. Microconditions are those conditions most immediately impacting the individual's involvement in the situation. Macroconditions are increasing social units represented by increasingly larger concentric circles moving outwardly around the individual evolving into macroconditions that may co-vary in numerous ways (Strauss & Corbin, 1998). The distinction between the two is artificial, and their influence is bidirectional (Corbin & Strauss, 2008). The following discusses how these conditions affect parents as they promote the health of their overweight or obese child.

Microconditions

Strauss and Corbin (1998) use the term microconditions to describe contextual elements that are "narrow in scope and possible impact" (p. 181). The investigator used this definition to describe contextual conditions at the level of the participant. Although the microconditions of the individual participant will be presented, the consequences related to these conditions are only narrow in definition in that they directly affect the action of making change within their microcosm. Ultimately, the consequences may indeed have far-reaching effects emphasizing the arbitrary line that separates microconditions from macroconditions.

Parental Style, Beliefs, and Upbringing
Consistent throughout the study were the participant's variations in approach to addressing their child's weight. Mothers and fathers used different styles, approaches, and techniques to make change and engage their child. Fathers approached making changes for their child as "black and white" and "fix it." It was simplistic and straightforward. Karen described her husband's approach:

> [His dad] is not as good at the educating part … just that you should not have cookies in the house, period. I shouldn't bring cookies home and shouldn't let [my son] have candy, you know. That kind of thing. [His dad] will say, William, you don't need that, you know. He is kind of like that with everything; it is more black and white for him.

Although this is through the lens of the mother, fathers confirmed they saw things differently as seen in the interview with Tom. He said:

There was one day I caught her on her third bottle [of soda] and I went and took it and dumped it down the drain. [My daughter said] you just wasted that. But [I said], you didn't need it. So, it's gone.

Despite the perspective of fathers to be more simplistic and straightforward, their actions were construed as more permissive by themselves and by mothers during a father–child interaction. Fathers were more likely to "give in" to their child, be a "pushover," the "weak link," resort to "bribery," "be inconsistent," and/or "buy affections" when compared to mothers. Fathers and male partners (i.e., fiancé or boyfriend) of mothers within the household were more likely to defer to the child's mother when it came to the ultimate decision-making process. For example, Mark stated, "My wife wears the pants around here, I guess, for lack of a better term." Similarly, fathers and mothers alike described moms as "the boss."

Parenting styles with mothers were more likely to approach and engage in making change through open dialogue, negotiating, and educating their child with regard to making better choices. Mothers presented an open dialogue as seen with Kammie and her daughter, "If you want a snack, you have to … let's talk about it and we'll make a choice about what is an appropriate snack for this time of day." Sharyl described her approach as a parent:

[We] just talk about, I guess education about, I guess it's like nutrition. Cause he will ask me, you know, how do I know whether to choose this or this and I'll try to help him with making good food choices.

Mothers were less likely to use directives, mandates, and bribery to effect change or engage their child. For several parents, their early experiences with food affected their attitudes toward food for their children. Growing up hungry or deprived made them less likely to moderate or restrict their child's food habits. For Anna, this played a large role in her ability to moderate her son's intake. She said:

Well my feeling is, if the kid is hungry, he's going to have something, whether it be an apple or an orange or a Twinkie. Because I don't always have apples and oranges or apples and bananas or whatever. I don't always have it. And—and I don't always have the Twinkies. But if they want something to tide them over for the next hour and a half, then they're going to get something because I grew up very hungry a lot of the time. And my kids are going to eat whether it's mealtime or it's not mealtime.

For Kammie, her childhood experiences with the strictness of her parents affected what foods she had in the house.

> Like [when] I grew up—my parents were very strict and we didn't have a lot of junk in the house and I remember like going to people's houses and being like obsessed with having a snack. And like, let's have a snack now, because I knew that they had—their parents bought chips and—you know, cookies and stuff that my mother wouldn't buy. And I was—when I had my own children, I'm like, I am not going to have the kid that comes to a play date and begs for food. Because—and I do think it comes from feeling deprived.

The interweaving of parenting styles, beliefs, and upbringing of the parent created and informed their perspective and provided the backdrop for subsequent decisions and actions made while pursuing change for their child.

Child Attributes

Equally important as the parental characteristics, are the native characteristics that the child brings to any interaction. Although parents, by definition, exert some type of control over their child, they are to an extent limited and influenced by the child's attributes, preferences, and wants. Parents described the nature of their child as being "difficult," "stubborn," "independent," "frustrating," or "strong-minded" while others described their child as "a pleasure," "he is a great kid," or "she makes it easy." For example, Alex portrayed his son as "frustrating as he simply will not do anything." In contrast, Peggy's daughter "is a pleasure. She is very easygoing." Parents who felt their children presented a more challenging disposition posed additional accommodations and, at times, barriers. Joyce described her daughter as "angry, she's irritable, and then the next minute she's the sweetest little thing. She loves me." These traits directly impacted their ability to make change, to engage their child, and to create teamwork.

Macroconditions

Strauss and Corbin (1998) define macroconditions as conditions "which are broad in scope and possible impact" (p. 181). Sociocultural norms and values, stigma, community and environment, economics, and the school system were identified as overarching global conditions affecting the process of making change for study participants.

Sociocultural Norms and Values

Cultural norms are behavior patterns, values, beliefs, and attitudes that are strongly ingrained in an individual's daily life. As a whole, these values and beliefs define the rules of society (Gardiner & Kosmitzki, 2005). They exist in the subconscious of everyday life and influence the actions and interactions of all individuals by affecting their perspective toward life. This perspective guides our social interaction within our self and among others (Charon, 2004). Within U.S. society, the mother has traditionally been the primary caregiver to the child. The mother cares for, rears, and educates the child, limiting the father's parental role. The findings from this study suggest that mothers assume the majority of the responsibility in two-parent households and all the responsibility in single-parent households. Mothers related, "[Dad] is just kind of there" or it is "mostly mom" when it comes to parenting decisions. Tom provided an example of this by bringing his wife to the interview since "she was the boss" when it came to addressing his daughter's weight. The context within these norms placed mom as the lead parent in the process of making change for each participant.

Within our culture, the symbol of the body is strongly linked to the internal characteristics of the person within (Reischer & Koo, 2004). Western societies have transmitted the cultural value of physical attractiveness based on body shape early in childhood. Individuals who are identified as thin are seen as nice, well liked, kind, and friendly (Feldman, Feldman, & Goodman, 1988). In contrast, individuals who are identified as fat are seen as lazy, cheaters, liars, and friendless (Feldman et al., 1988; Hill & Silver, 1995). The parental concern over the potential stigma faced by their child was of great concern and worry to participants. Mark related his concerns:

> I remember I had a date to the prom when I was in high school. It was a woman in our class who kind of—befriended me a lot. She just kind of flirted and, whatever, with me. She was about 300 pounds and she wasn't going to the prom. So I invited her to go. And I just feel—I felt bad for her. I don't want my daughter to be that way.

Other parents shared similar concerns. Barb

> thinks socially [it's] hard, because I think that you get a different sort of attention when you're obese. You know, you tend to be made fun of. I think there's a stigma.

Joyce further described the negative stereotype of fatness.

> I'm an adult, she's a child. So I can take the name calling from other people when I was heavier. When I was walking—whatever—oh, fat beeatch—you know people are cruel. But now she's only 13 and she goes to school and she gets it.

The value of thinness and the stigma of fatness that follows were found in children as well as parents. Parents described their children as associating fatness with stupidity and ugliness. This was evident in the following examples of what participants' children would say to them: "I'm fat. I'm ugly," "I'm fat. I'm stupid," "I'm fat and I look so terrible in this," and "You don't know what it's like to be fat." The pervasive overarching stigma attached to fatness, given the societal value on thinness, created worry and motivation toward change by the parent and, to a lesser extent, the child. This macrocondition served as the basis for worry and subsequent action on behalf of the parent.

Feeding practices and attitudes are learned and perpetuated within the environmental context of the culture in which one is reared (Gable & Lutz, 2000; Gardiner & Kosmitzki, 2005). Food plays a large role in defining family roles, rules, and traditions. It gives meaning to our social interactions. In this study, the role of food as a vital part of social interactions was apparent. Charlie was raised in an Italian family and the role of food can be seen in the following excerpt:

> I'm half Italian and basically my family was raised in an Italian environment, so food was always the necessity with everything. You don't feel good? Let's have something to eat. Somebody dies, let's have something to eat. Somebody gets married. Have something to eat. Try to at least finish your plate.

Heritage was only part of the influence on food culture. Parents described the context of social gatherings with food at the heart of the gathering. Cate said:

> [My son] went to a Halloween party last weekend and I watched as the mom had all the little sausage hot dogs and wrapped them in the blankets and brought out just like a tub of them and he came home and said, aw they were soooo good, I ate so many. It's frustrating, but I understand it. I . . . I understand being in that social situation and maybe not making the right choices.

Sharyl described a similar time with her son. She said:

> He'll go to a birthday party which I was at one time and his friends all
> had like four, five pieces of pizza dipped in ranch dressing, you know,
> I mean horrible stuff and, you know, I don't want him to be excluded
> from that kind of thing.

The belief that food is part of the social interaction posed a barrier to
making changes and promoting health for parents. The social gathering was
a mechanism for eating foods that would have otherwise been moderated.
For example, Marks described eating at his in-laws.

> Mark (M): [T]he kids' grandfather makes crepes and they're just
> spectacular. And they go there and he brags about how
> much each of them they've eaten—how many. He takes
> great pride in that....
>
> Investigator: Have you ever tried talking to them?
>
> M: I've considered it, but then again as I said earlier, they
> just take such great pride in how they cook and what
> they cook and how much the kids devour, and so I would
> struggle with popping that bubble.

Food, food choice, and the contextual condition of food in our society
and culture exerted strong influence on the parents and children. There was a
preconceived expectation on behalf of both parent and child of eating, eating
more, and eating more calorie-dense foods in social gatherings.

Community and Environment

The vast landscape of rural Vermont places small towns without a central-
ized community. There is no public transportation throughout much of the
state, and towns do not share fiscal responsibility for community resources to
a large extent. Community centers were either not easily accessible or available to parents. The physical environment played a variable role with regard
to the ability of children to be active. For example, Cate described her living
environment.

> It is right on the road and there is backdrop off to the river so there was
> not a lot of room to be outdoors ... um ... and we had two dogs at that
> point that ... that are different than the ones we have right now and to
> take them out for a walk meant putting them on a leash and there is a

certain little area that we could go into, so it wasn't like [my son] could go out and play with the dogs. You walked the dog and then you go back in.

There were no community resources available, which impacted the activity level of her and her son.

[T]here's not a real sense of community getting together and doing things. I don't know if that's because we're now out towards [the country] ... I don't know if the city is ... it's when he was grade school it seemed like there were a lot more things like that going on.

In contrast, Kylie and Charlie used the local community club as a means for spending time together and being active.

The kids like the different programs that they have there. They have like the queen room and the different little kids' rooms plus the gym time and the kids just really enjoy going there, really enjoy going to the one room where they have that dance thing where you have to do the steps. And [my daughter will] do that for like an hour, just doing the dance and that. And it's just they really like it, so it's something that they like. And they like going swimming at different times.

Parents living in suburban environments faced other barriers. For example, bicycling on the city streets presented safety concerns for their children. Kylie stated:

I've had to—you know, like ride around with my kids a lot and really focus on the idea that you may think other people see you—never, ever assume that they do. You need to be a very defensive bike rider.

The climate affected the activity level of children. The cold, long winters were hard for several parents. Kathy found "winters a bad time for us ... we tend to stay in more." Barb was concerned that "[She doesn't] know once the snow flies, whether we'll be able to get him [my son] outside." Charlie found summers easier to maintain his daughter's weight. He said:

Summers prove to be easy for being able to maintain on the lighter side with our kids. It's because they're just out and about and so much more active. As it gets colder, like now and going into the winter, you know, there's only—there's less and less activities that they can stay [in for].

The impact of the environment and community was variable among participants. From a global aspect, the type of environment in their lived world and/or the community resources available to the parents in this study affected their ability to promote physical activity.

Economics

The socioeconomic circumstances of the participants in this study were diverse. All but five participants described financial concerns with regard to healthy eating for their child. Foods such as fruits and vegetables were "more expensive," "didn't last," and didn't "fill them up." Single-parent households were more affected by financial hardship than two-parent households. For example, Joyce received government assistance and food stamps in which:

[She] gets $200 [worth of] food stamps a month to feed four people.

[My son] weighs 225 pounds, almost 230. He's a football player. He's big. [My other son]. My daughter. And me. And the food—in the middle of the month, I'll be going to Food Cupboard … when I don't have— run out of food. They give you what they give you. You know. Canned goods. Yeah, you can't pick and choose. It's canned goods. Some of them are outdated. They give you what they got, which is usually canned goods, a half-dozen eggs, rice, a thing of juice, and a little sausage if they have sausage. That's it. Scraping and struggling.

Other parents described similar concerns. Peggy felt "it's difficult just to, financially to eat healthier, you know. You can't, you don't have a lot of choices." If finances were not a concern, Kathy "would probably buy more of like the fresh fruits and vegetables and things like that, and less of the filler kind of stuff." Financial concerns were not restricted to food. Cate, a single mother, expressed the financial toll of many activities and sports for her child. For example, she said "Like the jujitsu is ten dollars a session … and … there's just, there are a lot of expenses if you want to go out and do a sport." She goes on to say:

I would love to be able to spend three or four hundred dollars and say, okay, we have this membership … and we're only to use … two of the things. And, you know, we may go once a week, we may go every couple of weeks. But to me we should just be walking if that's all we can really afford.

Two-parent homes were more likely to express generalized financial strain. Barb and Alex described, "added expenses" while Mark felt financially "it's stressful." Although Barb and Mark did not explicitly describe the financial concerns over foods and activities, there were financial strains that were taking a toll on the family economics as a whole.

School System
All the participants in this study, with the exception of Charlie and Kylie, whose daughter was homeschooled, had children in the public school system. Parental control was lessened to a great extent during school hours. The majority of parents found the schools posed a barrier to healthy eating. Barb found her son was able to "buy ice cream and Gatorade." Joyce reported her daughter had free access to "snack machines" and found her daughter ate "pizza every day." Anna described her son's possible lunches of "hotdogs," "cheeseburgers," "bags of chips," and "they have lots of desserts, big choices of desserts." Cate said her son would "come home and tell me he had a couple of hot dogs for lunch or he had a hamburger or nuggets." Julie spoke of her daughter's school as providing "greasy pizza," "burgers and chicken nuggets." Karen's son's school served similar items to the other children but moderated the portion size to be "healthy." She found this somewhat hypocritical:

> For the most part they are small portions so I am not too concerned about them. The only thing I don't like is that they preach healthy snacks and stuff. They don't want you send any chips to school, but every morning they have egg and cheese McMuffins or sausage and egg and cheese McMuffins every morning or muffins … and that's all they offer so he has that more than I would like him to have.

Participants consistently and clearly defined the healthy school lunch as the "salad bar." While some children had free access to the salad bar, others had to request a salad over the other lunches available. At Tom's daughter's school, this was a "numbers game." He explained:

> It's all this numbers game. They make a certain number of plates of salad for the first lunch; kids [get] "x" number. The second lunch kids [get] "x" number. So, if you want a salad today and you are the 57th person in line and they had 10 for your lunch there is a good chance you don't have salad for your lunch.

The only parent who felt her child was receiving a healthy lunch was Kathy. She said, "I think the lunches they give are pretty healthy, lots of vegetables and lower fat foods, really nice stuff." Alex had less of a concern since:

It came about the past 2 or 3 years we've eventually stripped them of selling soda, Powerade. So now it has to be nutritional food, water. So they lost that part and I think they're striving for any meals that are offered by the school to have nutritional value. And I believe candy may have also been eliminated as well.

Although most children had access to healthier choices such as the salad bar, the child chose what they ate. The parents were forced to step back and allow their child to make the choice. For example, Barb said,

They do have ice cream there and we don't send money in for ice cream. The money he took last week, I guess he told the school counselor that he was going to get some chips and some ice cream.

When Charlie's daughter was in public school, he found,

The kids would go in, and if they were given the freedom to take—buy what they want, they would buy just the snacks. And a couple of times we found out that, that's indeed what was going on.

Despite the concern by parents over the school lunches, several of the participants felt that schools were increasingly more health conscious. The parents who described this experience tended to have younger children who attended elementary school. For example, Kammie said:

I think they've done a great job in the schools as far as doing the best they can to push—to push healthy lifestyle.... Like sometimes at school they'll send home, you know, a chart like the five food groups. And this week, write every day the food groups that you [eat]—[my daughter] loves doing that stuff . . . [S]he'll take it out and, okay, you know, and an orange is one serving—she wants to figure out what—it's sort of just an awareness thing for schools to do. And she will do it. She wants to do it.

Karen described her school's approach to increasing physical activity:

[The school is] very, very health conscious. They have a, you know, health class. They promote walking to school. They have all these like little walk to school week, bike to school week. This is health week so bring your green vegetable. They are very, are always kind of reiterating it, you know, all year long really they have different [themes]. Jump rope for heart and who can jump … and they promote healthy eating. They send home notes saying, you know, this is a new recipe for some healthy granola mix or something and in the school newspaper every week is a healthy recipe. They send home notes, you know, just a generic note with a list of carrot sticks, cheese sticks, what's healthy for snacks in case some of [the parents] didn't know or whatever.

Sharyl, the mother of a middle school boy, noted that:

The school is, you know, they are all sort of becoming more aware of keeping kids healthy I think. Because this obesity is sort of an epidemic now so and that way it helped because as a whole I think schools were trying to make lunches healthier. I know when it first started in his school, they were offering, you know, [the] second helping.

Summary

The importance of the contextual conditions cannot be disregarded. The underpinning and interweaving of the micro- and macroconditions provided for a dynamic, fluid, and complex context for the process of making change. The overarching contextual conditions deepen and intensify the complexity as parents set forth on their goal. They were required to balance their actions within these contextual conditions as the prelude unfolds and evolves.

Core Concept: Discovery

All the participants in this study were aware their child was overweight when interviewed. These findings represent a retrospective look at how they came about knowing their child was overweight and what may have contributed to their child's weight gain. Together five subcategories were identified as attributes to the core category of discovery. They were predisposition, husky build, comparing to others, turning point, and HCP. During the discovery process, each of the subcategories served as a means of increasing parental awareness and, ultimately, confirmed that their child was truly overweight. For some parents this was a gradual process; for others, it was a sudden awakening. The interplay among the subcategories was widely variable for each participant. In certain circumstances these categories overlap, attesting to the complexity involved.

Predisposition

Most parents felt strongly there was some type of predisposition for their child being overweight or obese. Frequently cited was the role of genetics in both biological and adoptive parents. Biological parents talked about how their children looked like them growing up. For example, Kammie said, "I mean both my husband and I were short, pudgy kids. I mean I remember it was like right before I started my period that I like did that stretch out." For some parents, this was reassuring as they grew out of their own overweight body. For other parents, there was guilt associated with passing along non-desirable attributes. Sharyl compared her son and husband, "You can see his whole body is like my husband's." She spoke of her husband as saying, "Oh, he probably got that from me."

Family history was cited by several parents as placing their child at risk for weight gain and being overweight. For Kathy, "The whole family has a problem with it." Sharyl's husband's side "tends to have some obesity in it." Adoptive parents, Peggy, Kylie, and Charlie were more likely than biological parents to attribute a genetic predisposition to being overweight or obese. Adoptive parent, Peggy, felt:

> [Her daughter] may be predisposed in that she is going to be a big solid person. Because you can see it physically in her maternal uncles. Her birth mother at 5'11" is the shortest in her family. They are all over 6 feet …. Well, they're built like brick shithouses.

Kylie shared a similar view, "All our kids come from families that are very heavy. All of our children are thinner than they would probably be if they were with their birth families. Our younger daughter, her birth mother is probably 300 pounds." Charlie verified his wife's thoughts in a separate interview.

> She's very, very similar in that her [biological] mom was only about that much taller than what [my daughter] is now. And like I said, from the time we knew her, [her biological mother] never was thin. She fluctuated from being chubby to being fat, or overweight. I don't know how you want to put it.

Serena, the only grandmother interviewed, felt that even under the best circumstances her granddaughter was not going to be thin or of "normal weight." She described her as "10 [pounds] 2 [ounces] when she was born … So she was born a big—she started out her life as a big child." This was similar for Sara in that her child "was chunky back then [meaning 4 or 5 years old]" and Kammie described her daughter as "always be[ing] chubby, really since a toddler."

Collectively, parents identified different attributes that predisposed their child to being overweight or obese. Genetics and family history were the most common factors, although not the sole contributors to being overweight. As parents reflected on the reasons for their child's weight problems, they sifted through various possible factors that led to this problem thus giving them confirmation to their conclusions.

Turning Point

Most parents identified a time period in which they noticed their child's weight gain. For the majority of parents, this was a time of stress within the household or a difficult transition for their child. The age at which this occurred varied widely among participants and could not be attributed to any particular developmental period (i.e., puberty) in the child's life. Only Serena and Kylie felt that puberty "ha[d] made a difference increasing her weight" or had made it more noticeable. For Tom, Julie, and Anna, the transition from one school to another marked a period of stress and weight gain for their child. Julie and Tom described the transition to sixth grade as the time that contributed to their daughter's weight gain.

> [Our daughters] were in a different school. She went there in what third grade? They switched schools, so then there was the merging of the, you know, the two schools. Then the ones she was friends with since [then], you know, since preschool, they weren't necessarily best friends down there [at the new school]. Sixth grade was rough on her down there … in a social way.

Anna identified a similar time for her son.

> Well [my son] does have a speech impediment where sometimes he gets talking really, really fast and you can't understand a word he's saying. And he used to get picked on a lot by that, especially when he first went to the middle school. Because all the kids growing up through kindergarten all could understand him or say well, Bill, you just need to repeat that. And when he got to the middle school, not—they mixed in with the rest of the surrounding schools, children—And they didn't know to tell Bill to slow down. So he had to relearn that all on his own because he didn't have that reminder. But—so I think he just—I don't know—decided instead of talking, I'll eat.

For Alex, the period of his son's weight gain was less concrete but was in part due to increasing trouble at school and behavioral problems. Alex "[thought] there was some correlation or relation to what's been going on with regard to behavior issues at school [the past 1 or 2 years]."

A few parents cited a particular critical event within the household that contributed to their child's weight gain. Sara thought:

> It had to do with when [her daughter] was little, my dad was sick and the one thing he could not stand was her crying. That would set him off. That would upset him. I could bawl my eyes out and it had no effect. But if she was crying, forget it. He'd be like stressed out. So we would—if Alice wanted a candy bar, Alice got a candy bar. Because it wasn't worth—we were trying very hard not to stress my father out, so we knew that her being upset, upset him. So therefore, Alice became an extremely spoiled brat. If she wanted something, she got it.

The death of Sharyl's mother was the turning point whereby her son gained a disproportionate amount of weight. Sharyl felt that she was not available to her son and therefore was neither watching nor aware of what was going on with his weight. She said:

> It was the summer my mom died. He gained 14 pounds that summer. He spent a lot of time not with me. He was with my in-laws because I was at the hospital most of the summer and I, I didn't even see it until the end.

Peggy blamed her health as the source for "bad habits and weight gain." She found her child taking care of her and "not encouraging her [daughter] to be active because [Peggy] could not do it." Peggy went on to explain:

> A lot of this all happened at the same time when I was able, I got my new knees [from her joint replacement].... Because [my daughter] is very caring and has [been] taking care of me for many years because I was unable to get up and down the stairs to do things. She would get my ice packs for my knees and take care of me.

Joyce attributed family turmoil as a significant contributor for her daughter being overweight as seen in the following excerpt.

> Joyce (J):   [M]y husband was very abusive toward me and the kids. So we left and went to a shelter. [There was] a lot of moving around.

> Investigator (I):   And that was the time that you noticed [her weight gain]?

J: Mmmm.

I: What are your thoughts on how that contributed to her weight?

J: Um, the same as me. That's how I felt. I'm thinking, she doesn't—all of them don't express how they feel. They hold stuff in. That's why we're in family therapy right now trying to get—you know what I mean?—work on feelings. Because none of us say how we feel. We hide 'em. So trying to talk to her—she's just like I am. She's hurt. She's upset. And she eats the same way I did. All her patterns were just like me.

Many parents cited a distinct time period in which their child gained weight. Mark felt that his illness and health issues were the beginning of stress within the house. For Mark, there was a questioning of the impact something like his health could have on his daughter's weight. Although Kammie, Mark's wife, discussed this as a very stressful time she was unsure of the role this played in her daughter's weight gain but could not ignore it either.

The historical perspective of parents portrayed a vulnerable time period for children that contributed to weight gain and served as a source of awareness. The recollection of stress in the house whether gradual, abrupt, or persistent was a turning point that marked a different beginning, the onset of weight gain, and the difficult road to follow for study participants.

Husky Build

Throughout data collection, parents avoided using the words, overweight, obese, or fat to describe their child despite the awareness their child was overweight or obese. Descriptors such as "husky build," "chunky monkey," "man boobs," "a girl with curves," "potbelly," "chunky," "chubby," "big-boned," "pudgy," and "love handles" were used as refined or delicate ways parents described their children. The shape of the child served as a marker for the child's weight status for the majority of parents

For Karen, her son's "husky build" made her believe that he could have the "body stature that would put on weight easily." Similarly to Barb, Karen's son's body shape presented more of a questioning as if this actually could or would happen. She said, "He's really not fat. He is husky built, but he has the kind of protruding belly stance."

Sara described an incident while making clothing as providing an indicator of her child's body shape.

She was five [and] the dress that I made her was a size 10. And I was just like—of course, I had to alter it because it was too long. So I had to shorten it. But it was one of those, as I'm making this dress, going, no, you should not be this big. And then I thought, well, some of the other kids in her class were big, too. So I was like, okay, well, maybe it's not just me. You know. Or maybe it is just me. Maybe it's, you know—maybe the kids are big now.

Clothes shopping provided the awareness in which Julie realized her daughter had a weight problem.

Despite the polite circumlocutions attributed to the child's overweight body shape, no parent either identified or labeled his or her child as fat, overweight, or obese based solely on body habitus. The body shape served as an indicator but created more of a questioning stance for most parents. It presented a heightened awareness to the possibility their child was overweight or obese.

Joyce and Kylie provided contrary cases. Joyce described her daughter as "always [having] been thin, slender" and it was her shape that identified her daughter as having a weight problem. Joyce watched her daughter just "get bigger and bigger." For Kylie, her daughter's body shape led her to the belief her daughter was overweight. For these two parents, the body shape served as the predominant indicator of their child's weight status.

Comparing to Others

Many parents used comparison during the discovery process. Parents compared their children to the child's earlier years, siblings, peers, and themselves as they questioned the child's weight, searched for explanations as to why their child was overweight, or sought corroboration to whether or not their child was overweight or obese.

Several parents pointed out that their children were "skinny little kids," "used to be thin," or "had always been thin." The investigator discovered implicit meanings while listening to these participants. They conveyed a sense of wonder as to how and why their child was the one who gained weight. What followed was an ongoing comparative process between their overweight child and the child's siblings and/or the child's peers. For example, Sara questioned whether "maybe kids are bigger these days?" Frequently, parents compared one sibling's metabolism with that of the overweight child.

Parents compared body shapes of siblings. For the majority of the parents, this emphasized the possibility of their child being overweight. Anna described her son as "chunky around the middle and his twin brother is really thin. So it defines it more." Sara referred to her younger child as "skinny Minnie" and "having children who are polar opposites." Mark and Kammie both noted, in separate interviews, their younger daughter was thin and noticeably different than their overweight child. In contrast to this, Alex and Barb considered their other son too skinny, "you can see his ribs." Alex felt his "skinny" son needed to gain weight as compared to his overweight son. This was true for Karen. Here the body shape of her overweight child served to call parental attentions to the other son's thinness and to a lesser extent the overweight status of her child. Notably, these parents were clinically obese.

Parents with a single child used other comparative strategies. In the social setting, Sharyl compared her son's eating habits to that of his friends.

> Kolby will have two pieces [of pizza] tops. I mean the amount, it seems like the amount of food he eats is so much less and his, his activities is about the same, you know, I try to compare with other boys his age and, but yet … he's still overweight so what, you know, is it really genetics, you know, is there really nothing we can do?

Cate shared similar thoughts, "He has a lot of friends who are just, you know, 14 and skinny as a rail and they eat anything they want." The subcategory of comparing to others served a multitude of roles for parents. For some, it heightened the awareness their child was overweight. Yet for others, it was more an act of exploration, questioning, and/or searching that was integral to the process of discovery. Importantly, the investigator identified a palpable frustration and a sense of parental burden within this subcategory from which parental worry evolved.

Health Care Provider

The role of the HCP played a pivotal role in the discovery process for most parents. For several parents, the HCP confirmed the child as being overweight or obese. Kathy identified her child as being overweight merely from her HCP telling her so "because I trust her, and I trust her opinions." This was a terminating event and signaled the final event in the discovery process for many participants.

Parents described several ways in which their HCP discussed the weight of their child. The approach used by the HCP and the reaction by parents were worked out in various ways. For example, Kylie valued the directness of her HCP as validating what she already knew.

In contrast, both Sharyl and Julie described different experiences with the HCP's approach. They viewed the HCP as accusatory and that of casting blame. Sharyl described her interaction at her child's office visit.

> He was actually very mean. Well I felt like he was mean. Mean to me because he immediately … it seemed like he, you know, looked at me as a mom and said you need to stop giving him junk food and he needs to be more active and I'm like wait a minute, wait a minute, you know … I feel like I'm doing all these things and so that was hard…. He pretty much only said, you know, he can't gain any more weight so that he can grow taller and grow out of it.

Although Joyce and Sharyl referred to the interaction as unhelpful or accusatory, it significantly impacted their future actions in addressing their child's weight. Following their respective office appointments, both Joyce and Sharyl found new HCPs for their children.

Other HCPs were less explicit. In these instances, the HCP was less likely to use words such as overweight or obese. Their child was described as "heavier than according to what they should be," "not where they should be," or needing to "grow into it [his or her weight]." Anna described her son's physical:

> I believe it was a physical and they did the growth chart that they do. And they go over it with myself and Bill, and they did the same thing with Bob [twin sibling] and myself. And there was a big difference, because the boys—they talk back and forth. And so they just said, this is where you should be and you should eat more vegetables and get more exercise and no soda 9or cut down on the soda.

For Serena, the fact that the HCP did not mention the weight of her granddaughter created wonder and frustration. She found "you had 15 minutes to state your case" and her granddaughter's weight was not even addressed. "She couldn't believe it."

Regardless of the approach used by the HCP, participants found that this was a time that either identified or verified their child as being overweight. For many parents, this was of great consequence in the discovery process and it placed them in a position of having to make changes and address their child's weight and health.

Parental Buy-In and the Tipping Point: Linking Process Concept

Participant awareness was drawn from all the subcategories within the discovery process. Awareness that their child was overweight varied from gradual understanding to immediate recognition for parents. This process was far from linear. There was resurfacing evidence identifying the child as overweight, thereby increasing parental awareness. It was a reiterative process whereby parents may not have initially been accepting of this truth. Through input and social interaction, parents came to realize their child was overweight. There was a tipping point that occurred for participants when they moved from disbelief or questioning to acceptance that their child was truly overweight. Barb described this time for her.

> This past fall, actually, [my son] went in for a follow-up appointment with his pediatrician. And he said, you know, I'm really concerned about how much—how much weight he's gained. And he said, let's just go weigh him for the fun of it. And I can't remember—it was a significant increase from only a few months ago. I'm trying to think. So he would have had his well child check when he was 8. So—well, it would have been like a year ago. And I can't remember—I can't remember what the weight difference was, but it was quite remarkable. It was like, oh, my God. And so that's where it kind of really hit me then. All right, it's bad enough that we need to [address it].

For Sara, the tipping point was when she realized how much her daughter weighed.

> A 12-year-old shouldn't weigh 290 pounds. That's just—when my mom told me that my jaw hit the floor.

The tipping point for Joyce and Mark was less pronounced. Joyce kept watching her daughter "getting too big" within the context of her daughter "having a diabetic neck" while Mark didn't find any signs of his daughter's weight "letting up" or "plateauing." For the participants, these events did not occur in isolation. Ongoing and heightened awareness created, shaped, and completed the discovery process, and created a parental buy-in. It was the cumulative experiences and formal integration of the discovery subcategories, predisposition, turning point, comparing to others, and the HCP, that when combined, reached a pivotal personal level and ultimately demanded attention and action.

Other Core Concepts

The other core concepts are thoroughly discussed in Laurent (2014).

SUMMARY

Using grounded theory, the investigator discovered the true intent of participants was to promote the health of their overweight or obese child. Surprisingly, only a few participants identified weight loss as a strategy to achieving this goal. Importantly, it was only through the establishment of healthy eating, physical activity, and minimizing sedentary activities that child weight loss was sought after or considered acceptable by parents. Parental worry and concern for their child's health and well-being was the primary motivator for making healthful changes.

This study acknowledges the dynamic and fluid process of behavior change, given the increased complexity of the lived world and the stigma and comorbidities associated with obesity.

Current behavior change theories (Fishbein & Ajzen, 2010; Pender, 1996; Prochaska & Velicer, 1997; Rosenstock, 1974) describe the process of change through the lens of the individual by explaining how individuals create change for the self. The pathway to making change contributes to the body of knowledge in nursing and other disciplines by explaining how behavior change occurs within a dyadic relationship. The pathway to making change offers a novel theory of behavior change that focuses on the dependent parent–child relationship, not the individual as the sole aspect of change that exists in the literature today. Notable is the implicit, contextually driven, dependent relationship between the parent and child. The individual wants and needs of both parent and child must be reconciled for optimal healthful change to occur and be sustained. As a result, the parent–child dyad was transformed into a working team, a working team that created a healthier child, parent, and family.

The pathway to making change invites further scientific inquiry into the concepts of turning point and food intimacy. These concepts warrant future investigation to validate the role and relationship of stressful events and the development of food intimacy, explicate their relationship, and determine how they affect the development of overweight and obesity in children. The pathway to making change provides a substantive theory that explains how parents come to know their child is overweight and how they promote the health of their overweight or obese child. The findings from this study provide advanced practice nursing and other HCPs new insight on how to assist, guide, and support parents and children in their quest for health and provide further avenues for scientific inquiry yet to be previously identified.

REFERENCES

Adachi-Mejia, A. M., Longacre, M. R., Gibson, J. J., Beach, M. L., Titus-Ernstoff, L. T., & Dalton, M. A. (2006). Children with a TV in their bedroom at higher risk for being overweight. *International Journal of Obesity, 31*(4), 644–651.

Alaimo, K., Olson, C. M., & Frongillo, E. A., Jr. (2001). Low family income and food insufficiency in relation to overweight in U.S. children: Is there a paradox? *Archives of Pediatric and Adolescent Medicine, 155*(10), 1161–1167.

Baumrind, D. (1971). Current patterns of parental authority. *Developmental Psychology, 4*, 1–103.

Baur, L. A., & O'Connor, J. (2004). Special considerations in childhood and adolescent obesity. *Clinics in Dermatology, 22*(4), 338–344.

Blumer, H. (1969). *Symbolic interactionism: Perspective and method.* Berekley, CA: University of California Press.

Booth, S. L., Sallis, J. F., Ritenbaugh, C., Hill, J. O., Birch, L. L., Frank, L. D., . . . Hays N. P. (2001). Environmental and societal factors affect food choice and physical activity: Rationale. *Nutrition Reviews, 59*(3), S21–S36.

Borra, S. T., Kelly, L., Shirreffs, M. B., Neville, K., & Geiger, C. J. (2003). Developing health messages: Qualitative studies with children, parents, and teachers help identify communications opportunities for healthful lifestyles and the prevention of obesity. *Journal of the American Dietetic Association, 103*, 721–728.

Broughton, J. M. (1987). An introduction to critical developmental psychology. In J. M. Broughton (Ed.), *Critical theories of psychological development* (pp. 1–30). New York, NY: Plenum Press.

Bryant, A., & Charmez, K. (2007). Grounded theory research: Methods and practice. In A. Bryant & K. Charmez (Eds.), *The Sage handbook of grounded theory* (pp. 1–28). London, UK: Sage.

Charmez, K. (2006). *Constructing grounded theory.* London, UK: Sage.

Charon, J. (2004). *Symbolic interactionism: An introduction, an interpretation, an integration* (8th ed.). Upper Saddle River, NJ: Pearson Prentice Hall.

Chiva, M. (1997). Cultural aspects of meals and meal frequency. *British Journal of Nutrition, 77*(Suppl 1), S21–S28.

Christakis, N., & Fowler, J. H. (2007). The spread of obesity in a large social network over 32 years. *New England Journal of Medicine, 357*, 370–379.

CNN.com. (2003). Houston teams with McDonalds to fight fat. Retrieved November 22, 2006, from http://www.cnn.com/2003/HEALTH/diet.fitness/09/03/mc donalds.houston.reut/index.html

Corbin, J., & Strauss, A. (2008). *Basics of qualitative research* (3rd ed.). Los Angeles, CA: Sage.

Creswell, J. W. (2003). *Research design: Qualitative, quantitative, and mixed method approaches* (2nd ed.). Los Angeles, CA: Sage.

Darling, N., & Steinberg, L. (1993). Parenting style as context: An integrative model. *Psychological Bulletin, 113*, 487–496.

DeHart, G. B., Sroufe, L. A., & Cooper, R. G. (2004). *Child development: Its nature and course* (5th ed.). Boston, MA: McGraw Hill.

Dey, I. (1999). *Grounding grounded theory: Guidelines for qualitative inquiry.* London, UK: Academic Press.

Dietz, W. (1994). Critical periods in childhood for the development of obesity. *American Journal of Clinical Nutrition, 59,* 955–959.

Dietz, W. (1998). Health consequences of obesity in youth: Childhood predictors of adult disease. *Pediatrics, 101,* 518–525.

Dietz, W., & Robinson, T. N. (2005). Overweight children and adolescents. *New England Journal of Medicine, 352,* 2100–2109.

DiNapoli, T. (2008). Preventing and reducing childhood obesity in New York [Electronic Version]. Retrieved from http://www.osc.state.ny.us/reports/health/childhoodobesity.pdf

Epstein, L., Klein, K. R., & Wisniewski, L. (1994). Child and parent factors that influence psychological problems in obese children. *International Journal of Eating Disorders, 15,* 151–158.

Feldman, W., Feldman, E., & Goodman, J. T. (1988). Culture versus biology: Children's attitudes toward fatness and thinness. *Pediatrics, 81*(2), 190–194.

Fishbein, M., & Ajzen, I. (2010). *Predicting and changing behavior: The reasoned action approach.* New York, NY: Psychology Press.

Freedman, D. S., Shear, C. L., Burke, G. L., Srinivasan, S. R., Webber, L. S., Harsha, D. W., & Berenson, G. S. (1987). Persistence of juvenile-onset obesity over eight years: The Bogalusa Heart Study. *American Journal of Public Health, 77,* 588–592.

Gable, S., & Lutz, S. (2000). Household, parent, and child contributions to childhood obesity. *Family Relations, 49,* 293–300.

Gardiner, H. W., & Kosmitzki, C. (2005). *Lives across cultures: Cross cultural human development* (3rd ed.). Boston, MA: Pearson.

Glaser, B. (1978). *Theoretical sensitivity.* San Francisco, CA: Sociology Press.

Glaser, B. (1992). *Basics of grounded theory analysis.* Mill Valley, CA: Sociology Press.

Glaser, B. (1998). *Doing grounded theory: Issues and discussions.* San Francisco, CA: Sociology Press.

Glaser, B., & Strauss, A. (1967). *The discovery of grounded theory: Strategies for qualitative research.* Chicago, IL: Aldine.

Golan, M., Kaufman, V., & Shahar, D. R. (2006). Childhood obesity treatment: Targeting parents exclusively v. parents and children. *British Journal of Nutrition, 95,* 1008–1015.

Golan, M., & Weizman, A. (2001). Familial approach to the treatment of childhood obesity: Conceptual model. *Journal of Nutrition Education, 33,* 102.

Golan, M., Weizman, A. A., & Fainaru, M. (1998). Parents as the exclusive agents of change in the treatment of childhood obesity. *American Journal of Clinical Nutrition, 67,* 1130–1135.

Golley, R. K., Magarey, A. M., Baur, L. A., Steinbeck, K. S., & Daniels, L. A. (2007). Twelve-month effectiveness of a parent-led, family-focused weight-management program for prepubertal children: A randomized, controlled trial. *Pediatrics, 119,* 517–525.

Gortmaker, S., Must, A., Perrin, J. M., Sobol, A. M., & Dietz, W. (1993). Social and soci-oeconomic consequences of overweight in adolescence and young adulthood. *New England Journal of Medicine, 329*(14), 1008–1012.

Green, D., Creswell, J., Shope, R., & Clark, V. (2007). Grounded theory and racial/ ethnic diversity. In A. Bryant & K. Charmez (Eds.), *The Sage handbook of grounded theory* (pp. 472–492). Los Angeles, CA: Sage.

Hedley, A., Ogden, C. L., Johnson, C. L., Carroll, M., Curtin, L., & Flegal, K. M. (2004). Prevalence of overweight and obesity among U.S. children, adoles-cents, and adults, 1999–2002. *Journal of the American Medical Association, 291*(23), 2847–2850.

Hutchinson, S., & Skodol-Wilson, H. (2001). Grounded theory: The method. In P. Munhall (Ed.), *Nursing research: A qualitative perspective* (3rd ed.). Boston, MA: Jones & Bartlett.

International Obesity Task Force (IOTF). (2004). Appendix 2. Comparison of con-trolled trials undertaken to prevent obesity among children and adolescents. *Obesity Reviews, 5*(s1), 98–104.

Jarvie, G. J., Lahey, B., & Graziano, W. (1983). Childhood obesity and social stigma: What we know and what we don't know. *Developmental Reviews, 3,* 237–273.

Jiang, J. X., Xia, X. L., Greiner, T., Lian, G. L., & Rosenqvist, U. (2005). A two year family based behaviour treatment for obese children. *Archives of Disease in Childhood, 90*(12), 1235–1238.

Kerr, J., Rosenberg, D., Sallis, J. F., Saelens, B. E., Frank, L. D., & Conway, T. L. (2006). Active commuting to school: Associations with environment and parental concerns. *Medicine and Science in Sports and Exercise, 38*(4), 787–794.

Klesges, R. C., Stein, R. J., Eck, L. H., Isbell, T. R., & Klesges, L. M. (1991). Parental influence on food selection in young children and its relationships to childhood obesity. *American Journal of Clinical Nutrition, 53*(4), 859–864.

Laurent, J. (2007). *The experience of parents promoting health of their overweight or obese child: A mini study.* (Unpublished manuscript). Pittsburgh, PA: Duquesne University.

Laurent, J. (2010). *The pathway to making change: How parents promote the health of their overweight or obese child.* (Unpublished dissertation.) Pittsburgh, PA: Duquesne University.

Laurent, J. S., & Zoucha, R. (2014). Parents addressing health for their overweight or obese pre-adolescent. *Health Behav Policy Rev, 1*(2), 131–142.

Lincoln, Y., & Guba, E. (1985). *Naturalistic inquiry.* London, UK: Sage.

Lissau, I., & Sorensen, T. I. (1994). Parental neglect during childhood and increased risk of obesity in young adulthood. *Lancet, 343*(8893), 324–327.

Lobstein, T., & Jackson-Leach, R. (2007). Child overweight and obesity in the USA: Prevalence rates according to IOTF definitions. *International Journal of Pediatric Obesity, 2*(1), 62–64.

Lumeng, J., & Burke, L. M. (2006). Maternal prompts to eat, child compliance, and mother and child weight status. *The Journal of Pediatrics, 149*(3), 330.

Lutfiyya, M. N., Lipsky, M. S., Wisdom-Behounek, J., & Inpanbutr-Martinkus, M. (2007). Is rural residency a risk factor for overweight and obesity for U.S. children? *Obesity, 15*(9), 2348–2356.

Manis, J., & Meltzer, B. (1967). *Symbolic interactionism*. Boston, MA: Allyn & Bacon.

Must, A. (2005). Childhood overweight and maturational timing in the development of adult overweight and fatness: The Newton girls study and its follow-up. *Pediatrics, 116*(3), 620–620.

Myers, A., & Rosen, J. C. (1999). Obesity stigmatization and coping: Relation to mental health symptoms, body image, and self-esteem. *International Journal of Obesity & Related Metabolic Disorders, 23*, 221–230.

Myers, L., Strikmiller, P. K., Webber, L. S., & Berenson, G. S. (1996). Physical and sedentary activity in school children grades 5–8: The Bogalusa Heart Study. *Medicine and Science in Sports and Exercise, 28*(7), 852–859.

Nader, P. R., O'Brien, M., Houts, R., Bradley, R., Belsky, J., Crosnoe, R., . . . Susman, E. J.; National Institute of Child Health and Human Development Early Child Care Research Network. (2006). Identifying risk for obesity in early childhood. *Pediatrics, 118*(3), e594–e601.

Nemet, D., Barkan, S., Epstein, Y., Friedland, O., Kowen, G., & Eliakim, A. (2005). Short- and long-term beneficial effects of a combined dietary-behavioral-physical activity intervention for the treatment of childhood obesity. *Pediatrics, 115*(4), e443–e449.

Newman, B. M., & Newman, P. R. (2006). *Development through life: A psychosocial approach* (9th ed.). Belmont, CA: Wadsworth.

Nowicka, P., & Flodmark, C. E. (2008). Family in pediatric obesity management: A literature review. *International Journal of Pediatric Obesity, 3*(1 Suppl 1), 44–50.

Ogden, C. L., Carroll, M. D., & Flegal, K. M. (2008). High body mass index for age among U.S. children and adolescents, 2003–2006. *Journal of the American Medical Association, 299*(20), 2401–2405.

Paineau, D. L., Beaufils, F., Boulier, A., Cassuto, D., Chwalow, J., Combris, P., . . . Bornet, F. (2008). Family dietary coaching to improve nutritional intake and body weight control: A randomized controlled trial. *Archives of Pediatric and Adolescent Medicine, 162*(1), 34–43.

Pender, N. (1996). *Health promotion in nursing practice* (3rd ed.). Stamford, CT: Appleton & Lange.

Prochaska, J. O., & Velicer, W. F. (1997). The transtheoretical model of health behavior change. *American Journal of Health Promotion, 12*(1), 38–48.

Puhl, R. M., & Latner, J. D. (2007). Stigma, obesity, and the health of the nation's children. *Psychological Bulletin, 133*(4), 557–580.

QSR International Pty Ltd. (2008). *NVivo 8* [Computer software]. QSR International.

Reischer, E., & Koo, K. S. (2004). The body beautiful: Symbolism and agency in the social world. *Annual Review of Anthropology, 33*, 297–317.

Rhee, K., Lumeng, J. C., Appugliese, D. P., Kaciroti, N., & Bradley, R. H. (2006). Parenting styles and overweight status in first grade. *Pediatrics, 117*(6), 2047–2054.

Richmond, T. K., Field, A. E., & Rich, M. (2007). Can neighborhoods explain racial/ethnic differences in adolescent inactivity? *International Journal of Pediatric Obesity, 2*(4), 202–210.

Rosenstock, I. (1974). The health belief model and preventative health behavior. In M. Becker (Ed.), *The health belief model and personal health behaviors* (pp. 27–59). Thorofare, NJ: Charles B. Slack.

Snethen, J. A., Broome, M. E., & Cashin, S. E. (2006). Effective weight loss for overweight children: A meta-analysis of intervention studies. *Journal of Pediatric Nursing, 21*(1), 45–56.

Spurlock, M. (Producer). (2004). *Super-size me.* United States: Arts Alliance America.

Stein, R. I., Epstein, L. H., Raynor, H. A., Kilanowski, C. K., & Paluch, R. A. (2005). The influence of parenting change on pediatric weight control. *Obesity Research, 13*(10), 1749–1755.

Strauss, A., & Corbin, J. (1998). *Basics of qualitative research* (2nd ed.). Thousand Oaks, CA: Sage.

Stunkard, A., & Sorensen, T. (1993). Obesity and socioeconomic status: A complex relation. *New England Journal of Medicine, 329*(14), 1036–1037.

Sturm, R. (2004). The economics of physical activity: Societal trends and rationales for interventions. *American Journal of Preventive Medicine, 27*(3 Suppl), 126–135.

Trust for America's Health. (2009). F as in fat: How obesity policies are failing America [Electronic Version], from http://healthyamericans.org/reports/obesity2009/Obesity2009Report.pdf

United Health Foundation. (2009). America's health rankings. Retrieved March 10, 2010, from http://www.americashealthrankings.org/yearcompare/2008/2009/VT.aspx

Vermont Department of Health (VDH). (2000). Healthy Vermonter 2010. Burlington, VT: Vermont Department of Health.

Vermont Department of Health (VDH). (2006a). Fit and healthy Vermonters: Preventing obesity in Vermont [Electronic Version], 1–32. Retrieved October 7, 2008, from http://HealthVermont.gov/FitandHealthy.aspx

Vermont Department of Health (VDH). (2006b). *Obesity and health.* Burlington, VT: Vermont Department of Health.

Vermont Department of Health (VDH). (2008). *Health report 2008.* Burlington, VT: Vermont Department of Health.

Wang, Y., Beydoun, M., Liang, L., Caballero, B., & Kumanyika, S. (2008). Will all Americans become overweight or obese? Estimating the progression and cost of the U.S. obesity epidemic. *Obesity, 16*(10), 2323–2330.

Weiner, C. (2007). Making teams work in conducting grounded theory. In A. Bryant & K. Charmez (Eds.), *The Sage handbook of grounded theory* (pp. 293–310). Los Angeles, CA: Sage.

Whitaker, R., Deeks, C. M., Baughcum, A. E., & Specker, B. L. (2000). The relationship of childhood adiposity to parent body mass index and eating behavior. *Obesity Research, 8*(3), 234–240.

Whitaker, R., Wright, J. A., Pepe, M. S., Seidel, K. D., & Dietz, W. (1997). Predicting obesity in young adulthood from childhood and parental obesity. *New England Journal of Medicine, 337*(13), 869–873.

White, M. A., Martin, P. D., Newton, R. L., Walden, H. M., York-Crowe, E. E., Gordon, S. T., . . . Williamson D. A. (2004). Mediators of weight loss in a family-based intervention presented over the internet. *Obesity Research, 12*(7), 1050–1059.

Zimmet, P. (2000). Globalization, coca-colonization and the chronic disease epidemic: Can the Doomsday scenario be averted? *Journal of Internal Medicine, 247*(3), 301–310.

CHAPTER FIVE

APPLYING CONSTRUCTIVIST GROUNDED THEORY METHODS

Lorraine F. Holtslander

Very little is known about how a family caregiver transitions from a caregiver to a bereaved relative or about how caregiving impacts bereavement outcomes. As a practicing palliative home care nurse, I know firsthand how heavily caregivers are relied on and how few supports are available; even less so in bereavement. I chose for my dissertation research to study the vulnerable and underserved population of older women, bereaved after caregiving for a partner with advanced cancer. This research, built on my master's study, which was a grounded theory of hope for family caregivers while caregiving for a patient at the end of life (Holtslander, Duggleby, Williams, & Wright, 2005), used Glaser's grounded theory methodology (Glaser, 1978, 1992, 2001, 2005; Glaser & Strauss, 1967). This study revealed that the family caregiver's hope was focused on caregiving for her patient, and not on her own hope or well-being. Family caregivers often felt frustrated, angry, and sometimes experienced an erosion of their hope when dealing with health care professionals. At other times, health care professionals were very important sustainers of hope.

A passion and a distinct vision for the needs of this population were very important to sustain a long and grueling, yet extremely rewarding, research process. Family caregivers, most of whom are older women (Canadian Cancer Society Statistics, 2013; Martel, 2013), face a very uncertain future with a distinct lack of adequate and appropriate support from the health care system (Hudson, 2013). Older adults during bereavement face enormous challenges, including intense and prolonged suffering (Stroebe, Schut, & Stroebe, 2007) and distressing grief over an unpredictable length of time (Chentsova-Dutton et al., 2002).

Hope is a valuable psychosocial resource, very important to family caregivers in any situation (Duggleby et al., 2010), yet very little was known about the bereaved palliative caregivers' experience of hope, or how they manage the stressful adjustment from caregiving to bereavement. From previous research, both hope and grief are considered to be processes by nature (Cutcliffe, 2006; Folkman, 2013). Since grounded theory provides a methodology to generate theory that explains, at a broad, conceptual level, a process that has phases over time (Creswell, 2013), it was a well-suited approach. The overall goal of the research described in this chapter was to explore the experience of hope for older women who are bereaved palliative caregivers and to develop a tentative theory to explain how these women resolve their concerns relating to hope in their lives.

A constructivist, grounded theory approach (Charmaz, 2006) was used to study the hope experience, with the goal of an interpretive understanding of their actions and experiences within a complex social context. Acknowledging the philosophical and conceptual limitations of an objectivist approach to qualitative research, I decided that a constructivist grounded theory design, applying Charmaz's recommendations was a more personally appropriate methodological approach for this research. Constructivist grounded theory acknowledges subjectivity within every step of the research process, as well as the importance of social context as it impacts the experience of the participants.

Both the sensitizing concept of hope and the disciplinary perspective I had gained from many years of home care nursing provided a place to start the study (Charmaz, 2006). Grounded theory provided the tools to gain an insider's perspective, to explain and understand what is going on within a setting, around a particular event, and to conceptualize and theorize from the data (Morse, 2009), providing a consistent set of guidelines to meet my research objectives. The focus of this chapter is to explain how a graduate student could apply grounded theory methods through a real-life exemplar. The design of the study, a description of the findings, and the challenges and issues encountered are explained. For more information, the complete results of this grounded theory have been published elsewhere (Holtslander & Duggleby, 2009), as well as a comparative analysis of the psychosocial context of the participants of this study (Holtslander & Duggleby, 2010) and a content analysis of the written diaries the participants provided for this study (Holtslander & Duggleby, 2008).

DESCRIPTION OF THE STUDY

Purpose and Aims

The overall purpose of this research was to explore the experience of hope for older women who were bereaved following caregiving for a family member with advanced cancer. I wanted to develop an emerging, substantive theory that would explain how these women resolve their concerns relating to hope. The specific aims of the study were:

1. To explore the experience and processes of hope for the older woman who was bereaved after caregiving for her spouse with advanced cancer
2. To define hope for this population within their unique social context
3. To construct a substantive theory of the hope experience of the older, spousal, female, bereaved, palliative caregiver

Choosing a Sample Population

By building a purposive sampling framework for an initial sampling strategy I was able to gather rich data more efficiently and effectively. The purposive sampling framework was based on the age, gender, experiences, situations, and settings identified as important in the scientific literature and encouraged a range of diversity among the participants. These key parameters were identified as affecting the outcomes of caregiving on bereavement. For example, women recruited to the study had (a) a range of ages equal to and older than 60 years, (b) different lengths of caregiving time, and (c) various social support situations. The study's inclusion criteria for the sample were women (a) aged 60 and above, (b) who resided with and provided care for a spouse with terminal cancer who died within the past year to 18 months, (c) who were English speaking, and (d) who were freely consenting to be a participant in a research project about hope in bereavement. Exclusion criteria were those cognitively impaired, nonautonomous, or not able to give a free and informed consent.

Ethics and Approvals

This study was reviewed and received approval from my institution's behavioral ethics review board (as a minimal risk study) and operational approval from our local health region. Procedures for the protection of participants were strictly followed, including reporting all data in a group format. The study took place in the homes of the participants of a small, western Canadian city, over a 10-month time period.

Recruitment Strategies

The coordinator of volunteers for the local inpatient palliative care unit identified potential participants, based on the inclusion criteria, and asked them whether they would be willing to talk with a nurse researcher about the study. If they agreed, I contacted the participants by telephone and arranged to meet with them in their homes to explain the study and to obtain a written, informed consent. One participant chose to be interviewed in my office at the university, and this was accommodated.

Data Collection

Data collection was facilitated by a demographic form, face-to-face open-ended audiotaped interviews, written or audiotaped diaries completed by participants, and my field notes and memos. The interview questions were written and chosen to give the participants ample opportunities to provide their own insights about hope and included, What thoughts do you have about hope? What does hope mean for you right now? and Have you noticed any changes in your hope? The questions were altered as the study proceeded to become more focused on the emerging theory. Also, after the first interview, each participant was asked to write in a diary over a 2-week period. They were given a prepared booklet, with instructions for completion inside, including, What did hope feel like or look like today? Did you have any challenges to your hope today? and What did hope mean to you today? These daily writings gave unique insight into their daily challenges and experiences and provided further data about the benefits of writing in difficult situations (Holtslander & Duggleby, 2008). Field notes were made on the setting, including observed nonverbal behaviors and the general environment of the interviews. I used the techniques of memoing (Charmaz, 2006) to write and preserve my ideas about the findings throughout the entire data collection and analysis process.

Data Analysis

I was able to hire an experienced transcriptionist to transcribe the interviews verbatim. After each interview, the data were "cleaned" by listening to the interview and making any necessary corrections. The interview and written diary data were entered into NVivo software (QSR International) for the purposes of data storage and management. I completed data analysis after each interview, which meant applying Charmaz's (2006) described methodology for initial, focused, and theoretical coding.

Initial coding meant examining every part of the data line by line, searching for categories, concepts, actions, and patterns of behavior. Initial codes were extracted, which used the participants' language, or in vivo coding, to ensure the findings were closely grounded in the data. The next step, focused coding, meant the most frequent or significant initial codes were arranged, combined, integrated, and organized. Codes became categories and incidents. Theoretical coding involved analyzing the focused codes and specifying the relationships between the categories and concepts. The focused codes were integrated and organized into a logical, coherent emerging theory of the bereaved palliative caregiver's experience of hope. All processes and subprocesses were in vivo, meaning that a participant had used those exact words to describe her experience.

Constant comparison data analysis was also employed as a continual process of moving iteratively across all of the data, comparing data to the codes, categories, and incidents, to develop the initial codes, focused codes, and eventually to bring the theory together. Once the emerging theory was constructed, I returned to the data to ensure that all of the data were accounted for in the grounded theory.

Theoretical sampling strategies were used to narrow the focus of the data collection to the emerging categories and concepts in order to develop and refine them, add depth to their meanings, discover variation in the theory, and to define the gaps (Charmaz, 2006) to find a full range of experiences of hope during bereavement. If possible, follow-up interviews were conducted to focus specifically on the emerging ideas, categories, and processes to fully saturate the properties of the emerging grounded theory (Charmaz, 2006). As data analysis progressed, the questions were changed to become more focused on the main concern and basic social process.

Saturation was defined as theoretical completeness or until no new properties of the categories or theoretical insights were being gained (Charmaz, 2006), as the data collected were of sufficient richness and depth. Both purposive and theoretical sampling techniques were used to reach saturation after 30 interviews with 13 participants and 12 diaries, as well as my field notes and memos.

Rigor

Scientific rigor was sought through Charmaz's (2006) specific criteria of credibility, originality, resonance, and usefulness to produce a constructivist grounded theory that had fit, worked with the data, was relevant, and modifiable. Rich, in-depth data was gathered from multiple sources including interviews, participant diaries, and my field notes and memos, all of which were transcribed verbatim and coded line by line. The findings from the diaries and the interviews, and eventually the emerging theory, were confirmed for resonance with the participants at the second and third interviews. All theoretical findings were grounded in the data, and constant comparison and categorizing of the data ensured fittingness.

RESULTS

The findings of this study are based on the demographic characteristics of the participants in my study. I was able to obtain participants older than 60, including several women who were in their late seventies. This was helpful as a few were still active in the workforce or as volunteers while some were experiencing more of the debilitating physical challenges that often accompany older age. Sadly one participant was interviewed once and was admitted to hospital a few weeks later where she died of complications from heart surgery. She was in her late seventies and had been ignoring her own heart condition while providing 24-hour care for her husband. His death was a tremendous difficulty and her health greatly suffered. I conducted at least two interviews with the other 12 participants and returned to 5 participants a third time as they were such excellent informants who could provide feedback on the results and the emerging theory. I was able to obtain written diaries from 12 participants, which provided a great deal of insight into their daily lives. At the time of the second interview, most participants had found their own insights into hope, based on the writing they had done, and we were able to share these discoveries at the second and third interviews. Many continued to write, having found benefit, and I made sure to just photocopy their diaries and then return the original writing to each participant as soon as possible.

Developing a unique definition of hope for this sample was an important finding, meeting the second aim of the study. By analyzing the data over and over, and returning to the participants with the emerging results, I arrived at the following definition: "Hope was a gradual process of regaining inner strength and building self-confidence, to make sense of their totally changed situations" (Holtslander & Duggleby, 2009, p. 391). Specific quotes to support this definition included, "Hope meant having the courage and strength and self-confidence . . . ." For all the participants, hope was a process of learning ways to move forward, of finding the means to stay positive, and each participant said that hope was very important to them. They also stressed how each individual's journey through bereavement was unique and could not be compared in terms of time or specific recommendations or advice. A participant wrote in her journal, "It would be impossible to allow yourself to have any kind of life if you didn't have hope." Exploring what the participants hoped for was very interesting. They said they hoped to face each day with increasing strength, courage, and to find purpose in their completely changed life situations. As one participant said, "Hope meant that someday I could go from grief to joy, to be able to have pride and regain my self-confidence."

Each participant's hope was also for their very uncertain futures, their health, and for their extended families, which were so very important to them. Specifically they said that they hoped for good health, both physical and emotional. As a participant wrote in her diary, "At this time, my hope is that we will be able to face each new day . . . and being able to cope without him . . . the hope I have for my family is the same as it always has been."

The main concern was sought from and identified in the data as the concern that activated the basic social processes of hope. I was certain, based on direct quotes that were also supported by the data, that their recurring concern was "losing hope." I observed that each of the participants always had some level of hope, but it was low at times, shaky, and uncertain. Thinking back on the time of caregiving was especially challenging, and some experienced a loss of hope. As one said, "You go through the pain and the tears and the memories of how ill he was so vivid in your mind, and it kind of brings you back down a little bit, and, um, progress that you've made, you may have lost it [hope] for a little while."

Facing the overwhelming and uncertain future was further magnified by the many losses they were experiencing in addition to the loss of a spouse (such as losing their own caregiver, friend, driver, support, and comforter). Participants also felt they had lost their own identity as a married person and their loss of meaning and purpose as caregivers. Losing hope was described as, "I really don't want to go on, this really doesn't matter, I don't care." However, losing hope was what initiated the basic social process of "searching for new hope," based on each participant's tremendous inner strength and courage to face this uncertain future. Losing hope meant each participant had to find ways to "fill the void" and just "keep going."

The basic social process of "searching for new hope" was identified from the data as a way to describe the most important overall process, and involved a deliberate and unique process for each participant. One participant said, "Nothing comes easy, and you have to . . . work at everything . . . you know maybe there is some hope for me somewhere down the road." The subprocesses of searching for new hope were finding balance, finding new perspectives, and finding new meaning and purpose.

Arranging the theoretical model from the findings involved spending a lot of time in the data and conversations with my supervisor and committee. It eventually resembled a forward-moving spiral demonstrating the active, energy- and time-requiring, purposeful process of searching for new hope. The participants described how they were actively forcing themselves to do things to move ahead. One participant said, ". . . you kind of think to yourself well I've got to plan my day . . . I have to do something." As I analyzed the data, I was able to place each of the participants at various points in the spiral, based on her experiences, statements, level of hope, and ability to complete each of the processes. Each of course faced many setbacks to finding new hope, and the arrows of direction in the model indicate this movement. The participants described interconnected subprocesses of finding balance, finding new perspectives, and finding new meaning and purpose. The definitions of the subprocesses and processes within each are described below.

Finding balance emerged as a key process that was a struggle for some and an important launching point. Overwhelming difficult and negative emotions and experiences threatened finding balance. This quote described it nicely: "It's finding the balance. You know one day you can be so busy and then all of a sudden there's nothing." The ways to finding balance were finding hope in relationships, keeping busy, and releasing the pain. Not having supportive relationships, especially with family, was often a threat to balance. Keeping busy meant active distraction as one participant wrote, "Today, I will keep as busy as possible and hope that in doing so another day will go by." Painful emotions needed to be actively released, as one participant wrote in her diary, "No moping around—if loneliness overwhelms me and memories cause tears—have a good cry and cleanse your soul. Then get on with life."

Finding new perspectives meant facing new realities, realizing a need for refocusing, letting go, and finding specific ways to stay positive. Specifically, letting go of the past was very difficult, but participants found that through writing, talking with supportive people, and being grateful, they were able to arrive at unique solutions for doing that. One wrote, "I guess it's your own decision whether life is a bowl of cherries or just the pits! It was a great day, and although my heart aches for (spouse's name), I still feel good." Participants identified the need to be grateful as a step to hope. Often the participants would write about what they were grateful for. Other times they would reflect on what they had written earlier and wrote, "I just looked at it (the diary), and I thought my goodness, it's pretty glum, there wasn't too many up and up moments." Many participants wrote about how writing each day helped them to reflect and gain a new perspective. As one said, ". . . and then I found the more I wrote every day and I think some days I wrote a lot, I found it easier and I, I started feeling better."

Finding new meaning and purpose was the final subprocess that not all participants were able to arrive at, although it was a goal expressed by most. Participants found that participating in the study enabled them to find meaning and purpose from their situation, hoping they had been of help to me, and to others in similar situations. As caregivers, they received great rewards from helping others, and it made them feel better just to have contributed to my study. They were also reaching out to find others in need, as a way to find new hope. However, a sense of "taking control" of their lives was difficult and usually involved taking very small steps such as making lists and then completing small tasks. A participant joked, "Plan one thing for the day even if it's only taking out the garbage!" Several of the participants were at this place—reaching out to help their neighbors and planning new directions, travel, and volunteer activities. These processes of searching for new hope are shown as dynamic, interconnected, and active movement along the spiral, in order to begin to describe the very complex and context-based process of finding hope during bereavement.

CHALLENGES AND REWARDS

Although grounded theory methodology provides a very practical and well-defined approach, the whole endeavor requires a great deal of tenacity, persistence, creativity, and courage! Predicting exactly how a research project will be completed at the proposal stage is just not possible, and there will be inevitable obstacles, questions, and life events that need to be overcome with confidence and the support of a team. During the time of data collection and analysis, it was difficult not to become personally saddened by the hardships experienced by the participants, but I was able to debrief with my co-supervisor, Dr. Wendy Duggleby on many occasions. I need to acknowledge her expertise in grounded theory, her research wisdom, and amazing quick turnaround times with providing precious feedback on my writing. Avoiding distractions, procrastination, and following through on timelines and commitments with the support of your supervisor and committee will be key to your success. Specifically, data analysis, decisions about saturation, negative or contrast cases, and the constructivist aspects were areas of both challenge and benefit.

Data analysis was a constant process, all-consuming, and at times required a great deal of persistence, but was exciting when those wonderful "aha" moments would arrive. Insight could come at any time; thus a researcher journal, with field notes and memos, was essential to record these thoughts and feelings, any time of the day or night. I was very fortunate to have funding to pay an experienced transcriptionist to transcribe the interviews, as this is a very tedious process. However, after you receive the transcripts, you need to again listen to each interview and "clean" your data, by filling in any gaps missed by the transcriptionist. Uploading both the interview itself (as a digital file) and the typed transcripts into NVivo or another type of qualitative analysis software greatly facilitates organizing your data as well as the data analysis process; however, the software is not capable of doing the analysis for you!

Initial coding involves coding each part of the data, line by line, looking for processes, meanings, and actions of the participants that help to meet the objectives of the study. "Coding means categorizing segments of data with a short name that simultaneously summarizes and accounts for each piece of data" (Charmaz, 2006, p. 43). After each interview, line-by-line coding of each word, line, or section of data needs to be completed and becomes the first step in data analysis. Initial thoughts about actions and processes can be noted in memos and brought back to the participant at a subsequent interview for further discussion and insight. Questions or gaps may arise that could be discussed at subsequent interviews. When coding it is helpful to ask yourself, "What are these data a study of?" (Glaser, 1978; Glaser & Strauss, 1967). Charmaz recommends remaining open, staying close to the data, making simple, precise, short codes that are action words (or gerunds, such as "becoming" or "searching").

Be careful not to code for topics or themes; you are looking for processes, actions, and activities that relate to the concept you are studying. Personally, after I had hundreds of initial codes identified, printing out the list of codes facilitated focused coding as I searched for the most important or frequent initial codes with the ultimate goal of organizing, synthesizing, analyzing, and categorizing all of the data.

Incident coding helps you to identify patterns or contrasts that may become concerns or basic social processes in the conceptual analysis. A participant may have an innovative way of describing her experience that lends itself to an in vivo code that can become part of your theory. When integrated, the meaning of it will explain your data. Comparing your data with the emerging categories—that is the constant comparative process! Theoretical coding will bring all of the important focused codes into a theoretical model that explains all of the data, all of the experiences of each participant, and the influence of social context. The model needs to be well supported in all dimensions; each process is defined and supported by the data.

Frequent memo writing will help you to discover connections, comparisons, and incidents to be followed up in further data collection. After each interview, take time to write field notes on the setting and initial thoughts.

A very deep dwelling in your study, the lives of your participants, and in your data will yield a strong, interpretive understanding of the experience you are researching, leading to findings that you can be confident are well-saturated and grounded in data.

Saturation

Theoretical saturation is defined by Charmaz (2006) as the time in data collection when gathering more data about the categories reveals no new theoretical insights or properties of the emerging grounded theory. Because of the depth and richness of the experiences of the participants, as shared in their interviews and diaries, and the fact that I was able to conduct follow-up interviews with most of the participants, I claimed that theoretical saturation was reached with 13 participants. Returning to my supervisor with my tentative findings as well as presenting my results to my committee also helped determine when saturation was reached. When others can understand an experience more thoroughly and deeply, based on your findings, when the theoretical model seems significant, innovative, and well grounded, you can attest that theoretical saturation has been reached. Follow-up interviews, in which you show your theoretical model to your participants for confirmation, are also very important to reaching saturation. Participants may be able to help you "fine-tune" the model and identify gaps or whether the model adequately describes their experience. You need to choose to return to participants who are reflective and capable of giving that level of conceptual thought to your findings. Those participants who are struggling, or identified as contrast cases, will probably not be able to offer their insights into the full range of the processes of the emerging grounded theory.

Contrast/Negative Cases

This concept was discussed extensively with my supervisors and committee. I was able to identify that at least 3 of the 13 participants in my study were having a great deal of difficulty finding hope in their lives at the time of the interviews. I considered them to be my "contrast cases," a term preferred to "negative cases." Their experiences were unique and offered an insight and understanding of the full range of the social processes of searching for new hope. For the purposes of my study, a contrast case was defined as a participant whose experience seemed to challenge the emerging theory and processes of hope. This is similar to Charmaz's (2006) explanation of incorporating negative cases as a source of variation and thickness in the emerging theory. I analyzed further the experiences of these women and incorporated their experiences into the processes found within the emerging grounded theory. It seemed these three were struggling at the first process of "finding balance"; that dealing with overwhelming emotions and physical challenges limited their abilities to resume usual activities and build new relationships. All of the "contrast cases" expressed feeling that their own support system was inadequate, and difficult relationships, especially within their family members, were causing a loss of hope. Other aspects of the social context, such as their own physical health concerns and other secondary losses such as having to move or having experienced the loss of more than their spouse (such as one who lost her mother while caregiving for her spouse), also resulted in difficulty moving along the spiral. Difficulty finding balance, which was impeding finding new perspectives in a search for new hope, is exemplified in this participant's profound and honest statement, "I haven't found anything positive yet . . . it's [been] 1 year and I don't think I feel any more hopeful than I did . . . a year ago. I really don't."

Subjectivity

Charmaz (2006) suggests we construct our grounded theories through our past and present involvements and our interactions and interpretations throughout the study. From my experience as a palliative care nurse and my recent study of hope with caregivers of palliative care patients, I was aware of the challenges of caregiving, and I could only imagine the overwhelming difficulty of losing a life partner. However, I was truly surprised by the strength and courage of many of the participants to find new hope, meaning, and purpose in their situations. As I applied a constructivist approach to my grounded theory study, I was able to experience symbolic interactionism (Blumer, 1969) firsthand, as I asked the participants to think and talk about hope during their bereavement, which was a new concept for some of them to consider. Especially at the time of the second interview, I could observe and understand that thinking, talking, and writing about hope had an impact on the day-to-day lives of the participants. For example, one participant described how she wrote down a concern specific to the changes she needed to make at the bank regarding her account information. After she wrote this challenge down in her journal, she made an appointment at the bank and followed through by taking this step in her journey after the loss of her spouse. At our second interview, she had a very different outlook and a sense of renewed hope; it was obvious that a profound change had happened in her life. Each participant had a unique journey, based on rediscovering new hopes and letting go of her hope that her spouse would survive. Often this left her feeling uncertain and shaky, and hope related strongly to her self-confidence. I continue to be amazed by the uniqueness of each participant's experiences, and I feel honored and privileged to have had the opportunity to study, and even be a part of, her bereavement journey.

Carefully reflecting on my own experiences as a palliative home care nurse, my family values and beliefs it was important to explore how they may be impacting my findings. My own belief systems were difficult to extract from or immerse into the findings, especially a study of hope, which is highly individualized, complex, and based in a social context (Jevne, 2005). Through the process of completing this research, I discovered that my own hope was redefined, becoming much more meaningful as I could see how important relationships, especially with a life partner, and the loss can impact hope, how difficult it can be to rearrange your life after such a major loss. I try not to take these relationships for granted anymore.

IMPLICATIONS

Most health care systems are heavily reliant on the services of the family caregiver (CHPCA, 2004), and although both national (Ferris et al., 2002) and international guidelines for palliative care services (World Health Organization, 2002) mandate continuing support for bereaved family members, the evidence needed to provide effective and equitable bereavement support remains lacking (Holtslander, 2008; Hudson, Zordan, & Trauer, 2011). Research that provides an interpretive explanation of a complex and multifactorial process such as the experience of hope for older women, who are bereaved after caregiving for a spouse with advanced cancer, offers a practical means of building a program of research designed to support and promote health during bereavement. Each subprocess could be followed with ongoing research; for example, I completed a grounded theory of finding balance (Holtslander, Bally, & Steeves, 2011), as a way to develop a theory-based support intervention. Improving bereavement outcomes for older adults after caregiving for a spouse with cancer involves enabling the uptake of research results through innovative knowledge translation strategies and adapting successful caregiver interventions to distinct populations and groups and testing them for feasibility and effectiveness. Identifying caregivers at the highest risk for poor bereavement outcomes is another research priority.

SUMMARY

Staying consistent to a grounded theory methodology meant the data could be collected, analyzed, and transformed into an interpretive explanation (Sandelowski & Barroso, 2007) of the experience of hope for older women who are bereaved after caregiving for a spouse with advanced cancer. Constructivist grounded theory was a strong philosophical fit with my own approach to nursing, allowing me to acknowledge, examine, and describe complex social processes within the context they occur. Find an approach that has personal philosophical resonance and then maintain your commitment to follow the recommended steps with consistency from start to finish. The result will be a quality, credible, and rigorous set of findings of importance to nursing practice and research.

REFERENCES

Blumer, H. (1969). *Symbolic interactionism: Perspective and method*. Englewood Cliffs, NJ: Prentice-Hall.

Canadian Cancer Society. (2013). Canadian Cancer Statistics 2013. Retrieved October 2013, from http://www.cancer.ca/~/media/cancer.ca/CW/cancer%20infor mation/cancer%20101/Canadian%20cancer%20statistics/canadian-cancer -statistics-2013-EN.pdf

Canadian Hospice Palliative Care Association (CHPCA). (2004). VOICE in health policy. *The role of informal caregivers in hospice palliative and end-of-life care in Canada: A discussion of the legal, ethical and moral challenges*. Retrieved July 8, 2005, from http://www.chpca.net/informal_caregivers/VOICE_PROJECT-DISCUSSION _DOCUMENT-August2004-2.pdf

Charmaz, K. (2006). *Constructing grounded theory: A practical guide through qualitative analysis*. London, UK: Sage.

Chentsova-Dutton, Y., Shucter, S., Hutchin, S., Stause, L., Burns, K., Dunn, L., . . . Zisook, S. (2002). Depression and grief reactions in hospice caregivers: From pre-death to 1 year afterwards. *Journal of Affective Disorders, 69*, 53–60.

Creswell, J. W. (2013). *Qualitative inquiry and research design* (3rd ed.). Los Angeles, CA: Sage.

Cutcliffe, J. R. (2006). The principles and processes of inspiring hope in bereavement counselling: A modified grounded theory study—Part two. *Journal of Psychiatric and Mental Health Nursing, 13*, 604–610.

Duggleby, W. D., Holtslander, L., Kylma, J., Duncan, V., Hammond, C., & Williams, A. (2010). Metasynthesis of the hope experience of family caregivers of persons with chronic illness. *Qualitative Health Research, 20*(2), 148–158.

Ferris, F., Balfour, H., Bowan, K., Farley, J., Hardwick, M., Lamontagne, C., . . . West, P. (2002). *A model to guide hospice palliative care.* Ottawa, ON: Canadian Hospice Palliative Care Association. Retrieved from http://www.chpca.net /marketplace/national_norms/A+Model+to+Guide+Hospice+Palliative +Care+2002-URLUpdate-August2005.pdf

Folkman, S. (2013). Stress, coping and hope. In B. I. Carr & J. Steel (Eds.), *Psychological aspects of cancer* (pp. 119–127). New York, NY: Springer.

Glaser, B. G. (1978). *Theoretical sensitivity: Advances in the methodology of grounded theory.* Mill Valley, CA: Sociology Press.

Glaser, B. G. (1992). *Basics of grounded theory analysis: Emergence vs. forcing.* Mill Valley, CA: Sociology Press.

Glaser, B. G. (2001). *The grounded theory perspective: Conceptualization contrasted with description.* Mill Valley, CA: Sociology Press.

Glaser, B. G. (2005). *The grounded theory perspective III: Theoretical coding.* Mill Valley, CA: Sociology Press.

Glaser, B. G., & Strauss, A. L. (1967). *The discovery of grounded theory.* Chicago, IL: Aldine.

Holtslander, L. (2008). Caring for bereaved family caregivers: Analyzing the context of care. *Clinical Journal of Oncology Nursing, 12*(3), 501–506.

Holtslander, L., Bally, J., & Steeves, M. (2011). Walking a fine line: An exploration of the experience of finding balance for older persons bereaved after caregiving for a spouse with advanced cancer. *European Journal of Oncology Nursing, 15*, 6. doi:10.1016/j.ejon.2010.12.004

Holtslander, L., & Duggleby, W. (2008). An inner struggle for hope: Insights from the diaries of bereaved family caregivers. *International Journal of Palliative Nursing, 14*(10), 478–484.

Holtslander, L., & Duggleby, W. (2010). The psychosocial context of bereavement for older women who were caregivers for a spouse with advanced cancer. *Journal of Women and Aging, 22*(2), 109–124.

Holtslander, L., Duggleby, W., Williams, A., & Wright, K. (2005). The experience of hope for informal caregivers of palliative patients. *Journal of Palliative Care, 21*(4), 285–292.

Holtslander, L., & Duggleby, W. D. (2009). The hope experience of older bereaved women who cared for a spouse with terminal cancer. *Qualitative Health Research, 19*(3), 388–400.

Hudson, P. (2013). Improving support for family carers: Key implications for research, policy, and practice. *Palliative Medicine, 27*(7), 581–582. doi:10.1177 /0269216313488855

Hudson, P., Zordan, R., & Trauer, T. (2011). Research priorities associated with family caregivers in palliative care: International perspectives. *Journal of Palliative Medicine, 14*(4), 397–401.

Jevne, R. (2005). Hope: The simplicity and complexity. In J. Eliot (Ed.), *Interdisciplinary perspectives on hope* (pp. 259–291). New York, NY: Nova Science.

Martel, L. (2013). *Mortality: Overview, 2010 and 2011.* Ottawa: Ministry of Industry.

Morse, J. (2009). Tussles, tensions, and resolutions. In J. Morse (Ed.), *Developing grounded Theory: The Second Generation* (pp. 13–22). Walnut Creek, CA: Left Coast Press.

Sandelowski, M., & Barroso, J. (2007). *Handbook for synthesizing qualitative research.* New York, NY: Springer.

Stroebe, M., Schut, H., & Stroebe, W. (2007). Health outcomes of bereavement. *Lancet, 370*, 1960–1973.

World Health Organization. (2002). W.H.O. Definition of Palliative Care [Electronic version] Retrieved February 14, 2005, from http://www.who.int/cancer /palliative/definition/en

PSYCHOLOGICAL ADJUSTMENT OF CHINESE WOMEN WITH BREAST CANCER: A GROUNDED THEORY STUDY

Shirley S.-Y. Ching and Ida M. Martinson

The idea of studying the coping of cancer patients began when I (the first author) was working in the oncology ward of an acute hospital in Hong Kong. There is no doubt that cancer diagnosis and subsequent treatment have a significant impact on a patient's life and that of his or her family. However, I noted that cancer patients reacted to these impacts in different ways, ranging from facing the reality with a positive attitude to withdrawal or even suicide. As a nurse working closely with patients, I was curious to know what was happening to them, what affected their coping, and ultimately what nurses can do to enable them to cope with the demands of illness with strength and resilience.

With the purpose of understanding the coping process of Chinese women with breast cancer and exploring the factors affecting their use of coping strategies, the effects of coping strategies on outcome, changes in coping across time, and cultural characteristics, I adopted grounded theory methodology, which is philosophically rooted in symbolic interactionism (Blumer, 1969) in this study.

DESCRIPTION OF THE STUDY

Adopting the philosophical basis and methodology of the grounded theory, I conducted 35 interviews with 24 Chinese women suffering from primary breast cancer without metastasis. I followed and interviewed five women thrice, from diagnosis to 3 months after completion of treatment.

Reframing: Core Variable

We developed a model of psychological adjustment of Chinese women to the impact of breast cancer. "Reframing" was identified as the core variable in the adjustment process. With their awareness of the presence of breast cancer, the frame which women upheld to explain their assumptive world was no longer adequate to explain the situation. The women did not have a relevant reference to interpret or predict their experiences, and this resulted in a chaotic state. They needed to reconstruct a new frame (i.e., reframe) by forming an interpretation of the new situation. Reframing refers to the interaction among and organization of the ideas, thoughts, or concepts that were input after diagnosis. From the data, it was this new interpretation that affected the choice of coping strategies and resulted in different coping outcomes. One of the women summarized the process of psychological adjustment to illness as follows:

> After waiting for 4 months, the doctor told me that the tumor was not benign but malignant. I was shocked. Why? . . . I had much fear and worry . . . The social worker and nurses counseled me . . . they worked on my thinking . . . it was very helpful for me . . . There must be some worries and difficult times. You need to get through the struggling with your thoughts by yourself, . . . you have to work through your thoughts before you know how to cope and face it [breast cancer].

Terms such as "work on her thoughts," "struggling with thoughts," and "think in this way" reveal the women's effort to reconstruct a new frame on living with breast cancer during the reframing process. "Worked through her thoughts" was used by the women to describe the state of accepting cancer.

Reconstructing a new frame took a long time. From the data, it started when the women became aware of the possible diagnosis of breast cancer and did not end until they had integrated breast cancer into their life experience. During this period, the women experienced the stages of disclosure of diagnosis, treatment, and rehabilitation, which required corresponding psychological adjustments. From the data, there were three subprocesses in the reframing process through which the women were required to complete specific coping work (i.e., acceptance work in the appraisal process, sustaining work in the controlling process, and integration work in the assimilation process). Failure to complete the coping work in one subprocess may hinder the smooth transition to the subsequent subprocesses, in turn affecting the coping outcome. The categories, related concepts, properties, and dimensions are shown in Table 6.1 and are elaborated in the following sections that discuss modes of coping.

Table 6.1 *Appraisal Process, Controlling Process, and Assimilation Process, Courses of Action, Related Concepts, and Their Properties and Dimensions*

Mode of Coping		Fighting	Following the Natural Course	Struggling	Bearing
Context	Focus	Coping	Coping	Problem	Problem
	Approach	Active	Yielding	Active	Yielding
Appraisal process—Acceptance work					
Courses of action	Orientating to reality				
	Need to know	Great	Little	Great	Great/little
	Motivation to seek information	High	Low	High	Low
	Subjective positive interpretation	Yes	Yes	No	No
	Estimating impact of cancer				
	Method	Inference	Guesstimate	Guesstimate	Intuition
	Rule to delimit problem	Minimum risk	Minimum risk	Maximum risk	Maximum risk
	Assessing the ability to cope				
	Ability of self	Adequate	Adequate	Inadequate	Inadequate
	Ability of others	Adequate	Adequate	Adequate/ Inadequate	Inadequate

(continued)

Table 6.1 Appraisal Process, Controlling Process, and Assimilation Process, Courses of Action, Related Concepts, and Their Properties and Dimensions (continued)

Mode of Coping		Fighting	Following the Natural Course	Struggling	Bearing
Controlling process—Sustaining work					
Courses of action	Exercising control	Differential strategies according to nature of problems	Conforming	Forcing	Suppressing
	Creating sustaining forces	Yes	Yes	No	No
Assimilation process—Integration work					
Courses of action	Incorporating cancer into life — Orientation of cancer	Past	Past	Present	Present
	Resumption of "normal" life	Yes	Yes	No	No
	Vision for future	Positive	Positive	Grave	Grave
	Transformation	Yes	No	No	No
Consequence		Adapting	Surviving	Exhausting	Despairing

Context of Reframing

When analyzing the women's coping responses in the reframing process, we noted different patterns and found two contextual conditions, that is, focus and approach, to be discriminating in explaining the difference. "Focus" refers to the things that were at the women's center of attention. It affects the interpretation of a situation. It varied from focusing on "coping" (i.e., concentrating on the effort to deal with problems) to focusing on "problems" (i.e., being preoccupied by difficulties). "Approach" refers to the general method the women adopted in psychological adjustment. It varied from "active" (i.e., taking the initiative to assess the situation and adopt strategies targeted at changing the conditions) to "yielding" (i.e., conforming to the changes brought about by cancer and its treatment). We constructed a typology by using these two contextual conditions. Four modes of coping were discerned: "fighting," "following the natural course," "struggling," and "bearing."

In the next section, we describe the mechanism of psychological adjustment through which the women adopted different modes of coping and completed acceptance work in the appraisal process, sustaining work in the controlling process, and integration work in the assimilation process. Details of the women's coping responses in three subprocesses were elaborated in other two publications (Ching, Martinson, & Wong, 2009, 2012). The word "woman" in the following paragraphs refers to the participant of this study.

Fighting Mode

The fighting mode of coping was characterized by focusing attention on *coping* and the adoption of an *active* approach.

Appraisal Process

In *orientating to reality*, fighters needed to have psychological preparation for what would happen. They were motivated to seek information about cancer, treatment, and remedies but selective regarding the reliability of sources. Factual information from health care providers, books, and talks were preferred choices. In view of the uncertainty associated with cancer, fighters created a *subjective positive interpretation*, in which they tried to "underestimate" the impact of cancer and "overestimate" their ability to cope. This enabled them to collect evidence to support coping with a positive attitude. In *estimating the impact of cancer*, fighters more frequently used "inference" (i.e., reasoning based on factual evidence) and the "rule of minimum risk" (i.e., considering cancer-related risks that were very relevant, highly likely to happen, and with close immediacy). In *assessing their ability to cope and that of others*, fighters simply believed in and trusted their ability, as well as trusting their health care providers and advanced medical technology. With the use of these strategies, fighters interpreted the situation as manageable and were able to accept breast cancer. One fighter said:

> We need to open our eyes wide to observe other patients' conditions and hear what they say . . . If we believe that doctors can help us, we should have confidence in them. The pressure will be reduced if we become psychologically prepared . . . We need to rely on ourselves to face it [cancer].

Controlling Process

The strategies adopted by fighters were characterized by *differential strategies according to the nature of the problems* in the controlling process. In *exercising control*, fighters tried their best to control actual problems and to explore external help. For potential problems, fighters just "maintained hope for the best," and adopted a "wait-and-see" and "act-when-necessary" approach. Fighters created *sustaining forces* by identifying meaning in their experience to support them in facing challenges and persisting during times of suffering. The sources of sustaining forces included "striving for personally meaningful goals," "maintaining hope for recovery," "minimizing social disturbance" through "appraisal of social support" and "fulfilling role-related obligations," "self-reinforcement of courage," "appraisal of progress," and "appraisal of secondary gain." Fighters described their strategies: "My body is weakening . . . I drink Fructus Jujubae soup every day . . . I have adequate nutrition" and "I am not too worried about the potential side effects of chemotherapy . . . I believe I will be able to get through it . . . I am employing the strategy of crossing that bridge when I come to it."

Assimilation Process

With the influence of the appraisal and controlling processes, fighters were able to *incorporate their breast cancer experience into life* and accept it. Breast cancer was appraised as a past event; they were able to resume their "normal" life and adopt a positive vision for the future. *Transformation* occurred as the breast cancer experience prompted the fighters to examine the values, beliefs, goals, and directions that they had upheld before the diagnosis. Examples included "change in the relative importance of things in life," "increasing sensitivity to others' needs," "appraisal of the good in life," and "finding a new life orientation." After completion of treatment, one fighter said, "I am happy after resuming work. . . . Sometimes I think about it [the cancer experience]. It is already a past event."

Consequence

As fighters were able to accept breast cancer in the appraisal process, sustain their coping with a positive attitude in the controlling process, and integrate cancer into their life experience with positive transformation in the assimilation process, the consequence of their coping was described as *adapting*.

Following the Natural Course Mode

Following the natural course mode (the following mode) was characterized by focusing attention on *coping* and the adoption of a *yielding* approach.

Appraisal Process

In *orientating to reality*, followers had little need for information, as they relinquished control to advocates who managed their breast cancer (such as their grown-up children, significant others, or health care providers); they lacked the ability to understand the information given to them, or did not know what to ask. Similar to fighters, followers also created a *subjective positive interpretation* to support them and to cope with a positive attitude. Followers subjectively appraised the reality of being diagnosed with cancer as "I am not the only one," "There are others in the same boat," and through "normalization," and "causal attribution to fate." In *estimating the impact of breast cancer*, followers relied on the advocates without much consideration, simply believed that they would be cured, and compared their cancer experiences with past difficulties. They used "guesstimates" (i.e., reasoning based on suggested evidence) more often, and adopted the "rule of minimum risk." In *assessing the ability to cope*, followers relinquished control to advocates. However, they had confidence in their own ability to conform to the changes and endure the suffering. Followers interpreted the situation as manageable with the help of their advocates, and they were able to accept cancer. One woman who adopted the following mode stated:

> To feel at ease in all circumstances . . . just follow the natural course . . .
> To think in a way of letting go.

Controlling Process

Followers coped by *conforming* to changes in the controlling process. Similar to fighters, they also created *sustaining forces* that helped them to adopt a positive attitude and summon up the courage to confront difficulties. In *exercising control* for the management of breast cancer, followers did not have the knowledge necessary for controlling cancer; they followed the advice and arrangements of their advocates and adopted a "wait-and-see" and "act-when-necessary" approach after adhering to their advocates' advice. With help from their advocates, they were not powerless or desperate. One follower said, "I entrust myself to the doctors. They have the experience but I do not know much. They know what to do so I trust them."

Assimilation Process

Influenced by the appraisal and controlling process, followers were able to *incorporate the breast cancer experience into their life perspectives* by maintaining a sense of continuity between the past, present, and future, resuming "normal" life and maintaining a positive vision for the future in the assimilation process. Because the principle of following the natural course allowed much flexibility in coping, followers did not significantly evaluate, examine, or reflect on the values and attitudes that they upheld. Little *transformation* or psychological growth occurred in followers. One follower described her appraisal of breast cancer after completion of treatment:

> My children are really . . . very concerned about me when I am sick.
> I think I am very lucky. You ask me about the impact . . . I am not hurt.

Consequence

Followers were able to accept breast cancer in the appraisal process, sustain their coping with a positive attitude in the controlling process, and integrate cancer into their life but with little transformation in the assimilation process; therefore, the consequence of their coping was described as *surviving*.

Struggling Mode

The struggling mode was denoted by focusing attention on the problems of breast cancer and by the adoption of an active approach.

Appraisal Process

In *orientating to reality*, the strugglers were eager to seek information from health care providers or other patients about actual and potential problems (e.g., the curative rate, possible side effects, or difficulties). Strugglers used "guesstimates" more frequently to *estimate the impact of cancer,* as they had little basic knowledge about cancer. They estimated the impacts by assessing suggestive evidence or indirect cues from their encounters, comparing their condition with others and their own experience. Low tolerance of problems resulted in the adoption of the "rule of maximum risk" (i.e., considering cancer-related risks that were likely to happen, without giving much consideration to relevancy and temporal factors). This resulted in the initiation of problem-generating mechanisms, by which actual problems were counted and potential and new problems were expected. Strugglers *appraised their ability* to cope as inadequate because they overestimated the threat of cancer. They appraised the support from significant others as inadequate because of their focus on problems. With the use of these strategies, strugglers interpreted the situation as unmanageable by themselves and were unable to accept cancer. They did not create *subjective positive interpretation.* A struggler described her experience:

> My mind was filled with series of questions. Cancer is a horrible, incurable disease, . . . very frightened . . . I didn't know how to cope with it.

Controlling Process

To have "absolute control" of the problems, strugglers' coping strategies were characterized by *forcing* in the controlling process. Being driven by the urge to know more and to solve their problems, strugglers actively sought information to *control cancer.* However, because strugglers were not necessarily able to understand or evaluate the relevance of new information, such information might be a source of stress through anticipation, misinterpretation, and an inability to analyze and integrate it. Unreliable information might hinder the resolution of problems. With their appraisal of inability to cope, strugglers followed advice from others to control problems. Mismatches between strugglers' needs and the advice received, coping options limited by the advice, inability to choose among different advice options, and anticipation of new concerns might have resulted. Intolerance of problems also compelled strugglers to seek help from others to manage their concerns. While this provided temporary relief from irritability, it might also result in dependence and further impairment of their problem-solving ability. Driven by an urge to control their problems, strugglers might force themselves to do something against their wishes, and this might lead to reinforcement of irritability and conflicting feelings. Strugglers might blame themselves or others when feeling pressed by their problems. No creation of *sustaining force* was noted. One struggler said:

> I had great fear. The others told me that emotions were important for recovery ... I forced myself not to think too much. I struggled with myself.

Assimilation Process

Under the influence of their appraisal and controlling processes, strugglers failed to accept and *incorporate breast cancer into their life perspectives* during the assimilation process. As they appraised the threat of recurrence and metastasis as very significant, cancer was a present event, and their future was grave. The compulsion to take measures to prevent potential problems hindered strugglers from resuming "normal" life after treatment completion. Little positive *transformation* was noted, as they spent much of their energy dealing with their problems and seldom examined and evaluated the values and beliefs that they upheld. One struggler stated her worry after completion of treatment:

> Now my situation is just like that before surgery ... you know removing the lymph nodes might have a significant effect ... I believe this.

Consequence

Because strugglers could not accept cancer in the appraisal process, forced themselves to have absolute control of problems in the controlling process, and failed to integrate cancer into their life perspective in the assimilation process, the consequence of their coping was described as *exhausting*.

Bearing Mode

The bearing mode was delineated by focusing attention on the *problems* and adoption of a *yielding* approach.

Appraisal Process

Bearers had little motivation to seek information and *orientate to reality* because of the short period of time from diagnosis to commencement of treatment, the lack of information given by health care providers, and their self-inhibition in information seeking as a result of emotional disturbance. Bearers *estimated the impact of breast cancer* as high, and were in a state of powerlessness. The "rule of maximum risk" was used. They appraised "intuitively" from their preconceptions about cancer, overestimated the impact, and underestimated their ability to cope. No creation of *subjective positive interpretation* was noted in bearers. Bearers did not make much effort in *assessing their ability to cope.* They sought help from health care providers to manage their problems. As a result of all these conditions, bearers interpreted the situation as unmanageable and were unable to accept cancer. One bearer described the state of bearing as inability to face the situation:

> If an event happens but one is unable to think of a way of letting go . . . backing oneself into a corner through sheer stubbornness . . . only thinking in one way.

Controlling Process

The strategies they adopted in the controlling process were characterized by *suppressing.* In the controlling process, bearers needed to know what was happening and what would happen to *control cancer.* However, they avoided seeking information and knowing more about cancer to limit their cognitive and psychological disturbance. Because of their high threat appraisal and strong sense of powerlessness in coping, bearers had no choice but to follow the advice of powerful others and adopt suppressing strategies to control cancer. However, there was the potential for new problems to arise when others' advice did not fit their needs, and they lacked the preparation required for coping and adjusting to negative changes, despite available remedies. Similar to strugglers, bearers focused their attention on problems, and some of them even sought external help. No creation of a *sustaining force* was noted. One bearer described her experience:

> The doctor instructed me to be admitted for operation . . . I could not change the situation . . . I could do nothing . . . I had nothing to say . . . Could I tell him that I did not want the operation? In fact I was scared when I heard about cancer.

Assimilation Process

Influenced by their appraisal and controlling process, bearers failed to accept and *incorporate breast cancer into their life perspectives* during the assimilation process. Because they appraised the threat of recurrence and metastasis as high and experienced a strong sense of powerlessness and lack of control, cancer was appraised as a present event, even years after completion of treatment. They were unable to resume "normal" life and saw their future as grave. Little *transformation* was noted in their powerless state. One bearer said:

> I anticipate about it [recurrence] . . . most of the patients will have an undesirable outcome. It is a matter of time.

Consequence

Because bearers were unable to accept cancer in the appraisal process, they focused on problems and had a sense of powerlessness in the controlling process. They failed to integrate cancer into their life perspective in the assimilation process. The consequence of bearers' coping was described as *despairing*.

In this study, the four modes of coping refer to a dynamic state in which coping strategies were used as dictated by women's interpretations of the situation. Some women did change from one mode of coping to another when their interpretation changed.

CONCEPTUAL AND METHODOLOGICAL ISSUES

We reviewed the literature during the conceptualization stage of the study, with three focuses: (a) illness experience of women with breast cancer, (b) conceptualization of illness experience and coping, and (c) qualitative research methods, with special attention to their philosophical basis and the development of grounded theory. We were able to identify the knowledge gap and significance of the study and were reminded of the essence of qualitative research and grounded study before conducting the study.

From the literature review on illness experience, we knew that breast cancer patients can now live longer with this life-threatening disease but are suffering from treatment side effects that affect their daily living (Schmid-Buchi, Halfens, Dassen, & van den Borne, 2008). Since stress is inevitable in this situation, coping makes all the difference in the adaptation outcome. Assisting cancer patients to cope with the demands has become an emerging challenge for health care professionals in the coming decade. This brings us to the realization of the need to understand the coping process of cancer patients at different phases of cancer care.

We then reviewed the literature on conceptualization of the illness experience and coping to learn more about the existing understanding and provide broad directions for exploration. Illness experiences were conceptualized by medical versus psychosocial models (Maes, Leventhal, & De Ridder, 1996) and dispositional (Burgess, Morris, & Pettingale, 1988) versus contextual (Ali & Khalil, 1991) approaches, and models have been proposed (Lazarus & Folkman, 1984). However, there were inherent limitations that did not provide a comprehensive understanding of coping (Maes et al., 1996; Skinner, Edge, Altman, & Sherwood, 2003). Researchers advocated longitudinal designs (Calhoun & Tedeschi, 2006) with the use of unstructured or semi-structured interviews as more sensitive methods to understand patients' illness experience and cultural implications.

In the choice of method for investigation, we considered a few important criteria. First, in order to identify the essence of coping from a woman's point of view, the method should facilitate exploration of all the concerns of a woman's life and allow her to comment on the aspects that are significant in the coping process. Second, the method should facilitate the exploration of the rationales and conditions that affect the use of coping strategies and their effects on the outcome of coping, as this is one of the gaps and weaknesses in the coping research done in the past. Third, changes in the coping process across time should be detected. Final, the method should allow an exploration of the cultural characteristics inherent in the coping process. With these considerations in mind, we adopted the grounded theory methodology, which aims to explore the "process" question in social settings (Denzin & Lincoln, 1994).

We conducted a literature review using qualitative methodology, in contrast with quantitative methodology, as the means of inquiry into the phenomenon. Madeleine Leininger (1985) explained that qualitative methodology focuses on the description and analysis of values, essences, and meanings that encompass the totality of an experience in a natural context. An open, inductive, and flexible discovery approach with no predetermined judgment is used to study cultural, social, environmental, and philosophical processes and phenomena. People are frequently involved to obtain full and accurate "truth," including both subjective and objective data. The researcher is the main instrument. Field study tools included observation guides, open-ended interviews, documents, direct participation, and many others. Diverse and creative modes of analysis, such as content, symbolic, interactional, and ethnographic, are adopted to fit the context and purpose of the research.

Symbolic interactionism is a social psychological and sociological theory with roots in American pragmatism (Schwandt, 1997). As stated in Herbert Blumer's work in 1969, symbolic interactionism was/is grounded in three basic premises, which are (a) human beings act toward things on the basis of the meanings that the things have for them; (b) the meaning of such things is derived from the social interaction that one has with one's fellows; (c) these meanings are handled in, and modified through, an interpretive process used by the person in dealing with the things encountered. With these philosophical premises in mind, no assumptions should be made regarding the impact of any situational conditions on the participants. Strauss and Corbin (1994) noted that some users did not carry out the important procedures properly, as they did not understand them, deliberately did not aim at developing theories, and claimed to use the grounded theory method only because their studies were inductive. Benoliel (1996) found that some researchers only used interview data in their studies, while others did not pay attention to the basic premises of symbolic interactionism and did not account for social structural influences on the experiences of the respondents. With awareness of all this possible diffusion, we emphasized the basic premises of symbolic interactionism when conducting the study and adhered to the core procedures (i.e., constant comparative method, theoretical coding, theoretical sampling, and memo writing; Glaser, 1978; Glaser & Strauss, 1967; Strauss & Corbin, 1998). We appraised the essences of qualitative methodology. We understand the importance of adopting an open, inductive, and flexible discovery approach with no predetermined judgment in the exploration. The conceptualization and proposal writing stage lasted for 1 year.

SAMPLE

Because permission was only granted for us to review the medical records of women who consented to participate in this study, physicians and nurses in the hospitals recruited participants who had been diagnosed with breast cancer and were sufficiently articulate to share their experience. To control the effect of generality for both the scope of the population and the conceptual level of the theory (Glaser & Strauss, 1967), we included other sampling criteria such as being Chinese, being 18 years of age or above, having been diagnosed with primary breast cancer without clinically confirmed metastasis to other organs, having no previous diagnosis of cancer, and being cognizant of the diagnosis of cancer. We contacted the women referred by the two hospitals either by phone or face-to-face interaction.

We conducted 35 interviews with 24 Chinese women suffering from breast cancer. We followed and interviewed five women thrice, from diagnosis to 3 months after completion of treatment. During the process of recruiting participants, we encountered the problems of theoretical sampling and refusal of interview. Theoretical sampling is a method of sampling whose purpose is to go to places, people, or events that will maximize opportunities to discover variations among emerging concepts in the data and to densify categories in terms of their properties and dimensions (Strauss & Corbin, 1998). With no direct access to the women before they consented to join the study, we relied on the physician and nurses to select the participants. In some cases, the participants might not have the required characteristics or behaviors to verify the hypothesis, but their interview data were useful in increasing the diversity of the data or illustrating other hypotheses in the substantive theory. Continuous communication and constant reminders from us to the physician and nurses were essential. Some women refused to be interviewed because they disliked the use of a recorder, were unwilling to be interviewed again before completion of treatment, or were persuaded by family members not to disclose too much to others. My explanation on the purpose of recording during interview and maintaining the anonymity and confidentiality of the data relieved the concerns of most of the women.

SETTING

The physicians and nurses recruited the participants in surgical clinics, surgical wards, and oncology outpatient departments where the women had been checked for abnormality in the breast, undergone surgery, and received radiation therapy and chemotherapy. An interview appointment would be made at a time and place that was convenient to the participants. If they indicated no preference, I would conduct the interviews in their homes to allow me to observe their living environment and interaction with family members. Out of the 36 interviews, we conducted 17 in the women's homes. The other interview locations included meeting rooms in the wards and clinics, the hospital canteen, my office, and the office of the Kai Fong Association. The interviews lasted from ½ hour to 3 hours. The average was 1½ hours. The meeting rooms in the hospitals and my office provided a quiet and comfortable environment for the women to share their experience. However, I encountered interruptions by family members when interviewing in the women's homes. Adult family members were usually very cooperative, but there were incidents in which young children clung to their mothers and requested food and their attention during the interviews. I stopped the interviews for a short while so that these women could take care of their children first. I believe these moments gave me precious chances to observe the interaction of the women and their family members in their daily living and understand their coping in the real context.

I made minor modifications to the interview arrangements of two women. One woman only consented to be interviewed and recorded by telephone, as her family members were opposed to her participation in the study. Another woman requested to be interviewed by telephone because she was emotionally disturbed. Without a recorder, only field notes were written as part of the data. This woman provided an excellent illustration of coping during emotional disturbance.

INSTRUMENTATION

With the broad aim of finding out what happened when women coped with breast cancer, we developed a broad interview guide to remind us about the topics that would be explored (i.e., cancer experience, problems, responses to impacts, facilitating and hindering factors, and changes brought about by cancer) and to maintain the consistency of the data collected. The researcher is often considered as an instrument in qualitative studies (Janesick, 1994). Maintaining flexibility and theoretical sensitivity was essential during the interview. It was impossible to begin the interview with no planning on the content of discussion, but I had to maintain an insight on seeking diversity or illustrating the emerging categories, properties, and dimensions from the data and understand the meaning of the women's experience. I continuously modified the interview guide based on the interview findings.

DATA COLLECTION AND DATA ANALYSIS

Interviews

I started the interviews by inviting the women to tell me what had happened from the detection of an abnormality in their breast to the time of interview. I found this narrative account to be very helpful, as it was an easy and natural way to start the conversation, provided groundwork for further discussion as I did not have access to the women's medical records before the interview, allowed the women to "speak in the context" because they could tell their story according to their stream of thoughts, and enabled them to give a more detailed description of the relationship among the different components in the coping process. I used probing and follow-up questions to clarify the details of their story. I was then able to stay open and keep in mind the current categories (Glaser, 1978; Strauss & Corbin, 1998) in theoretical sampling. As data collection proceeded, I continuously modified the interview guide to elicit information about concepts in the emerging theory. I agreed with Janesick's (1994) notion that trust, rapport, and authentic communication patterns with participants must be established. The women who participated in this study were informants, but at the same time they were patients who needed attention and care. With empathetic understanding, the women knew that they were being cared for and respected, and this increased their sense of security when they shared their experience, struggle, and the meaning of the events.

With the use of grounded theory, we collected and analyzed data simultaneously. Data collection gave input for data analysis, and data analysis gave direction for data collection (Glaser, 1978). I interviewed participants who were recruited based on theoretical relevance. The goal of analysis was to generate an emergent set of categories and their properties that fit, worked, and were relevant for integrating into a theory (Glaser, 1978). We followed the three levels of sampling procedures (i.e., open sampling, relational and variational sampling, and discriminate sampling), which are directed by the logic and aim of the coding procedures (i.e., open coding, axial coding, and selective coding) of grounded theory (Strauss & Corbin, 1998). The interplay between theoretical sampling and theoretical coding is summarized below.

Open Sampling and Open Coding

At the beginning, I used *open sampling* with the intention of seeking diversity in the data and uncovering potentially relevant categories along with their properties and dimensions. I conducted interviews with women at different stages of their breast cancer experience (i.e., newly diagnosed, receiving treatment, and in rehabilitation) and with a variety of demographic and medical information (e.g., age, educational level, place on the cancer trajectory, etc.). As I analyzed more interview data, I realized that the women's coping responses were affected by conditions other than their demographic characteristics. I then looked for differences in their personalities, their use of cognitive or behavioral strategies, and the support from their family members, as suggested by the data. Shortly after the interview, I transcribed the interviews word by word in Chinese to maintain the semiotic meanings of the data and imported them into QSR NUD*IST (Non-numeric Unstructured Data, Index Searching and Theorizing) computer software versions 3 and 4 for analysis. In order to enable the display of Chinese characters, I used the computer software TwinBridge Chinese Partner Version 4.5 (TwinBridge Software Corporation, 1997). In *open coding*, I examined each word, line, sentence, and paragraph (Glaser, 1978). From the beginning of data analysis, I kept the following few questions in my mind at all times: What are the data about? Which category, property, and dimension does this incident illustrate? Does it fit into an existing category or illustrate a new phenomenon? Coding was done by comparing the similarities and differences in context both within the same women and among different women. I used descriptive codes and in vivo codes to label each piece of data. QSR NUD*IST provided high sortibility and flexibility, which allowed me to code each piece of data into as many codes as possible to ensure the best fit and to visualize and modify the name and content of the nodes on the coding tree. At first, I made the mistake described by Strauss and Corbin (1998), summarizing instead of conceptualizing when labeling the phenomena. I grouped the coping strategies according to criteria that were familiar to us (i.e., cognitive, emotional, and behavioral; and problem-focused and emotion-focused). I then found that this coding method provided little ability to detect the difference between the use of coping responses among the women, to understand the phenomenon, and to move the analysis toward a higher level of abstraction. I recoded all the data according to the women's intentions underlying the use of coping strategies (i.e., accepting cancer and controlling cancer). I also encountered difficulty in deciding when to stop seeking diversity in data collection.

Narrowing down the focus for exploration before knowing the breadth of the phenomenon might cause a researcher to miss the essence of the problem. Open sampling came to an end when there were very few new data identified from the interviews. I coded all interview data by using open coding.

Axial Coding and Relational and Variational Sampling

I used *axial coding* to put the data back together by using theoretical codes. Theoretical codes conceptualize how the substantive codes may relate to each other as hypotheses to be integrated into a theory (Glaser, 1978). When the women gave accounts of their coping experience, they always described the cause–consequence relationship among different elements. After several interviews, I revisited the data collected from a few women who were more willing to share by using the paradigm model. I adopted *relational and variational sampling* to validate the hypothesis noted in the data. In order to densify the categories and verify their interrelationship, I interviewed participants who (a) had similar responses, intervening conditions, and outcomes to confirm the relationship between the categories; (b) did not respond in that particular way or under the influence of that particular intervening condition to validate whether the relationship existed only under a specific condition; and (c) were negative cases, to confirm the relationship did not exist or that the opposite condition would occur if the particular condition did not exist. In addition, we noted limited power in the detection of change across time as the women tried to tell the whole story at one point in time. We had difficulty pinpointing the exact time at which some elements of the coping process, identification of the transition from one psychological phase to another, or change in pattern of coping within the cancer experience had occurred. Some women could not recall experiences they had had long before, and their feelings and impressions about their earlier experience might have been modified by the outcome of their coping and later experience.

We then decided to recruit, follow, and interview women at the time of diagnosis, during treatment, and about 3 months after treatment. We constantly communicated with nurses and physicians, who had a better understanding of the women, in recruiting participants. By continual comparison and development of the categories and subcategories along the dimension level, we identified patterns in the women's coping. For example, women were uncertain about what would happen (causal condition) after diagnosis. To cope with the demand (phenomenon), they would orientate to reality by seeking information (action). Dimensions for the seeking of information spanned from more (detailed information) to less (no information). It was these earned distinctions in the theory that provided the concepts with operational meanings for application (Glaser, 1978). Then we explored the variations in the phenomenon by comparing each category and its subcategories at the dimensional level for different patterns in the data. With a similar causal condition, phenomenon, and intervening condition, the women who coped by adopting an active approach (context) tended to seek more detailed information, while those who adopted a yielding approach (context) tended to seek much less information. Of those who adopted an active approach and sought detailed information about cancer, not all were able to remain calm and gain psychological comfort (consequence). We noted that some of the women sought information because they wanted to know what they could do to cope (context of focusing on coping), while others worried about the problems (context of focusing on problems).

To move a step further, when taking the other coping strategies into consideration, we noted patterns in the use of coping strategies. We set up hypotheses on the relationship among categories only when they were clearly indicated in the data and no postulations were made before data collection. We verified the hypotheses in the subsequent interviews. The tracing of the cause that led to a difference in the use of different strategies and coping outcomes finally resulted in identification of the reframing as the core category as related meaningfully to other categories and reoccurring frequently in the data. Both the inductive and deductive approaches were employed to arrive at this conclusion.

Discriminate Sampling and Selective Coding

With the aim of validating categories and their relationship and filling in any gaps, we adopted *discriminate sampling* by follow-up interviews or rereading and reanalyzing the existing data to pick up pieces of data that had gone unnoticed in the early stage of data analysis. This was very helpful, as it was difficult to gain an in-depth understanding of the women in the field setting and identify specific illustrations before the interviews. In *selective coding*, I delimited the coding to only those variables that related to the core category (i.e., reframing), their properties, and dimensions and integrated them to form a theory. I applied the paradigm model again. I started with "rich" interviews from each pattern identified. I reviewed the existing transcripts and collected new and detailed data in subsequent interviews. I went back to the same women to collect a specific piece of data that would only be found in women adopting a specific mode of coping, and it was very helpful.

Under the specific impact of breast cancer (causal condition), reframing took place in the form of reconstructing new frames (phenomena). The focus and approach of coping were identified as the properties of the reframing process. A typology was constructed to illustrate the four modes of coping formed by the dimensions of these two variables and consisted of fighting, following the natural course, struggling, and bearing (context). Under the complex interaction of various conditions that affected the focus and approach of coping, the women completed various types of work in the reframing process: acceptance work, sustaining work, and integration work (action/interaction), each with specific manifestations and consequences that were shown by dimensions.

Finally, I reviewed the existing transcripts, sorting memos to fill in any gap in the theory. Selective coding came to an end when theoretical saturation was achieved and no additional data could be identified in the incoming data; all variations in contributing conditions, coping responses, and outcome were explained by the framework. When this state was reached, 35 interviews with 24 women had been analyzed. A substantive theory was developed to describe the psychological adjustment of Chinese women to breast cancer.

Memos, Diagrams, and Tables

Memos are an indispensable tool for theory development. In this study, we constantly documented and reviewed our thoughts and ideas, development of the categories and their properties and dimensions, relationships, or hypotheses in the theoretical memo. Directions for the theoretical sampling and topics to be explored in the subsequent interviews as the theory emerged for the data were recorded in the operational memo. Data accounting sheets and paradigm model tables were used to display the data in tabular form for easy comparison and visualization of the similarities and differences. Carefully constructed paradigm model tables were found to be particularly useful when comparing the details related by the components of the paradigm model. During data analysis, numerous diagrams were used to capture the causal relationship of the elements in the coping process to conceptualize abstract concepts.

ESTABLISHING TRUSTWORTHINESS

We adopted the four assessment criteria that were put forward by Lincoln and Guba (1985) for the naturalistic paradigm to address trustworthiness. In this study, we enhanced *truth value/credibility* through prolonged engagement and continuous interaction with the women with breast cancer and reflection on my understanding of the phenomenon during the 20 months of data collection. We conducted peer debriefing by describing the analytic trail with nursing research students and supervisors throughout the study to clarify and explore their thoughts. Negative case analysis was used to verify specific relationships between the categories.

At the end of the interviews, we incorporated member checks on the categories and their relationships with the women who provided the data or the women who participated in the subsequent interviews. After the member checks, the findings were either verified, modified with additional information, or disproved and subjected to further exploration. *Applicability/ transferability* was enhanced as we developed the categories together with their properties and dimensions to provide contextual details about the events in the coping process. We also provided thick descriptions to enable someone interested in making a transfer. Seeking diversity in the data in open sampling also specified and enlarged the scope to which the conclusion of the study might be applied.

We ensured *consistency/dependability* with an audit trail that recorded details of the process of data collection and analysis and the findings from transcripts, demographic and medical information sheets, different types of memo, tables, diagrams, field notes, and case summaries. We established *neutrality/confirmability* by leaving an audit trail with details of the data collection and analysis and verification of the findings with the women to confirm that it reflected their interpretation accurately and to identify any subjective input from us. Documenting the observed facts and our subjective impressions separately helped to ensure confirmability.

ETHICAL CONSIDERATIONS

For ethical considerations, we adopted measures at various stages of the study to minimize any potential risk that might arise. During the recruitment of participants, I contacted each woman personally and explained the purpose of the study, the voluntary nature of their participation, the right to withdraw at any time without affecting their treatment and care, the necessity of follow-up interviews, and the use of a recorder before they signed a consent form. They were given my phone number for clarification of any query concerning the study. During data collection, I always tried to avoid evoking psychological disturbance in the women. In exploring some issues that were more sensitive, I tried to ask superficial questions first and used probing when the women talked about related issues. I respected the women's wishes if they chose to avoid discussing certain issues during the interview. A psychologist was invited to give advice and provide counseling services to the women if signs of increased psychological disturbance were identified. No such referral was required. During data analysis, the confidentiality of the information and data of this study was ensured throughout the research process by putting the transcripts and related documents in a locked filing cabinet and strictly limiting their access to the researcher only. Anonymity was maintained by assigning codes to each woman and each interview and not including their names in any transcripts or documents. Their personal information was recorded on a form that was kept separate from the other documents. After completion of the study, all the transcripts and related documents were destroyed.

DISSEMINATION

During the process of data collection and analysis, we compared the discoveries from the data to working on a jigsaw puzzle. We identified pieces of data on the women's coping, explored their relationship with other pieces of data, and related them to the bigger picture of their psychological adjustment to the impact of breast cancer from diagnosis to completion of treatment and thereafter. After putting all the pieces of the jigsaw puzzle together, we then moved from conceptualization of the phenomenon to the identification of a storyline that was comprehensive yet easy to follow. We tried different ways and finally decided to follow the evolution of the process of psychological adjustment (i.e., from the appraisal process to the controlling process to the assimilation process) and then explained the women's responses to adopting different modes by relating to their coping focus and approach.

We included the codes identified from the data to provide details of different manifestations of the coping phenomenon. For example, the fighters and followers created a subjective positive interpretation, believing that "I am not the only one" and "There are others in the same boat." We also captured key quotations to enable the readers to gain a better understanding of the women's considerations. Summarizing tables and diagrams served as road maps and were helpful in guiding our writing and the reading of the manuscripts. The writing-up process lasted about 6 months.

SUMMARY

Based on the substantive model of psychological adjustment of Chinese women with breast cancer, we emphasized the importance of understanding women's interpretation of the situation. Adaptive coping depends on enabling women to complete the coping work inherent in different stages of the cancer experience—that is, facilitating acceptance after diagnosis, creating a personally meaningful sustaining force when facing problems caused by cancer and its treatment, and finally integrating the cancer experience into their life. The interventions of health care providers must be specific to the women's mode of coping and time on the cancer trajectory in order to address their needs.

To summarize the process of conducting the study using the grounded theory method, we believe it was a challenging but very satisfying experience. Curiosity and sensitivity guided us in exploring the phenomenon during data collection and analysis. Patience and persistence were essential as we reread and recoded the verbatim transcripts throughout the data analysis. Continuous collaboration with the clinical staff ensured theoretical sampling. Support from supervisors and fellow students was indispensable. We learned courage and sincerity from the women who shared their experiences with us. Because our development of the model was grounded in the data, we are confident that it fits, works, and is relevant to the psychological adjustment of Chinese women with breast cancer.

REFERENCES

Ali, N. S., & Khalil, H. Z. (1991). Identification of stressors, level of stress, coping strategies, and coping effectiveness among Egyptian mastectomy patients. *Cancer Nursing, 14*(5), 232–239.

Benoliel, J. Q. (1996). Grounded theory and nursing knowledge. *Qualitative Health Research, 6*(3), 406–428. doi:10.1177/104973239600600308

Blumer, H. (1969). *Symbolic interactionism: Perspective and method*. Berkeley, CA: University of California Press.

Burgess, C., Morris, T., & Pettingale, K. W. (1988). Psychological response to cancer diagnosis—II. Evidence for coping styles (coping styles and cancer diagnosis). *Journal of Psychosomatic Research, 32*(3), 263–272.

Calhoun, L. G., & Tedeschi, R. G. (Eds.). (2006). *Handbook of posttraumatic growth: Research and practice*. Mahwah, NJ: Lawrence Erlbaum Associates.

Ching, S. Y., Martinson, I. M., & Wong, T. K. S. (2009). Reframing: Psychological adjustment of Chinese women at the beginning of the breast cancer experience. *Qualitative Health Research, 19*(3), 339–351. doi:10.1177/1049732309331867

Ching, S. Y., Martinson, I. M., & Wong, T. K. S. (2012). Meaning making: Psychological adjustment to breast cancer by Chinese women. *Qualitative Health Research, 22*(2), 250–262. doi:10.1177/1049732311421679

Denzin, N. K., & Lincoln, Y. S. (1994). Introduction: Entering in field of qualitative research. In N. K. Denzin & Y. S. Lincoln (Eds.), *Handbook of qualitative research* (pp. 1–17). Thousand Oaks, CA: Sage.

Glaser, B. G. (1978). *Theoretical sensitivity*. Mill Valley, CA: The Sociology Press.

Glaser, B. G., & Strauss, A. L. (1967). *The discovery of grounded theory: Strategies of qualitative research*. New York, NY: Aldine de Gruyter.

Janesick, V. J. (1994). The dance of qualitative research design: Metaphor, methodolatry, and meaning. In N. K. Denzin & Y. S. Lincoln (Eds.), *Handbook of qualitative research* (pp. 209–219). Thousand Oaks, CA: Sage.

Lazarus, R. S., & Folkman, S. (1984). *Stress, appraisal, and coping*. New York, NY: Springer.

Leininger, M. M. (Ed.). (1985). *Qualitative research methods in nursing*. Orlando, FL: Grune & Stratton.

Lincoln, Y. S., & Guba, E. G. (1985). *Naturalistic inquiry*. Beverly Hills, CA: Sage.

Maes, S., Leventhal, H., & De Ridder, D. T. D. (1996). Coping with chronic disease. In M. Zeidner & N. S. Endler (Eds.), *Handbook of coping: Theory, research, applications* (pp. 221–251). New York, NY: John Wiley & Sons.

QSR NUD*IST (Versions 3 & 4) [Computer software]. Thousand Oaks, CA: Scolari.

Schmid-Buchi, S., Halfens, R. J. G., Dassen, T., & van den Borne, B. (2008). A review of psychosocial needs of breast cancer patients and their relatives. *Journal of Clinical Nursing, 17*(21), 2895–2909. doi:10.1111/j.1365-2702.2008.02490.x

Schwandt, T. A. (1997). *Qualitative inquiry: A dictionary of terms.* Thousand Oaks, CA: Sage.

Skinner, E. A., Edge, K., Altman, J., & Sherwood, H. (2003). Searching for the structure of coping: A review and critique of category systems for classifying ways of coping. *Psychological Bulletin, 129*(2), 216–269. doi:10.1037/0033-2909.129.2.216

Strauss, A., & Corbin, J. (1994). Grounded theory methodology: An overview. In N. K. Denzin & Y. S. Lincoln (Eds.), *Handbook of qualitative research* (pp. 273–285). Thousand Oaks, CA: Sage.

Strauss, A., & Corbin, J. (1998). *Basics of qualitative research: Techniques and procedures for developing grounded theory* (2nd ed.). Thousand Oaks, CA: Sage.

TwinBridge Chinese partner 4.5: CD-ROM version: User's guide. (1997). Monterey Park, CA: TwinBridge Software Corp.

CHAPTER SEVEN

THE INTEGRATION OF GROUNDED THEORY WITHIN CLINICAL ETHNOGRAPHIC RESEARCH

Denise Saint Arnault

In the mid-1990s, the wife of a Japanese auto industry employee in Detroit became the focus of public scrutiny, when tragically, during postpartum psychosis, she drowned her baby (Fetters, 1997). The intercultural dialogue between the Japanese community and the clinical community that followed highlighted the critical need to understand how symptoms interact with social and cultural factors to affect help-seeking for Asians. I was a medical anthropology student, a clinical nurse specialist in psychiatric nursing, and an advanced Japanese language student, when my tutors beseeched me to get involved and help the Japanese community understand what happened. Most of the newspaper reports and the TV news insisted that the Japanese had a large supportive community, acknowledged that this woman had been under the care of a medical practitioner throughout her pregnancy, and that her mother had come to live with her for some time before the birth. Because I was in a position to interface with both the Japanese and the psychiatric and the primary care communities about this phenomenon, I went to work, educating students and the Japanese community about how culture can affect mental illness. However, the question that plagued me, and became the focus of my research, was how this could occur in such a "close" community. I wondered how culture affects communication of distress and the provision of help. To understand this phenomenon, I took a clinical ethnographic perspective. This perspective is helpful for practitioners who are also anthropologists because they sit between a cultural and a clinical community and are therefore in a position to merge the skill sets from each role to create a new set of insights. This chapter focuses on a clinical ethnographic project that used mixed methods to understand the interaction between culture and help-seeking. I describe how I embedded the grounded theory methodology into a larger project that integrated theories from medical anthropology and social psychology into a framework for a triangulated clinical ethnographic investigation of help-seeking for distress in a community of Japanese women in a particular expatriate community.

RESEARCH PROBLEM

Asian Americans are a fast-growing ethnic group in the United States (U.S. Census Bureau, 2001; U.S. Department of Health and Human Services, 2001). The Asian population grew faster than the total U.S. population between 1990 and 2000 (U.S. Census Bureau, 2001). Michigan has a large Japanese population because many Japanese have immigrated to work in the automotive industry and related businesses, bringing their families with them. There are between 6,000 and 8,000 Japanese families affiliated with this industry alone, with a population in 2000 of over 12,000, and the Japanese population in surrounding counties ranging from 4.2% to 8.3% of the total population (U.S. Census Bureau, 2001).

Characteristics of the Asian population that may put them at risk for mental illness include separations from their extended families; intergenerational conflict, family system, and role relationship changes; acculturation conflict related to strong ethnic identification; lack of English language proficiency; employment problems; and discrimination. While it is true that any given immigrant or ethnic population varies along a continuum of less to more acculturated to the host cultures, we believe that the starting point for understanding how culture affects symptoms, illness, and help-seeking is to focus on less acculturated groups. This is important for two reasons. First, less acculturated immigrants are most vulnerable to the risk factors outlined above. Second, we do not yet understand how less acculturated immigrants experience symptoms or what help-seeking options they access or employ.

Despite the overlapping risk factors and prevalence rates, there is convergent evidence that Asians underutilize mental health services regardless of the service type or their regional population density (Sue, 1999; U.S. Department of Health and Human Services, 2001). The consequences of underutilization include high illness prevalence and high illness severity (Sue, 1999; U.S. Department of Health and Human Services, 2001). Studies that have examined the factors that may cause this underutilization of mental health services have found the following: the tendency to endorse somatic rather than emotional and interpersonal problems; stigmatization of psychiatric disorders and the desire to avoid shame and loss of face; differences in language, culture, and ethnicity that present barriers to health care access; and a culturally based lack of understanding of western-defined psychiatric disorders. These studies have also found that Asians may favor help-seeking through primary care and other physically oriented self-help channels, combined with social support. Physically oriented self-help includes the use of natural remedies and professional help such as herbalists, acupuncturists, massage, exercise, and chiropractors (De Wester, 1996; Kirmayer, 2001; Lock, 1987b; Maeno, Kizawa, Ueno, Nakata, & Sato, 2002; Simon, VonKorff, Piccinelli, Fullerton, & Ormel, 1999; Waza, Graham, Zyzanski, & Inoue, 1999).

THEORETICAL UNDERPINNINGS

There is a debate in qualitative research about how much theory should be used to inform inquiry. This "atheoretical" stance is incredibly important to help the researcher avoid premature or inappropriate framing of the phenomenon or leading a participant along a line that captures only part of his or her experience. However, it is naïve to think that one can truly approach a project without a theoretical frame. These perspectives inform how we make sense of the world and are always present. I took the approach that I *did* have disciplinary perspectives, and that I *was* engaged with theory. For me, the task was to clarify and explicate what those were and specifically how they framed my perceptions of the phenomenon of interest. As we will see, I used the theory to make sense of the field during the fieldwork phase of my research. I also used the theory to help me narrow the scope of inquiry.

At the time I carried out the study (1995–1998), there was a substantial body of works in the two areas that informed my inquiry (Saint Arnault, 1998). One area was social psychology, which explained how culture became part of the individual consciousness and how individual-level cultural knowledge guided perception and behavior. I selected the cultural model perspective from this field. The other area was medical anthropology, which described how culture can be viewed with regard to illness. In my work, I took the perspective that cultural expressions of distress were specific ways that the group understood and gave meaning to expressions of need, defined normalcy, and how culture shapes professional definitions of mental illness. Below, I synthesize these theoretical underpinnings. These underpinnings were the *container* that held my clinical ethnographic investigation and created a kind of frame within which the grounded theory component of this project was carried out.

Culture is a group-level phenomenon that includes the beliefs and values, behavioral practices, and social institutions within the social environment or milieu. This collection of expectation patterns is often referred to as cultural models (Holland & Quinn, 1987; Markus, Kitayama, & Heiman, 1996; Moscovici, 1988). As such, a given cultural model has expectations for its members. The categories of expectations broadly include ideal values, motivations and goals, status-related social roles, and preferred social behaviors. The perspective for my research was that of symptom experiences, symptom interpretations and evaluations, the dynamics within the social structure, and help-seeking as "filtered through" cultural models. Cultural models direct a person's attention to the aspects of his or her experience that need attention. I knew that the Japanese had a rich understanding of subtle changes in the body, so I made sure I had open-ended questions about physical and emotional distress (Ohnuki-Tierney, 1984).

Research in anthropology has explored how cultural models include cultural theories about how the body and mind function. These are ethnophysiological models, and research has explored how, once a sensation is noticed, it is evaluated in terms of its normalcy and severity. A physical sensation or emotion is labeled a "symptom" when it is a sign of an abnormal state, disturbance, illness, or pathology. These are cultural interpretations, and are based on past experience by the self and others within one's family and reference group. Along with symptom labeling, individuals evaluate the level of severity. Sometimes, this initiates an internal inventory of other important or co-occurring symptoms. Often symptoms are experienced as a collection, constellation, or cluster (Kirmayer, 2001). Culture models provide shared conceptualizations about the body, the nature of the healthy self, and when symptoms signify a condition outside the range of normal health (mentally ill). Moreover, culture defines whether people believe that mental illnesses are dangerous, incurable, or cause poor social skills. Specifically, cultural models provide templates that interpret the cause of, as well as the social significance of, distress symptoms. Research has shown that Asians may attribute their somatic symptoms to social and environmental causes, as well as underlying physical pathology, and that this may explain the tendency for Asians to primarily use medical care and social support for their distress (Guarnaccia, Rivera, Franco, & Neighbors, 1996; Hinton, Um, & Ba, 2001; Jenkins, Kleinman, & Good, 1991; Kirmayer, 1993; Kirmayer, Dao, & Smith, 1998; Kirmayer & Young, 1999; Kleinman, 1988, 1996, 2003; Pang, 1998). Therefore, in my help-seeking inquiry, I included questions about causes of distress as well as social significance and meaning.

Ethnographic studies have explored somatic distress in Asians in more detail. In a review of interactions between Chinese physicians and their patients, Ots found that both physicians and patients related internal organs with emotions, and carefully examined bodily perceptions (Ots, 1990). For example, the liver was seen as the cause of headaches, epigastric pain, hypertension, and anger, while the heart was related to anxiety, uncertainty, and fear. In a sample of Koreans with depression, Pang found that emotions were connected with bodily sensations and internal organs. These patients described how their experiences of physical distress were related to emotions in a holistic, symbolic way, such that depression was described as a symptom cluster that included anger, physical pain, and social discord (Pang, 1998). Finally, Lock interviewed physicians and middle-class women in Japan to document and explain *futeishūso* (nonspecific physical complaints). *Futeishūso* includes symptoms such as coldness, shoulder pain, palpitations, and nervousness. Both the physicians and patients in her study related these symptoms with social discontent, problems with the autonomic nervous system, pelvic inflammatory disease, and general personality sensitivity (Lock, 1987b).

Help-seeking occurs within the social context. Cultural models influence the social structure of a society, which broadly includes the power relationships and power elements between individuals, families, groups, and political institutions. Social structure directs how people distribute resources, divide labor, and acquire and distribute wealth. Social structure also constrains the actions of individuals, even in the smallest gestures, speech patterns, manners of dress, and emotional displays. The social structures of Asian cultures have been influenced by Confucian philosophy, in which interpersonal relationships are of primary concern. Within this philosophy, there is a focus on the family as the primary vehicle of support and nurturance of the individual. Research has documented that Asians share Confucian collectivist values about mental illness that stigmatize or that cast shame onto the families of those who experience mental illness (Association of Asian Pacific Community Health Organizations, 1995; Iwamasa & Hilliard, 1999; Lin & Cheung, 1999; Ma, 1999). Research has shown that many Japanese favor reliance on the primary family or group for emotional support (Fetters, 1998) and that they simultaneously fear stigmatizing or shaming the family if they use professional mental health care (Alem, Jacobsson, Araya, Kebede, & Kullgren, 1999; Atkinson & Gim, 1989; Bekker, Hentschel, & Fujita, 1996; Flum, 1998; Hom, 1998; Kagawa-Singer, Wellisch, & Durvasula, 1997; Kim, 1998; Kim, 2003; Narikiyo & Kameoka, 1992; Ono et al., 2001; Suan & Tyler, 1990; Yeh, Inose, Kobori, & Chang, 2001). Moreover, people generally match the treatment they seek to their beliefs about the cause of the distress (Chrisman & Kleinman, 1993). These data directed me to include questions about multiple types of help-seeking.

These collectivist rules can also discourage the open display of emotions and may also sanction the expression of negative emotion to maintain social and familial harmony. Asians may therefore deny the experience and expression of emotions or may conform to social emotion display rules that favor showing somatic rather than emotional or interpersonal distress (Kirmayer, 2001; Kleinman, 1982, 1983, 1988; Lin, 1996; Lock, 1987a; Ohnuki-Tierney, 1984). In addition to group solidarity, Confucian philosophy specifically structures society along hierarchical-status lines. The hierarchical dimension is present whenever there are differences in gender, age, social status, education, and a host of other status-related indicators. In my research, therefore, I asked women whom they felt they could and could not discuss their distress with and why.

MIXED-METHOD RESEARCH DESIGN

This research sought to clarify how culture defines and shapes both help-seeking and social exchange. Specifically, it explored how Japanese women temporarily residing in the United States with their husbands seek help and provide social support within their Japanese community. The project had three phases. First, I carried out 1 year of fieldwork both in Japan and in Michigan. Next, I carried out a 1-year grounded theory study with 25 women living in the Japanese community in Michigan. The final part of this project began after the grounded theory building. I further tested the hypothesized relationships among the concepts discovered in the analysis in a short survey of the Japanese women. Seventy-eight women took my survey, and the data further confirmed the theoretical propositions developed in my theory. This chapter briefly reports the importance of, and use of, fieldwork in a clinical ethnographic project and how this fieldwork and the literature review interacted to inform my grounded theory study.

My fieldwork in Japan included living in an apartment in Tokyo and several homestays. I paid close attention to the roles of women and the ways that they exchanged support and help in their communities. I talked with women on trains, in public baths, at nursing schools, and with my various homestay "mothers." I also met with nurses and physicians to understand distress and help-seeking for Japanese women living in Japan. Next, I carried out fieldwork in Michigan. I "hung out" at restaurants and grocery stores,

Saturday schools (these are culture and language schools set up by the education ministry in Japan), did English tutoring at several women's homes, had Japanese tutoring at several more women's homes, and talked with English as a second language (ESL) tutors. I met with nurses, doctors, the Japanese consulate, and many women from the Japanese business community. These experiences, coupled with my literature search, provided the framework for the grounded theory portion of the project.

Despite all that I now knew about Japanese culture, language, and Japanese women's lives, the gap in knowledge was immense. From the review of the literature (described above) and the fieldwork, I was able to narrow down beginning domains of inquiry. These domains included the importance of *both* physical and emotional forms of distress, cultural rules about emotional expression, the varieties of ways that the Japanese promote health, and the complexities of the social structure. My fieldwork experiences in Japan and Michigan also helped me understand the characteristics of the sample. I now knew that a woman's husband's position was important for their social status, the Japanese did not organize around churches, that the Saturday school was an important part of a woman's life, and that the family's affiliations were with other families according to the company (Toyota, Mazda, and Nissan). I knew that I needed to sample from all of the auto companies, as well as diverse age groups. I also knew that age, social status, and the age of children would be highly correlated because of the promotion structure of the Japanese employment system. Furthermore, some women did not want to affiliate with the auto company families, so I recruited them through grocery stores and ESL classes. I came to realize during fieldwork that the Japanese "community" was not a community, but very many small pockets or groups. Students, and women coming with their husbands for academics or banking, had different characteristics than those coming for the auto companies, so I included only a few to verify what I was seeing. Finally, I learned that my research team, especially my translator for the interviews, could not be part of the auto company because of the women's concerns for their confidentiality.

GROUNDED THEORY METHOD

The research design for the theory-building portion of this study used grounded theory methodology proposed by Strauss (1987). The general design proceeded according to my understanding of the grounded theory process depicted in Figure 7.1. All portions of the process were iterative

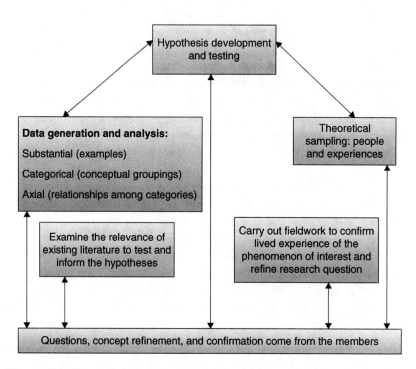

Figure 7.1 *Grounded theory embedded within a mixed-method project.*

(the double arrows). At the base is the community that should generate the relevant research questions, refine its own concepts, and confirm or revise hypotheses. To engage the communities during the preparatory stages, I used theoretical and ethnographic material and fieldwork. I knew that the processes of data generation, analysis, and sampling were simultaneous and that these three activities had the aim of hypothesis development and testing. My understanding was that this process was carried out by the community itself. Thus, I approached the process as a facilitator. I created a forum wherein members of the community could inquire about, and teach me, the important concepts and how they were connected. My initial question asked how the Japanese community organized themselves to provide places for women to receive information, social interaction, and social support and to get help when needed. Semi-structured, individual interviews included questions about social networks, social organization, and social interactions among Japanese women.

A university human subject review board approved the research plan before data collection. All of the interviews were carried out by me, with a Japanese translator who gave verbatim translation of my questions and the participant's responses during the interview. The initial sample began with five participants who attended a public lecture I gave to the community about the American mental health system. Snowball sampling generated another eight women from various auto companies. The remainder of women was recruited either with recruitment fliers posted in grocery stores, bookstores, and restaurants or fliers received from ESL instructors, childbirth classes, or Japanese Saturday-school staff.

Interested women initiated phone contact with the researcher, and interviews were scheduled at a location of their choice. With few exceptions, the researcher and translator conducted interviews in the women's homes, and all but three of the women were interviewed in Japanese. At the time of the interview, confidentiality was assured both orally and in a written informational letter retained by the participants. Interviews ran 2 to 3 hours in length and all but three were taperecorded. Most interviews were conducted with only one participant; however, we arrived at one interview to find three women eager to discuss themselves and their situation together as a group.

Theoretical sampling generated a diverse sample of women who could help test the hypothesis generated in previously coded data. The first five women from the lecture were primarily in their 30s with young children. However, one of the women was a higher status woman married to a middle manager, and she helped me understand the ways that rank affected giving and receiving help. Snowball sampling was purposive, and I asked women to tell people they knew about the study who met the sample characteristics needed for the theory generation. For example, I asked the young women to connect me with other young women who were with other companies or to introduce me to their "boss's wife." I asked the middle manager's wife to connect me with women who did not have children or who were new to the community. The "boss's wife" connected me to other older women with status, who had also been in the community much longer. Data collection stopped after 25 interviews because analysis reached theoretical saturation (i.e., the interviews were yielding no new information or insights; Strauss, 1987).

The average age of the sample was 36 years, with a range from 25 to 59 years. Twenty-four percent either had no children or had preschool-aged children, 40% had school-aged children, and the remainder (36%) had grown children either living in Japan or attending college in the United States. The average length of time they had spent abroad, including the present international venture, was 6 years, with a range from 1 to 14 years. The women in the sample held conferred status from their husbands' positions within their companies. About one third of the sample were of high status (i.e., vice presidents' or presidents' wives), and two women were of middle status (i.e., managers' and administrative assistants' wives). More than one third of the

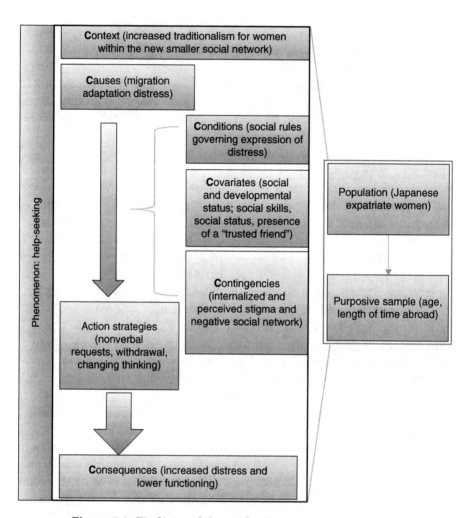

Figure 7.2 *Findings of the study organized by the six Cs.*

sample (40%) were wives of engineers, whereas the remainder (12%) were either wives of professors or executives outside of the automotive industry.

The general structure of the interviews was the same for all participants. First, participants were asked for demographic information. Next, they were asked to explain their daily life and their social network and compare and contrast their lives in the United States and Japan. Next, they were asked to describe three occasions in which they needed help and asked for it. They were then asked to describe three occasions in which they needed help and did not ask. Data analysis and theory generation were carried out after each interview, and additional questions and clarifications were added to the interview based on the previous analyzed interview. Even though the interview was translated at the time of the interview, a native Japanese speaker transcribed and translated the Japanese women's descriptions after each interview. A second native speaker translated the first three interviews to establish the reliability of the transcriptions. Data coding used NUD*IST data management software (Qualitative Solutions and Research, 1997).

Theory generation began with the research question: How do the Japanese women organize themselves, and how does that organization facilitate or decrease help-seeking? As I began to discern the answers to these questions, I would "inquire of the data" how any given woman's experience was the same or different from the last woman's experience. I used the six Cs (Figure 7.2) as my guide: conditions, context, causes, contingencies, covariates, and consequences (Strauss, 1987). In the early stages, it was difficult to see the subtle differences among the women. Larger, more striking patterns stood out. But within about six interviews, I was able to discern some of the variables that modified social organization and help-seeking. The question about "needing help but not seeking it" proved extremely helpful. Women began to help me understand the rules that regulated their interaction, and the expression of need.

FINDINGS

The findings of this research are published elsewhere (Saint Arnault, 2002). In brief, this research found that social structure and social rules for expression of distress and need constrained help-seeking and provision of social support for the women in the interviews. They spoke of the Japanese as the reference group that they identified with and that, in Japan, they would typically have only one primary reference group (Saint Arnault, 2004). They said that the Japanese have a cultural value about mutually interdependent relationships with the people in their primary reference group and their family, and that conceptually they share responsibility for support and security with all of the members. This group was referred to as *uchi*, which loosely translates as "the inside," "the home," "the house," or one's primary group. The women affirmed that they owed obligations to their uchi and sought to keep harmony within their primary reference group.

The women taught me that smooth functioning within the group requires a person to sensitively and accurately perceive each context and one's role within it. In practice, appropriate behavioral styles and norms about social exchange in a given situation depend on this accurate perception of relative social distance between any given two participants (*kejime*). Communication and social exchange between intimates (*uchi*) include relatively free expressions of emotions and help-seeking for needs (*honne*), and by nonverbal, unrestrained exchange of support (*amae*). Social distance decreases this intimacy, prompting people to communicate using polite deference (*enryo*) in order to avoid offending the higher status person.

Finally, the social structure described by the women served to modify and inhibit support-giving and help-seeking. For example, the women explained that Japanese culture has rules about reciprocity between nonintimates. One such rule is the edict that each favor incurs a reciprocal exchange. This reciprocity is not necessarily directly repaid between participants but can be repaid to other important people; neither does the favor have to be repaid in kind. Another reciprocity or help-seeking norm is to ask for help only within one's intimate social group. Therefore, people need to be self-reliant to avoid overtaxing limited support reserves. Appropriate role behavior includes indirect communication of personal needs and limited negative and positive emotional expression outside of one's intimate social circle. Behaviors that foster conflict or indicate deviance are frowned on and may result in ostracism.

The research generated the hypothesis that Japanese expatriate spouses felt unable to freely express emotional distress within their general social network because of hierarchical barriers and cultural rules dictating reciprocity in the exchange of social support. Specifically, this research was able to develop a Japanese cultural model of social exchange that varies significantly from the Western model (Saint Arnault, 2002).

For the purposes of this chapter, it is instructive to return to the six Cs and to organize the findings accordingly. Here, I take all of the material and attempt to help the reader see how the six Cs are distinct, interactive, and clarifying. In this model, the phenomenon of interest is *help-seeking*, and the *population* is Japanese expatriate women, from which a *purposive sample* was included. The *context* for these women was the migration situation, and within that, the women explained that there was an increase in "traditionalism"; in this migration context, women were expected to be good Japanese wives. The *causes* of help-seeking for distress for the women were the stress of adapting to this new social network. The factors that modified that distress were the *conditions, covariates,* and *contingencies*. The *conditions* were the social rules governing the expression of distress. This was modified by a variety of factors, including social status, developmental status, social skills relevant to this new situation, and the presence of a trusted friend. *Contingencies* included internalized and perceived stigma about the distress they were experiencing, as well as the amount of negativity in the women's immediate social circle. *Action strategies* the women used to communicate need included nonverbal requests, social withdrawal, and "passive" coping strategies such as changing their thinking about their situation. The *consequences* of not asking for help and not receiving help included increased distress and lower levels of functioning.

SUMMARY

The culturally based rules, norms, and practices for these Japanese women help to explain why the news media and the general American community think of the Japanese as a "close-knit" community. The cultural rules about being interdependent, and providing general support for others within the primary reference group, leave the appearance of closeness. It is true that the community has social structures that provide advice, security, and general support. However, as with any culture, there are specific rules and norms for behavior in general, and expression of distress and need specifically. This study adds to the literature about variations in the expression of distress and need that are critical to understand when providing care for immigrants.

This exemplar of grounded theory shows how this method can be used as part of larger research designs. I emphasize the need for people to "do their homework" before embarking on a grounded theory project. Specifically, I suggest that we understand and declare what our position is within existing theoretical perspectives. Next, I emphasize the role of fieldwork in cultural studies. Finally, I try to situate the fieldwork and grounded theory design as a kind of clinical ethnography that can help provide middle range theory that can facilitate culturally relevant practice.

REFERENCES

Alem, A., Jacobsson, L., Araya, M., Kebede, D., & Kullgren, G. (1999). How are mental disorders seen and where is help sought in a rural Ethiopian community? A key informant study in Butajira, Ethiopia. *Acta Psychiatrica Scandinavica Supplementum, 100*(Suppl 397), 40–47.

Association of Asian Pacific Community Health Organizations. (1995). *Taking action: Improving access to health care for Asians and Pacific Islanders.* Oakland, CA: Author.

Atkinson, D. R., & Gim, R. H. (1989). Asian-American cultural identity and attitudes toward mental health services. *Journal of Counseling Psychology, 36*(2), 209–212.

Bekker, F. J., Hentschel, U., & Fujita, M. (1996). Basic cultural values and differences in attitudes towards health, illness and treatment preferences within a psychosomatic frame of reference. *Psychotherapy & Psychosomatics, 65*(4), 191–198.

Chrisman, N., & Kleinman, A. (1993). Popular health care, social networks, and cultural meaning: The orientation of medical anthropology. In D. Mechanic (Ed.), *Handbook of health, health care and the health professionals* (pp. 569–590). New York, NY: The Free Press.

De Wester, J. (1996). Recognizing and treating the patient with somatic manifestations of depression. *Journal of Family Practice, 43*(6 Suppl), S3–S15.

Fetters, M. (1997, Winter). Cultural clashes: Japanese patients and U.S. maternity care. *Japanese International Institute, 17.*

Fetters, M. D. (1998). The family in medical decision-making: Japanese perspectives. *Journal of Clinical Ethics, 9*(2), 132–146.

Flum, M. E. (1998). Attitudes toward mental health and help-seeking preferences of Chinese, Japanese, and Korean international college students. *Dissertation Abstracts International Section A: Humanities & Social Sciences, 59*(5-A), 1470.

Guarnaccia, P. J., Rivera, M., Franco, F., & Neighbors, C. (1996). The experiences of ataques de nervios: Towards an anthropology of emotions in Puerto Rico. *Culture, Medicine & Psychiatry, 20*(3), 343–367.

Hinton, D., Um, K., & Ba, P. (2001). A unique panic-disorder presentation among Khmer refugees: The sore-neck syndrome. *Culture, Medicine & Psychiatry, 25*(3), 297–316.

Holland, D., & Quinn, N. (Eds.). (1987). *Cultural models in language and thought.* New York, NY: Cambridge University Press.

Hom, K. L. (1998). Investigating the influence of individualism-collectivism and acculturation on counselor preference and attitudes toward seeking counseling among Asian-Americans. *Dissertation Abstracts International: Section B: The Sciences & Engineering, 58*(8-B), 4451.

Iwamasa, G. Y., & Hilliard, K. M. (1999). Depression and anxiety among Asian American elders: A review of the literature. *Clinical Psychology Review, 19*(3), 343–357.

Jenkins, J. H., Kleinman, A., & Good, B. J. (1991). Cross-cultural studies of depression *Psychosocial aspects of depression* (pp. 67–99). Hillsdale, NJ: Lawrence Erlbaum Associates.

Kagawa-Singer, M., Wellisch, D., & Durvasula, R. (1997). Impact of breast cancer on Asian women and Anglo American women. *Culture, Medicine and Psychiatry, 21,* 449–480.

Kim, H. H. W. (1998). Asian-American students: Ethnicity, acculturation, type of problems and their effect on willingness to seek counseling and comfort level in working with different types of counselors. *Dissertation Abstracts International Section A: Humanities & Social Sciences, 58*(9-A), 3417.

Kim, W. (2003). Ethnic variations in mental health symptoms and functioning among Asian Americans. *Dissertation Abstracts International Section A: Humanities & Social Sciences, 63*(8-A), 3004.

Kirmayer, L. J. (1993). Culture and psychiatric epidemiology in Japanese primary care. *General Hospital Psychiatry, 15*(4), 219–223.

Kirmayer, L. J. (2001). Cultural variations in the clinical presentation of depression and anxiety: Implications for diagnosis and treatment. *Journal of Clinical Psychiatry, 62*(Suppl 13), 22–28.

Kirmayer, L. J., Dao, T. H. T., & Smith, A. (1998). Somatization and psychologization: Understanding cultural idioms of distress. In S. O. Okpaku (Ed.), *Clinical methods in transcultural psychiatry* (pp. 233–265). Washington, DC: American Psychiatric Press.

Kirmayer, L. J., & Young, A. (1999). Culture and context in the evolutionary concept of mental disorder. *Journal of Abnormal Psychology, 108*(3), 446–452.

Kleinman, A. (1982). Neurasthenia and depression: A study of somatization and culture in China. *Culture, Medicine & Psychiatry, 6*(2), 117–190.

Kleinman, A. (1983). The cultural meanings and social uses of illness: A role for medical anthropology and clinically oriented social science in the development of primary care theory and research. *Journal of Family Practice, 16*(3), 539–545.

Kleinman, A. (1988). *Rethinking psychiatry: From cultural category to personal experience.* New York, NY: Free Press.

Kleinman, A. (1996). How is culture important for *DSM-IV? Culture and psychiatric diagnosis: A DSM-IV perspective* (pp. 15–25). Washington, DC: American Psychiatric Press.

Kleinman, A. (2003). Introduction: Common mental disorders, primary care, and the global mental health research agenda. *Harvard Review of Psychiatry, 11*(3), 155–156. Retrieved from http://her.oupjournals.org

Lin, K.-M. (1996). Asian American perspectives. In J. E. Mezzich & A. Kleinman (Eds.), *Culture and psychiatric diagnosis: A DSM-IV perspective* (pp. 35–38). Washington, DC: American Psychiatric Association.

Lin, K.-M., & Cheung, F. (1999). Mental health issues for Asian Americans. *Psychiatric Services, 50,* 774–780.

Lock, M. (1987a). Introduction: Health and medical care as cultural and social phenomena. *Health, illness, and medical care in Japan: Cultural and social dimensions* (pp. 1–23). Honolulu, HI: University of Hawaii Press.

Lock, M. (1987b). Protests of a good wife and wise mother: The medicalization of distress in Japan. *Health, illness, and medical care in Japan: Cultural and social dimensions* (pp. 130–157). Honolulu, HI: University of Hawaii Press.

Ma, G. (1999). Access to health care for Asian Americans. In G. Ma & G. Henderson (Eds.), *Ethnicity and health care: A socio-cultural approach* (pp. 99–121). Springfield, IL: Charles C. Thomas.

Maeno, T., Kizawa, Y., Ueno, Y., Nakata, Y., & Sato, T. (2002). Depression among primary care patients with complaints of headache and general fatigue. *Primary Care Psychiatry, 8*(2), 69–72.

Markus, H. R., Kitayama, S., & Heiman, R. J. (1996). Culture and "basic" psychological principles. *Social psychology: Handbook of basic principles* (pp. 857–913). New York, NY: The Guilford Press.

Moscovici, S. (1988). Notes towards a description of social representations. *European Journal of Social Psychology, 18*(3), 211–250.

Narikiyo, T. A., & Kameoka, V. A. (1992). Attributions of mental illness and judgments about help seeking among Japanese-American and White American students. *Journal of Counseling Psychology, 39*(3), 363–369.

Ohnuki-Tierney, E. (1984). *Illness and culture in contemporary Japan: An anthropological view.* Cambridge, UK: Cambridge University Press.

Ono, Y., Tanaka, E., Oyama, H., Toyokawa, K., Koizumi, T., Shinohe, K., ... Yoshimura, K. (2001). Epidemiology of suicidal ideation and help-seeking behaviors among the elderly in Japan. *Psychiatry & Clinical Neurosciences, 55*(6), 605–610.

Ots, T. (1990). The angry liver, the anxious heart and the melancholy spleen: The phenomenology of perceptions in Chinese culture. *Culture, Medicine & Psychiatry, 14*(1), 21–58.

Pang, K. Y. C. (1998). Symptoms of depression in elderly Korean immigrants: Narration and the healing process. *Culture, Medicine & Psychiatry, 22*(1), 93–122.

Qualitative Solutions and Research. (1997). QSR NUD*IST 4: User Guide. Victoria: Scolari.

Saint Arnault, D. (1998). *Japanese company wives living in America: Culture, social relationships, and self.* (Dissertation). Detroit, MI: Wayne State University.

Saint Arnault, D. (2002). Help seeking and social support in Japanese company wives. *Western Journal of Nursing Research, 24*(3), 295–306.

Saint Arnault, D. (2004). The Japanese. In M. Ember & C. Ember (Eds.), *The encyclopedia of medical anthropology* (Vol. 2, pp. 765–776). New Haven, CT: Yale University.

Saint Arnault, D., & Sakamoto, S. (2001). Raw data.

Simon, G. E., VonKorff, M., Piccinelli, M., Fullerton, C., & Ormel, J. (1999). An international study of the relation between somatic symptoms and depression. *New England Journal of Medicine, 341*(18), 1329–1335.

Strauss, A. (1987). *Qualitative analysis for social scientists.* Cambridge: Cambridge University Press.

Suan, L. V., & Tyler, J. D. (1990). Mental health values and preference for mental health resources of Japanese-American and Caucasian-American students. *Professional Psychology: Research & Practice, 21*(4), 291–296.

Sue, S. (1999). Asian American Mental Health. In W. Lonner & D. Dinnel (Eds.), *Merging past, present, and future in cross-cultural psychology* (pp. 82–89). Lisse, Netherlands: Swets and Zeitlinger.

U.S. Census Bureau. (2001). The Asian and Pacific Islander Population in the United States: March 2000 (Update) (PPL-146). Retrieved August 21, 2004, from http://www.census.gov/population/www/socdemo/race/api.html

U.S. Department of Health and Human Services. (2001). *Mental health: Culture, race and ethnicity—A supplement to mental health: A report to the surgeon general.* Rockville, MD: Public Health Service, Office of the Surgeon General.

Waza, K., Graham, A. V., Zyzanski, S. J., & Inoue, K. (1999). Comparison of symptoms in Japanese and American depressed primary care patients. *Family Practice, 16*(5), 528–533.

Yeh, C., Inose, M., Kobori, A., & Chang, T. (2001). Self and coping among college students in Japan. *Journal of College Student Development, 42*(3), 242–256.

CHAPTER EIGHT

GROUNDED THEORY STUDIES OF CAREGIVING AND LONG-TERM CARE DECISION MAKING IN RURAL AFRICAN AMERICAN FAMILIES

Yvonne D. Eaves

Qualitative research has finally received recognition as a credible paradigm for scientific inquiry and is increasingly used in health care research (Sandelowski, 2004). Grounded theory (GT) continues to be one of the more popular methods used by qualitative health researchers. Competence in GT is particularly important (Watkins, 2012) if the substantive theories developed from GT research are to contribute to the improvement of health outcomes for the groups that participate in these studies. However, we cannot always carry out exactly what we learn from qualitative research textbooks and courses. The unfolding nature of qualitative inquiry requires "competence in the field"—experiential skills in which we adapt our qualitative training to the actual conduct of research. Therefore, the purposes of this chapter are to (a) describe how GT was used in two separate studies on caregiving and long-term care (LTC) decision making and (b) explicate in detail the critical techniques of the method that required adaptation while simultaneously remaining true to the tenets of GT.

DESCRIPTION OF THE STUDIES

Two completed studies are used in this chapter as exemplars of GT research. The first study, "Caregiving in Rural African American Families for Elderly Stroke Survivors" (Eaves, 1997), was a dissertation study. The second study "Caregiving Transitions: Long-Term Care Decision-Making in Rural African American Families" (Eaves, 1999a), was funded 2 years after the completion of my dissertation. I selected these two studies as exemplars for this chapter because at the time of the dissertation study I considered myself to be a novice qualitative researcher and grounded theorist; by the second study, I was able to build on the knowledge and methodological skills gained in the first study.

Study 1: Caregiving in Rural African American Families for Elderly Stroke Survivors

The purpose of this study was to examine and interpret the process of caregiving from the perspective of African American families living in rural settings who were caring for an older adult family member who had suffered a recent stroke. The specific aims of Study 1 were to:

1. Identify, explain, and interpret those aspects of the caregiving process that have a major impact on interrelationships within rural African American families caring for elderly relatives, specifically, the type of care given and received; the amount of caregiving shared between family members; and the impact and influences of the caregiving process on individual family caregivers, the care recipient, and the family as a whole.
2. Develop a substantive theory of family caregiving that can be applied to rural African American families caring for an elderly family member who has sustained a recent stroke.

Study 2: Caregiving Transitions: Long-Term Care Decision Making in Rural African American Families

The overall purposes of Study 2 were twofold: (a) to identify and explain transitions that occurred over a 2-year course of the caregiving process and (b) to examine the family decision-making process of rural African Americans who relinquished their caregiving roles and placed their elderly relative in an LTC facility (Eaves, 1999a). The specific aims were to:

1. Identify, explain, and examine transitions in African American families that occur over a 2-year course of the caregiving process that may lead to placement of an elderly relative in LTC.
2. Examine the family decision-making process of rural African Americans who relinquish their caregiving roles and place their elderly relative in an LTC facility.

3. Examine the consequences (effects) and impact of institutionalization of the older adult on individual family members, particularly, primary and secondary caregivers, the older adult, and the family as a whole.

4. Develop a substantive theory (explanatory model) of family decision making that could be applied to rural African American caregiving families who decide to place their elderly relative into an LTC facility.

Conceptual Issues

The literature was reviewed a priori for both studies to determine the state of the science for caregiving in African American families, in rural families, and for stroke survivors. The literature was also reviewed to find out what was known and unknown about caregiving transitions, namely, how families figured out that they could no longer care for their older relative at home and how they made decisions about LTC placement. It was important to know this information prior to data collection to plan the methodology of the study, especially what data to collect and what questions to ask when interviewing study participants. In addition, knowing the state of the science of the particular research area allowed me to make a sound argument for the significance of the two studies both in the dissertation proposal stage and in grant applications. Seeking National Institutes of Health (NIH) grant funding influenced my initial planning for both studies because I had to adhere to the NIH grant application guidelines. This required me to describe, a priori, the significance of each study, what new knowledge might be gained from the proposed study, participant recruitment, sampling, data collection, and data analysis procedures. Therefore, the methodology for both studies was well planned a priori, although my grant applications always included the caveat that methodological strategies might change during the actual conduct of the studies because of the inductive and cyclical nature of qualitative research. Thus, I learned how to write qualitative grant proposals in what seemed to be the linear mode reviewers were accustomed to at the time. However, I was also able to be honest to the GT method by allowing diversions from the methodology put forth in the grant application to procedures that were in keeping with the GT method and the naturalistic paradigm.

Theoretical Framework

The theoretical framework that guided the two studies was symbolic interactionism. I chose this framework because I was exposed to symbolic interactionism as the basic underpinning of GT during my doctoral education.

Symbolic interactionism is a theory about human behavior that focuses on the meaning of events to people in natural or everyday settings. Additionally, it is an approach to the study of human conduct and human group life (Chenitz & Swanson, 1986).

Symbolic interactionism stems from the earlier works of John Dewey, Charles Horton Cooley, Robert Park, W. I. Thomas, and George Herbert Mead. Although there existed some debate among interactionists in terms of the meaning and significance of certain concepts related to symbolic interactionism, Mead's formulation in his book *Mind, Self, and Society* is considered to be the classic view (Bogdan & Taylor, 1975). While Mead's works focused on the general processes of social interaction, the task of relating his premises to concrete and everyday life experiences was left to his followers, namely Herbert Blumer, Everett C. Hughes, Howard Becker, and Blanche Geer (Bogdan & Taylor, 1975). Of these, Herbert Blumer's work on symbolic interactionism has been the most widely received.

Blumer (1969) cited three basic premises that expanded the theory of symbolic interactionism. The first premise is that "human beings act toward things on the basis of the meanings that the things have for them" (p. 2). These things may include objects, other human beings, institutions, ideals, beliefs, activities of others, and situations or any combination of these (Blumer, 1969; Chenitz & Swanson, 1986). The second premise states that "the meaning of such things is derived from, or arises out of, the social interaction that one has with one's fellows." The third and final premise is that "these meanings are handled in, and modified through, an interpretative process used by the person in dealing with the things he encounters" (Blumer, 1969, p. 2).

Transitions Theory

During the 3-year period of Study 2, I became aware of another theoretical framework, transitions theory (Meleis, Sawyer, Im, Messias, & Schumacher, 2000), that was a good conceptual fit for my area of research and the study-specific aims. A transition is a "passage from one life phase, condition, or status to another" (Chick & Meleis, 1986, p. 239). The transition process involves both the disruption that the transition brings and the person's responses to this interference. Major tenets of transitions theory are that changes in individuals' health and illness status create a process of transition, and persons in transition are more vulnerable to risks that may adversely affect their health (Meleis et al., 2000). The occurrence of a "transition is precipitated by a significant marker event or turning point that requires new patterns of response" (Schumacher, Jones, & Meleis, 1999, p. 2).

For Study 2, the marker event or antecedent was the illness episode that precipitated family caregiving and included the type, pattern, and properties of the transition. In the case of LTC placement, the type of transition is classified as a developmental, situational, and health transition. For example, an illness event may interfere with the older adult's functional status, bring about the need for relocation to a relative's home or LTC facility, and affect the person's health status. Such events bring about transitions for family caregivers and their older adult care recipients.

It is important to note that I used symbolic interactionism and transitions theory as a means of conceptualizing and guiding my understanding of the caregiving and decision-making processes and the caregiving and care recipient transitions that arise from these processes. I did not use concepts, terms, or variables from the frameworks to label or categorize data or to base my interpretations of the data. I followed a purely inductive approach to data analysis and interpretation that resulted in substantive theories that emerged from the analysis.

METHODOLOGY

Design

Both projects were longitudinal, descriptive, and exploratory studies that used the qualitative research method of GT. The primary reason for using the GT method in the two studies was my belief that caregiving is a process that develops, changes, and endures over time. Part of this process is the various transitions that occur during a period of caregiving for both the caregiver and the care recipient. Such transitions may also lead to secondary processes such as the decision-making process about LTC placement. In addition, one study aim was to develop substantive theory. GT was the most appropriate qualitative method to use for Study 1 and Study 2 because GT focuses on (a) process and trajectory, resulting in identifiable stages and phases (Morse, 2001); (b) discovery and analysis of social and social psychological processes that tie the stages and phases together (Glaser & Strauss, 1967); (c) analytic processes that prompt discovery and theory development rather than verification of preexisting theories; and (d) the processes and products of research that are shaped from the data rather than from preconceived logically deduced theoretical frameworks (Glaser & Strauss, 1967).

I have received several inquiries about why the studies described in this chapter were not ethnographic designs. Often people assume that if a qualitative study has a sample from a particular diverse racial or ethnic group, the appropriate design to follow is ethnography. However, I argue that the design has to fit the purpose and aims of the study. Ethnography is the method of choice when the researcher seeks to describe and interpret patterns of behavior of a cultural or social group or a system (Fetterman, 1998). Thus, ethnography is a description of a culture or subculture that emphasizes the cultural perspective (Wolf, 2012). Although aspects of the rural environment and historical experiences of southern African Americans are evident in the narratives of caregiving from participants in my studies, the primary objective of the research was not the cultural perspective but the process of caregiving and decision making in regard to LTC placement.

Sample

For both studies, purposeful sampling was used initially to select "information-rich cases." These cases provided "in-depth understanding" (Patton, 2002, p. 46) about caregiving for older adult stroke survivors in the case of Study 1 (Eaves, 2006) and caregiving and LTC decision making in Study 2. As the studies progressed, theoretical sampling was used for continued selection of families based on the information already obtained and further information that was needed to adequately address the aims of each study (Eaves, 2006). Because I study caregiving as a family process, the selection criteria for each study required that older adult care recipients and their primary and secondary caregivers agree to be in the studies. Thus, the unit of analysis was the family. Study 1 included 8 rural African American caregiving families that consisted of 8 stroke survivors, 8 primary caregivers, and 18 secondary caregivers. Eleven rural African American caregiving families, comprising 12 older adults and 11 primary caregivers, participated in Study 2. There were 12 care recipients but 11 primary caregivers because the only male caregiver in Study 2 provided care to both parents. It was difficult to recruit secondary caregivers in Study 2 because most of the adult children in these families had moved away from their rural birth towns, usually for employment reasons.

Recruitment of families that met the selection criteria was difficult in both studies. In Study 1, four major barriers to recruitment were identified. Two of these barriers were related to the study design, including the requirement that more than one family member participate in the study and that families be followed and participate in interviews over a 2- to 4-month period. The third barrier was the common observation that vulnerable populations, particularly minority groups, are less likely to participate in research studies due to mistrust of the scientific community, which is historically connected to the Tuskegee Syphilis Experiment. Finally, I was unfamiliar with southern culture and the state where the study was conducted, having relocated there only 9 months prior to the start of recruitment (Eaves, 1997, 1999b). To resolve these barriers I developed a "multi-step recruitment process" that involved the use of an intermediary such as a medical social worker to identify potential participants and a visit to the community hospital or rehabilitation center to meet the care recipient and/or primary caregiver before their discharge to home, to provide them with a written and verbal description of the study. If the stroke survivor and/or primary caregiver expressed a willingness to participate in the study, I telephoned them once the stroke survivor was discharged to home and scheduled a date and time for the first interview. Even with close adherence to the multi-step recruitment process, it took 9 months to enroll the first family, although 3 months later eight families had been recruited (Eaves, 1997, 1999b). The multi-step recruitment process has been described in detail in a previous publication (Eaves, 1999b).

In Study 2, I had planned to employ the multi-step recruitment process developed in Study 1, namely, the use of intermediaries. However, for Study 2, I had to expand recruitment efforts to different rural counties and hospitals because of personnel changes at the community hospitals used for recruitment in Study 1 and the inability to receive institutional review board (IRB) approval at one of the hospitals. Eventually, using different networks and establishing a relationship with a long-time resident of a rural county who referred to herself as a community advocate proved successful in recruiting families for Study 2. This community advocate in turn assisted the principal investigator in establishing a relationship with an African American physician who practiced at a clinic located in an area designated as medically underserved. After establishing partnerships with a rural community hospital and the medical center where the physician was on staff, IRB approval was obtained from both of these agencies as well as the university IRB where I was employed. However, once again I had to acquaint myself with rural counties new to me, learn my way around, and become familiar with new locations. I also had to build trusting relationships with the "community advocate" and physician. These tasks were extremely time intensive, yet an essential part of the project. It took 17 months to build these new relationships.

Setting

For both studies, interviews and focused observations took place in care recipients' and caregivers' homes. Participants were given the option of being interviewed in their homes or another place of their choice that would afford a level of privacy and be convenient for them and the interviewer. However, all participants chose to be interviewed in their homes. Care recipients and caregivers were not required to live in the same dwelling to be eligible for either study. Thus, there were times when I interviewed participants in the same family at different homes; this was especially true for secondary caregivers.

Ethical Considerations

At the time of Study 1 (my dissertation) I had relocated and was working at a university different from where I was a doctoral student. Therefore, I had to obtain IRB approval for the study from both the university where I was a doctoral student and the university where I was employed. In addition, I obtained approval from the appropriate boards of the community hospitals and rehabilitation centers where participants were recruited; these were usually medical review boards.

Because I proposed to interview older adult care recipients and their caregivers, the IRBs required me to develop different consents for these two categories of participants. I also followed this protocol in Study 2. In both studies, written informed consent was always obtained during the first home visit prior to the start of the first interview. I always give older adults the option of reading the consent themselves or having me read the consent to them. Most elect for me to read the consent to them. I find this a useful strategy to combat literacy issues and impaired vision.

Service or volunteer personnel from rehabilitation centers of rural hospitals served as intermediaries for the initial contact with potential participating caregivers and care recipients. Intermediaries had no vested interest in recruitment; thus they were able to relay an invitation to participate without bias or coercion. Data collection did not begin until human subjects' approval had been granted by both the university where I was enrolled as a doctoral student and the university where I was employed and the community hospitals or rehabilitation centers that agreed to refer clients for recruitment into the study.

Study 1 and Study 2 occurred before the widespread use of digital voice recorders and USB flash drives; therefore, cassette tapes were used to record interviews, and computer diskettes were used to store transcripts. Once transcribed, transcripts were copied from discs to a desktop PC that was password protected and located in my university office. In order to maintain anonymity, identification numbers were assigned to each participant and family, and were used in all written records of the study including interview transcripts and field-note forms. Identification numbers were also used on cassette labels, computer diskettes, and when naming computer files.

Confidentiality is of the utmost concern when conducting qualitative family research with rural residents. I learned to be careful not to divulge information one family member had shared during an interview with another family member who I interviewed at a later time. This is crucial in establishing trust with participants, especially because family caregivers often criticize the level and quality of care provided by another family member. Similarly, it is important not to divulge interview data with intermediaries and staff from health care agencies where recruitment takes place. Finally, privacy and protection of data and information are also important when interacting with members in small, rural communities. I do not promise participants anonymity, because in small towns residents notice outsiders and often recognize when researchers visit certain homes. I do, however, promise confidentiality of data and not to identify data when findings are disseminated.

Instruments and Rigor

A detailed instrument guide was developed for Study 1, and revised for use in Study 2. For Study 2, I also developed a one-page demographic form to record age, gender, and primary and secondary health diagnoses for both care recipients and caregivers. The relationship of the care recipient to the caregiver was also recorded on this form. In Study 1, I asked these questions as part of the first interview but found it difficult to go through all the first interviews to record these data in order to summarize the sample characteristics.

I also developed a field-note form to record the focused observations that occurred during the interview sessions. Field notes covered at least the following four topic areas: (a) physical setting or environment; (b) context of the situation; (c) theoretical insights that the researcher may have during or after the field experience; and (d) emotional feelings, thoughts, and reflections experienced by the researcher. Additionally, the field notes included any other information that I obtained during the field experience that was not covered in the four previously described areas.

Rigor was established by achieving credibility—the primary criterion for judging the truth value of qualitative research (Lincoln & Guba, 1985). Credibility assesses whether the results of the research accurately reflect the experiences of participants or the context situation under study (Whittemore, Chase, & Mandle, 2001). Data (different data sources), theory (multiple perspectives to interpret data), and methodological triangulation (multiple methods—e.g., interviews and focused observations; Denzin, 1989) were used to increase credibility in both studies (Eaves, 1997, 2006).

Data Collection Procedures

In both studies, data were generated through interactive interviews and focused observations in caregivers' or care recipients' homes. Three or four interviews were conducted with each primary and secondary caregiver and stroke survivor during a 4- to 8-month period in Study 1 (Eaves, 1997, 2006) and with primary caregivers and care recipients over a 19-month period in Study 2. There was only one instance in which I did not interview an older adult, and this occurred in Study 1. In this instance, the care recipient's stroke had left her in a semi-comatose state, and she was unable to participate in an interview. The interviews were "semi-structured and followed an interview guide composed of open-ended questions. Probes and follow-up questions were used to elicit in-depth responses and narratives, and participants were encouraged to explain abstract responses with concrete stories" (Eaves, 2006, p. 272). In both studies, different interview questions were posed to care recipients and primary and secondary caregivers. For example, care recipients were asked to reflect on perceptions of the illnesses from which they suffered and on the care they received from family members. Primary caregivers were asked why they chose to care for their family member, who helped them with caregiving tasks, and how nursing home placement decisions were made. Secondary caregivers were asked to describe how often they participated in caregiving and the specific caregiving tasks they performed when relieving the primary caregiver. Focused observations centered on caregiving tasks that naturally occurred during the interview sessions and interactions with support networks. Interviews typically lasted 30 minutes to 2 hours, with an average of 1 hour. All interviews were audio-recorded, and field notes were handwritten, typed, or dictated within 24 hours of the interviews.

Timeline

In keeping with the norms of NIH applications, stringent timelines were created for both studies during the grant preparation stage. Study 1 was funded via a Minority Dissertation Research Grants in Aging mechanism from the National Institute on Aging/NIH for a 1-year time period. However, because of recruitment difficulties in Study 1, I requested and received a 1-year no-cost extension. Although it took 9 months to recruit the first family, during the next 3 months all eight families were recruited. Thus, data collection, data analysis, and defense of my dissertation occurred during the second year.

Study 2 was submitted and funded as a 3-year grant. Even so, it took 17 months to build new relationships with the community advocate and physician who assisted in recruiting families for the study. Indeed, this affected adherence to the original project timeline, and more importantly, it affected the longitudinal design of the study, which initially called for following some families for 2 years following hospital discharge, to study caregiving over time and observe whether transitions to nursing home placement actually occurred. In both studies, recruitment difficulties impacted theoretical sampling and the simultaneous and cyclical nature of data collection and data analysis, which is one of the major hallmarks of GT research.

Data Analysis

Audiotapes of the interviews and written or dictated field notes were transcribed verbatim. After three unsatisfactory transcriptionists, I hired an experienced transcriptionist who was referred to me by a colleague. This transcriptionist was a southern native, and she had no difficulty in understanding the linguistic style and speech of rural African Americans. She also had years of experience transcribing interview data for other qualitative health researchers. Initially, I checked the accuracy of her transcribed interviews against the audiotapes, hardly ever found a mistake, and found very few instances in which she left a phrase or sentence out because she could not decipher it. In general, I found that if this transcriptionist could not decipher a comment on tape, neither could I; thus, eventually I stopped checking her transcriptions for accuracy. Once hired, I used this transcriptionist for both Study 1 and Study 2. I even had her go back and transcribe the interviews from the earlier transcriptionists because they were fraught with mistakes and missing data.

The transcribed interviews and field notes were merged together to create one large pool of data. Qualitative text analysis software was used to code, categorize, and organize data. In Study 1, MARTIN (Diekelmann, Lam, & Schuster, 1991) software was used, and ATLAS.ti was used in Study 2. Data analyses incorporated the Glaser and Strauss (1967) constant comparison technique and a synthesis approach to GT analysis derived from the works of Charmaz (1983), Chesler (1987), and Strauss and Corbin (1990).

This synthesis technique was developed in Study 1 (Eaves, 1997) when, as a novice qualitative researcher, I felt lost in data analysis and had difficulty following the analytic techniques put forth by different grounded theorists. I adhered to this synthesis technique for GT data analysis, which is described in detail elsewhere (Eaves, 2001), in both studies.

Dissemination

I have disseminated the findings from both studies at regional, state, national, and international scientific conferences. I have several publications from Study 1. My major struggle with publishing articles from Study 1 was reducing chapters from a dissertation to journal page requirements. Because of this, I elected to publish the major findings—the substantive theory of rural African American family caregiving for elderly stroke survivors—in a journal that did not specify page length. However, the topic of stroke was a good fit with the focus of the journal—*Journal of Neuroscience Nursing*—and during the revision of the article, I still had to cut several pages prior to full acceptance for publication. The order in which I published manuscripts was important. As it happened, *Nursing Research* had a call for a special issue on caregiving in which I was able to publish a paper on my multi-step recruitment process. Next, I decided to submit a paper on my synthesis technique for GT data analysis because there was no way I could fit this content into the same paper that I reported the major study findings. Having this paper published required a lot of perseverance as I submitted it to three journals before it was accepted; this spanned about 3 years. In the end, this methodological paper was accepted without revisions; I only had to convert the narrative abstract to a structured abstract, and the editor changed certain words to British English spelling. This paper (Eaves, 2001) has been cited more than any of my other publications, and I have had many researchers (especially doctoral students) in several countries contact me about the synthesis technique for GT data analysis reported on in the article.

By now I should have published the findings from Study 2 but have not. I did, however, submit a manuscript and after completing the revisions found that it far exceeds the journal page limit. I hope to pull it out of the drawer in the near future and extensively cut it (or have someone else edit and shorten it) so that I can resubmit it. Unfortunately, I have missed the opportunity to have it considered as a revised manuscript and will have to enter it as a new submission to the same or a different journal. This, of course, is something we are all taught not to do, but in the real world it does happen.

SUMMARY

According to Charmaz (2006), "GT methods consist of systematic, yet flexible guidelines for collecting and analyzing qualitative data to construct theories 'grounded' in the data themselves" (p. 2). The keyword here is "flexible." Such flexibility allows GT researchers to adapt traditional techniques of the method or to develop or create new techniques, such as the multi-step recruitment process and the synthesis technique for GT data analysis described in this chapter, that do not violate the original approach and tenets of GT. Such developments usually emerge during the actual conduct of research in response to a problem that has arisen. For example, the multi-step recruitment process was developed when I encountered difficulty recruiting participants for Study 1. However, this process did not hinder my ability to employ purposive sampling, although it was more difficult to adhere to the strict textbook description of theoretical sampling. New developments help us to conduct GT research in a practical and realistic manner. Indeed, over time, these "lessons learned" advance our skills in GT and allow us to study difficult or sensitive topics and to include groups in our research that have been traditionally difficult to recruit (e.g., ethnic/racial minorities and older adults). I encourage novice and seasoned researchers to advance GT methods by recognizing when and how to make sound adjustments to textbook techniques to accomplish study aims and thereby construct substantive theories that will assist us in improving health outcomes for the groups in our studies.

REFERENCES

Blumer, H. (1969). *Symbolic interaction*. Englewood Cliffs, NJ: Prentice Hall.

Bogdan, R., & Taylor, S. J. (1975). *Introduction to qualitative research methods*. New York, NY: Wiley-Interscience.

Charmaz, K. (1983). The grounded theory method: An explication and interpretation. In R. M. Emerson (Ed.), *Contemporary field research: A collection of readings* (pp. 109–126). Prospect Heights, IL: Waveland Press.

Charmaz, K. (2006). *Constructing grounded theory: A practical guide through qualitative analysis*. Thousand Oaks, CA: Sage.

Chenitz, W. C., & Swanson, J. M. (1986). *From practice to grounded theory: Qualitative research in nursing*. Menlo Park, CA: Addison-Wesley.

Chesler, M. A. (1987). *Professionals' views of the dangers of self-help groups: Explicating a grounded theoretical approach* (Center for Research on Social Organization, Working Paper Series). Ann Arbor, MI: University of Michigan Department of Sociology.

Chick, N., & Meleis, A. I. (1986). Transitions: A nursing concern. In P. L. Chinn (Ed.), *Nursing research methodology: Issues and implementation* (pp. 3–15). Menlo Park, CA: Addison-Wesley.

Denzin, N. K. (1989). *The research act* (3rd ed.). Englewood Cliffs, NJ: Prentice Hall.

Diekelmann, N. L., Lam, S. L., & Schuster, R. M. (1991). *Martin v. 2.0 user manual*. Madison, WI: University of Wisconsin.

Eaves, Y. D. (1997). *Caregiving in rural African American families for elderly stroke survivors*. (Unpublished doctoral dissertation). University of Michigan, Ann Arbor, MI.

Eaves, Y. D. (1999a). *Caregiving transitions: Long-term care decision-making in rural African American families*. Minority Investigator Supplement to Parent Grant # NR04716, National Institute of Nursing Research, Advancing Minority Aging Research Efforts, Resource Center on Minority Aging Research.

Eaves, Y. D. (1999b). Family recruitment issues and strategies: Caregiving in rural African Americans. *Nursing Research, 48*(3), 183–187.

Eaves, Y. D. (2001). A synthesis technique for grounded theory data analysis. *Journal of Advanced Nursing, 35*(5), 654–663.

Eaves, Y. D. (2006). Caregiving in rural African American families for older adult stroke survivors. *Journal of Neuroscience Nursing, 38*(Suppl. 4), 270–281, 330.

Fetterman, D. M. (1998). *Ethnography, step by step* (2nd ed.). Thousand Oaks, CA: Sage.

Glaser, B. G., & Strauss, A. L. (1967). *The discovery of grounded theory*. Chicago, IL: Aldine.

Lincoln, Y. S., & Guba, E. G. (1985). *Naturalistic inquiry*. Beverly Hills, CA: Sage.

Meleis, A. I., Sawyer, L. M., Im, E. O., Messias, D. K., & Schumacher, K. (2000). Experiencing transitions: An emerging middle-range theory. *Advances in Nursing Science, 23*(1), 12–28.

Morse, J. M. (2001). Situating grounded theory in qualitative inquiry. In R. S. Schreiber & P. N. Stern (Eds.), *Using grounded theory in nursing* (pp. 1–15). New York, NY: Springer.

Patton, M. Q. (2002). *Qualitative research and evaluation methods* (3rd ed.). Thousand Oaks, CA: Sage.

Sandelowski, M. (2004). Using qualitative research. *Qualitative Health Research, 14*, 1366–1386.

Schumacher, K. L., Jones, P. S., & Meleis, A. I. (1999). Helping elderly persons in transition: A framework for research and practice. In E. Swanson & T. Tripp-Reimer (Eds.), *Life transitions in the older adult: Issues for nurses and other health professionals* (pp. 1–26). New York, NY: Springer.

Strauss, A., & Corbin, J. (1990). *Basics of qualitative research: Grounded theory procedures and techniques*. Newbury Park, CA: Sage.

Watkins, D. C. (2012). The importance of conducting research that doesn't "count." *Health Promotion Practice, 13*(2), 153–158.

Whittemore, R., Chase, S. K., & Mandle, C. L. (2001). Validity in qualitative research. *Qualitative Health Research, 11*, 522–537.

Wolf, Z. R. (2012). Ethnography: The method. In P. L. Munhall (Ed.), *Nursing research: A qualitative perspective* (5th ed., pp. 285–338). Sudbury, MA: Jones & Bartlett Learning.

CHAPTER NINE

WOMEN'S EXPERIENCES OF CORONARY ARTERY BYPASS GRAFT SURGERY: A GROUNDED THEORY STUDY

Davina Banner

Researchers are faced with many challenges when embarking on a research project, including refining the research problem, delineating theoretical perspectives, and developing rigorous methods. Qualitative research has become an increasingly important form of inquiry within the health and social sciences and is underpinned by a diverse range of philosophical traditions and approaches (Marshall & Rossman, 2011). Grounded theory (GT) is a popular qualitative methodology that has been used extensively in nursing and health care disciplines (Charmaz, 2006; Mills et al., 2006a, 2006b).

Grounded theory methodology has evolved considerably since its advent and has roots in ethnography, symbolic interactionism, and more recently, the constructivist paradigm (Annells, 1996; Charmaz, 2006; Mills et al., 2006a; Strauss & Corbin, 1998). The methodology involves both inductive (theory that reflects observed relationships as they emerge from the data) and deductive (as theoretical data emerge they are constantly compared and validated in the data, further data collection, and finally through comparison with the literature) approaches to analysis. This goes beyond pure description to provide explanatory models and substantive theory that explains "what is going on" (Charmaz, 2000; Glaser & Strauss, 1967; Strauss & Corbin, 1998). Grounded theory is highly relevant to nursing and provides the opportunity to explore the contexts, experiences, and processes of health and illness.

This chapter reflects on some of the challenges and processes experienced when undertaking my first GT study exploring women's experience of coronary artery bypass graft (CABG) surgery. The chapter begins with a brief overview of my study followed by a discussion of selecting methods for human inquiry, practical concerns in GT studies, and developing rigorous GTs.

THE STUDY

My GT journey began during my undergraduate nursing studies, when as part of my dissertation, I developed a research proposal focused on the examination of stressors in women with coronary heart disease (CHD). Even during this early exposure to research, GT stood out as a rigorous methodological approach that had the genuine potential to drive high-quality research that could enhance clinical care and patient outcomes. It was over the course of my first 18 months in clinical practice that my intrigue in issues of women, heart disease, and cardiac surgery continued to grow. I developed a basic research proposal, sought advice from experts in a local university, and quite by surprise found myself embarking on a PhD study (Banner, 2010a). During the initial planning stages, I was encouraged to read widely and explore different theoretical perspectives, but consistently returned to GT. Following this period of preparation, I refined my research proposal and set about initiating the research study by gaining access to the study population and obtaining ethical approval.

CHD is a "modern epidemic" (Lockyer & Bury, 2002) and a leading cause of morbidity and mortality worldwide (World Health Organization, 2013). Traditionally CHD has been regarded as a disease primarily affecting men, but CHD remains the leading cause of death for women. Women are known to have worse outcomes of CHD than their male counterparts. Explanations include the poor recognition of cardiac symptoms by health care providers and women themselves (British Heart Foundation, 2003, 2006), delayed help-seeking, less frequent use of diagnostic testing, and treatment delays (DeVon, Hogan, Ochs, & Shapiro, 2010; Grace et al., 2003; Maynard, Every, Martin, Kudenchuk, & Weaver, 1997; Rosenfeld & Gilkeson, 2000; Vodopiutz et al., 2002; Willingham & Kilpatrick, 2005). CABG surgery is a surgical procedure undertaken to restore coronary blood flow, decrease symptoms, and improve myocardial functioning. Women are a sicker population at the point of surgery, having significantly higher mortality rates and levels of postoperative complications (Ayanian, Guadagnoli, & Cleary, 1995; King, McFetridge-Durdle, LeBlanc, Anzarut, & Tsuyuki, 2009; Redecker, Mason, Wykpisz, & Glica, 1996; Stramba-Badiale et al., 2006). The aim of this study was to explore the experiences of women undergoing CABG surgery in order to improve the management and outcomes for women.

A constructivist GT approach was adopted to capture the illness experiences of women through their CABG journey. Thirty women were recruited from two urban teaching hospitals in the United Kingdom. Eligibility included women who could read and understand English, were aged above

18 years, and were undergoing first-time CABG surgery. An initial convenience sample was recruited to gain a general understanding of experiences, with theoretical sampling being undertaken in response to the emerging theoretical data (Charmaz, 2006). Sample size was determined by theoretical saturation, or the point at which no new major themes emerged (Strauss & Corbin, 1998).

Grounded theory methodology advocates rigorous simultaneous data collection and analysis (Strauss & Corbin, 1998). Semistructured interviews were undertaken preoperatively and at 6 weeks and 6 months postoperatively. Interviews were tape-recorded and transcribed and were conducted either at the hospital clinic, participants' home, or via telephone. Interviews lasted on average 90 minutes, and participants were encouraged to speak openly about all aspects of their illness experience. A pilot study was undertaken initially to consolidate research training, collect preliminary data, and identify any pitfalls in the research process. Interview data were contextualized through informal observations of the main clinical areas, and theoretical memo analysis was undertaken to foster theoretical sensitivity. Basic clinical and demographic information was collected to define the study sample and guide theoretical sampling.

Interviews were systematically coded and constantly compared (Strauss & Corbin, 1998). An initial line-by-line analysis of the data was undertaken to discover subtle nuances and identify important words or phrases (Charmaz, 2006). Following this, conceptual groups or themes were identified through open coding. These became more abstract and explanatory through axial coding. Recursive data collection provided the freedom to pursue interesting leads (Strauss & Corbin, 1998). During the final stages of analysis, selective coding was employed to examine the interrelationships between categories and to uncover core categories. Through this prolonged immersion with the data and an ongoing dialogue with participants, a substantive theory explaining the public–private dialogue of normality emerged (Banner, 2007, 2010b). Amalgams of computerized (using ATLAS.ti) and manual techniques were used to facilitate data analysis.

A substantive theory of the public–private dialogue of normality emerged demonstrating that participants faced lifestyle disruptions as they attempted to privately normalize and integrate physical and functional limitations, while minimizing a public display of illness. During the preoperative period, participants experienced difficulties recognizing and acting on symptoms and endured physical and emotional distress while waiting for CABG surgery. Following surgery, women experienced functional limitations, which forced them to relinquish normal activities and roles. As recovery progressed, women came to accept their changed health status and renegotiated state of normality. The findings increase understanding about the modifications that women undergoing cardiac surgery make as part of living with a long-term condition and the support needed to develop innovative gender-sensitive health education programs and services.

The outcomes of this research study were communicated in peer-reviewed journal articles (Banner, 2010b; Banner, Miers, Clarke, & Albarran, 2012) and other conference and health care presentations. While these traditional knowledge translation approaches present the key findings of a study, there is rarely the opportunity or adequate space to review underlying methodological, practical, and theoretical considerations. This chapter provides a practical review of some of the key processes undertaken as part of this study, starting with the process of selecting a method for human inquiry.

SELECTING A METHOD FOR HUMAN INQUIRY

Researchers are faced with many considerations and decisions when embarking on a research project. During the early stages of a project, researchers typically engage in an extended process through which an idea or problem becomes conceptualized, methods are delineated, and the practical elements of the project (such as proposal development, ethics, and funding applications) are explored and addressed. Grounded theory methodology has evolved considerably since its advent, and numerous versions of GT have emerged, including constructivist and feminist approaches. Such elaborations and evolving perspectives can give rise to methodological uncertainty and confusion (Mruck & Mey, 2010). A clear grasp of the philosophical foundations and methodological principles is critical for the development of a robust and rigorous qualitative research study (Kramer-Kile, 2012; Vasilachis de Gialdino, 2009).

While developing my research proposal, I contrasted a range of methodologies (GT, ethnography, phenomenology, and mixed methods) to assess their suitability and appropriateness. For example, I was attracted to ethnography through its focus on understanding cultures within complex social environments. I anticipated that this would provide important contextual insights but that the reliance of observational methods was not feasible given that I would be exploring women's experiences over a long period of time and within a range of environments. Throughout these considerations, I consistently returned to GT.

My decision to adopt GT was governed by five factors: (a) the methodology directs the researcher to undertake detailed and meticulous analyses of experiences and contexts; (b) GT studies develop substantive theory that could inform practice and policy, and improve patient outcomes; (c) GT is particularly useful to examine phenomena for which little other research exists (Strauss & Corbin, 1998); (d) the approach fit well with my own philosophical position; and (e) the methodology is widely used in nursing and health and is characterized by well-defined methodological approaches to analysis. This was particularly attractive to me as a novice researcher. In any circumstance, researchers must choose their approach wisely based on a consideration of their philosophical position, the focus of the research problem, and the practical aspects of the research, including researcher skill level, time available, and resources.

Upon examining the diverse range of GT models, I felt most aligned with the constructivist approach (Charmaz, 2006). The constructivist ontological perspective asserts that multiple socially constructed realities exist, as opposed to a singular truth or objective reality. Constructivist beliefs are rooted in a relativist ontology whereby reality or truth is not governed by fixed laws. Research framed by this approach typically involves the collection of diverse, detailed data that are studied from the position of both the participant and the researcher (Guba & Lincoln, 1989). The historical evolution of GT methodology has seen a conceptual shift from the earlier positivist and interpretivist positions toward the constructivist approach (Annells, 1996; Norton, 1999). A constructivist GT approach sees the researcher as an active participant in the research process, as opposed to a passive observer. Through this approach, multiple perspectives are identified, and the position of the research is examined through an ongoing reflexive process (Annells, 1996; Bryant & Charmaz, 2007; Charmaz, 2006; Rice & Ezzy, 1999).

UNDERTAKING GROUNDED THEORY STUDIES: PRACTICAL CONSIDERATIONS AND PROCESSES

Grounded theory is a complex methodological approach with varied theoretical roots and practical considerations. Like other studies, negotiating access and gaining the appropriate approvals are key steps in the research process. This section presents some of the practical considerations experienced while initiating the study, collecting rich data, sampling, analyzing data, and theorizing and mapping.

Initiating the Study

The initial setup of a research study is time-consuming and requires research-ers to conceptualize and articulate the research process in a comprehensive proposal and to successfully progress through a range of academic and reg-ulatory processes before they are able to undertake the research itself. These include undertaking required preparatory courses, seeking funding, and acquiring approval from ethics committees. As part of this, researchers must also gain access to the study population.

Gaining Access

To access a sample of women undergoing CABG surgery, I obtained sup-port from the cardiac surgery consultants and research leads in each of the study sites. A steering committee of local decision makers and clinicians was established to assist in accessing and recruiting the study sample, as well as guiding knowledge translation activities upon completion of the study. A comprehensive information package and invitation letter was sent to each consultant surgeon and key stakeholders in the study sites. This included a summary of the research, patient information, and consent sheets and curric-ulum vitae. Each consultant surgeon was asked for permission to approach his or her female patients for inclusion into the study. All hospital consul-tants granted permission to access their patients. Following this, I connected with local cardiac surgery waiting list coordinators to review participant eligibility and to negotiate effective mechanisms for recruitment.

Gaining Ethical Approval

Once these approvals were in place, I then submitted applications to five regional UK research ethics and regulatory committees (including local data protection officers, hospital research and development departments, local research ethics committees, and the university ethics committee). Each com-mittee required completion of a specific application form. This process was time-consuming, challenging to coordinate, and was a source of delay.

Getting Started

Once these preparatory processes were complete, I was able to work directly with the cardiac surgery waiting-list coordinators to identify potential partic-ipants. As new patients were screened for surgery, the coordinators provided eligible patients with the study information package and, if the patient agreed, collected their contact information. This information would be collated, and I would meet with the waiting list coordinators on a weekly basis to review the referrals and select potential participants. Once a prospective participant had received information about the study, I made a follow-up call to introduce myself, answer any questions, and seek informed consent. Participants were asked to sign a consent form and return it in a stamped envelope. Once the form was received, I was able to begin with data collection.

Collecting Rich Data

To develop robust GT studies, the researcher must gather rich data. The process of collecting data in GT studies is inherently nonlinear and evolves over the course of the research in response to data analysis (Charmaz, 2006). In-depth semistructured interview formed the main body of data collection for this study, while informal observations of the main clinical areas (to contextualize the study) and an analysis of basic clinical and demographic data (to define the study sample) were also undertaken. In this section, I focus on my experience of qualitative interviewing.

In-Depth Interviews

Qualitative interviews are powerful and versatile tools that gather rich data necessary for qualitative inquiry (Rubin & Rubin, 2011). Interviews are well suited to the GT methodology as they can foster the discovery of "life worlds" by exploring context, metaphors, and meanings of experiences (Banner, 2010b; Charmaz, 2006; Stroh, 2000). Interview methods are diverse and vary depending on the nature of questioning and their degree of structure. Interviews may be structured, whereby a predetermined set of questions are used to gather data, or unstructured, during which experiences are explored more broadly (Banner, 2010b; Rubin & Rubin, 2011). Both approaches may lack the flexibility and sensitivity required of GT studies. Semistructured interviews form the middle ground and include the use of broad guiding questions and probes, while allowing sufficient flexibility to pursue interesting leads (Struebert & Carpenter, 2007). The semistructured interview method is most fitting with GT and constructivist approaches by facilitating the exploration of assumptions, interpretations, meanings, and stories of the participant in detail (Charmaz, 2006).

A key facet of qualitative interviewing is the development of appropriate and sensitive questions to guide the data collection process. Adequate preparation and planning are required to ensure that the questions are appropriate and fitting to the approach and project and that the language is free from jargon and nonleading (Banner, 2010b; Rubin & Rubin, 2011). This is particularly important for researchers with established clinical or professional backgrounds who may find it challenging to approach a topic in a fresh way (Banner, 2010b). Other dynamics, such as age, gender, and context, which may impact on the interview process, must also be considered (Charmaz, 2006; Docherty & Sandelowski, 1999; McDougall, 2000). Researchers frequently develop interview guides to help facilitate the interview process and to satisfy the demands of those assessing the research (such as ethics committee or supervising committee). Interview guides can provide a useful framework, but caution must be taken to ensure that the interviewer remains flexible and sensitive to the emerging data.

In-depth interviewing may initially appear simplistic in nature, but in reality, it is inherently complex and employs a wide range of communication and interpretative techniques (Banner, 2010b; McNair, Taft, & Hegarty, 2008; Powney & Watts, 1987). Practice interviews can assist researchers to hone their skills and iron out any inconsistencies in the research process. These may be undertaken with volunteers, peers, or family members. Through these practice experiences, a researcher can become familiar with equipment (such as voice recorders), test the suitability of the interview environment for noise and interruptions, and review interview questions (Banner, 2010b). Early in my graduate studies, I gained firsthand experiences of some of these issues. During a practice interview, I experienced both equipment failure and excessive noise that led to an inaudible recording and a subsequently incomplete interview transcript. This taught me the importance of having a contingency plan in place and the need to generate detailed field notes to "fill in" any missing data. As well as the practical elements of data collection, these practice experiences can support the researcher to critically examine his or her use of language, and interviewing skills in general. Such exercises can illuminate the inadvertent use of leading language, discomfort when examining sensitive topics, or a failure to follow up on interesting leads. Ongoing reflection and reflexivity to examine, question, and sensitize the researcher in the data collection process are essential to the development of a robust GT (Cupchik, 2001; Hertz, 1997; Koch & Harrington, 1998).

Sampling in Grounded Theory Studies

Sampling is a critical component of a GT study and encompasses the mechanisms through which prospective participants are identified and recruited.

In GT studies, the sample is not predetermined; rather sampling occurs in response to the emerging theoretical data (Strauss & Corbin, 1998). In this study, both convenience and theoretical sampling approaches were utilized. Convenience sampling involves the recruitment of any suitable prospective participant and leads to a wide and diverse sample (Hutchinson, 2001). This initial sample provided a baseline for the study and provided a general insight into the experiences of women undergoing CABG surgery. I was cautious not to begin theoretical sampling too early, to avoid prematurely honing or limiting data collection. Once these general experiences were captured, I began theoretical sampling in response to the data analysis. Theoretical sampling involves the selective recruitment of participants to explore specific variables and gain greater conceptual comprehensiveness (Charmaz, 2006; Strauss & Corbin, 1998). Through this approach, the researcher is able to hone the data collection to follow interesting leads and develop meticulous conceptualizations and analyses. This is in contrast to other methodologies in which analysis occurs mainly once data collection is complete (Charmaz, 2006).

A sample of 30 women was recruited for this study, with the majority being selected through theoretical sampling. Theoretical sampling was driven by numerous emerging areas of interest, including the selective recruitment of those who lived alone or had limited social support, those requiring urgent surgery, and those with a recent diagnosis of CHD. Waiting list coordinators were key supports during theoretical sampling, as they were able to prescreen prospective participants based on these interests. In this study, sampling continued until saturation occurred, that is, the point where no further themes were generated. The sample size was fairly large for a qualitative study, which is typical of many GT studies (Morse, Swanson, & Kuzel, 2001; Sandelowski, 1999). Documenting and reflecting on sampling decisions, through reflexive accounts and theoretical memos, is critical to undertaking a rigorous GT study.

Analyzing Data

The GT methodology is characterized by systematic data analysis and coding techniques. Grounded theory studies are inherently complex, nonlinear, and entail the concurrent collection and analysis of data. Coding is undertaken throughout to label, group, and compare emerging data. As the research progresses, coding becomes increasingly focused, and comprehensive explanations and substantive theories of phenomena are constructed.

Four types of coding are undertaken in GT studies: microscopic analysis, open coding, axial coding, and selective coding. Microscopic data analysis is the process of examining the data on a line-by-line basis. Open coding involves the abstract labeling of data into conceptual groups or themes. Themes are generated according to specific properties and dimensions. While open coding deconstructs the data to form distinct, fragmented categories, axial coding encompasses the reconstruction of data to form categories that are linked to achieve precise, dense, and accurate explanations of the phenomena under study (Strauss & Corbin, 1998). Axial coding signals a departure from analytical description to abstraction. Throughout this process, constant comparison is undertaken as a method of contrasting and juxtaposing the data. Different participants, situations, times, and events are compared to tease out similarities and differences. This sharpens the analysis and promotes the comprehensiveness of the emerging theoretical data. Finally, selective coding involves the identification of the core category that links all other categories. During selective coding, the researcher works to refine this theoretical scheme as a means of achieving consistency and constructing theory that is grounded in the data.

At each part of these coding processes, theoretical memos are generated. Theoretical memos are an important aspect of GT studies and provide an audit trail for the research process, tracking emerging theories and capturing the reflexive aspects of the research study. The memos are produced throughout the course of the study, to support data analysis, keeping the researcher engaged with the data, and documenting ongoing ideas, thoughts, and challenges (Charmaz, 1990; Strauss & Corbin, 1998). They become analyzed as data in themselves and are used extensively during the writing-up period to capture important aspects of the research journey and theory development.

Effective Data Handling

A hybrid of manual and computerized analysis approaches was used during the study. During my initial data collection, I utilized manual techniques to undertake the microscopic and open coding. This included using hand coding with colored pens to delineate different codes, and cutting and pasting segments to build preliminary themes. As I progressed through open coding, these manual techniques became impractical as a result of the already large volumes of data and difficulties in tracking the analysis. I soon transitioned to the use of computer-aided qualitative data analysis software (CAQDAS).

Since the 1980s, numerous software packages (such as the Ethnograph, NUD*IST, ATLAS.ti, and NVIVO) aimed at assisting qualitative data analysis have been developed and have been widely adopted throughout a range of disciplines. However, the increased use of CAQDAS is not without criticism;

this has been accused of promoting positivist approaches that objectify and quantify analysis (Kelle, 1995, 1997; Lee & Fielding, 1991; Seidel, 1991; Seidel & Kelle, 1995). However, such criticisms can be misleading as they fail to recognize the complex theoretical processes integral to qualitative research, with technology merely "facilitating" as opposed to actually "doing" the analysis (Kelle, 1997). In GT studies, the researcher must remain flexible and sensitive to the data and should not be restrained by technology. The use of CAQDAS can facilitate analysis by supporting the coding and retrieval of data, and in some cases, can assist in the development of theoretical models (Banner & Albarran, 2009; Coffey, Holbrook, & Atkinson, 1996; Fielding, 1994). However, the researcher must ultimately immerse himself or herself in the data to achieve conceptual depth and robust theory.

The decision to adopt a computer-assisted approach to data analysis presents the researcher with the challenge of finding a suitable package. In this early study, I used ATLAS.ti to support data analysis. This decision was based on a number of factors: (a) availability of software, (b) skills gained during an analysis training session provided as part of my graduate studies, and (c) the functions of the program were consistent with the analysis techniques of this GT study.

Initially, I found it challenging to use the software, but my confidence and proficiency increased rapidly. I found the code and retrieve functions of the software to be invaluable during microscopic and open coding and made the constant comparison of data reasonably easy. It was not until I began axial coding and constructing more abstract relationships through coding, that I struggled with the computerized approaches. I had attempted to use some of the theory building and hypertext functions of the software but soon ran into difficulties. I became increasingly concerned that my unskilled use of these theory-building functions could hinder my creativity and could potentially push me to prematurely establish theoretical relationships. Through a prolonged period of immersion with the data, I returned to some manual techniques and utilized an amalgam of manual and computerized analysis techniques according to the analysis under way. Through this process I was able to start mapping relationships as a means of constructing theory. I utilized digital photography to capture these and reflexive accounts to track my decision making.

Theorizing and Mapping

The aim of GT methodology is to produce a theory that explains "what's going on." Definitions of theory vary considerably with the diverse epistemological and ontological positions, even within GT itself. The classical GT approach advocates the generation of theory through rigorous comparative and verification techniques (Glaser, 2002a; Glaser & Strauss, 1967). This reflects the positivist underpinnings of the classical GT methodology whereby the researcher remains objective and neutral (Charmaz, 2006). Strauss and Corbin's (1998) and Charmaz's (2006) later constructivist approach to GT asserts that theory is generated from the interpretations and constructions of the researcher and the participant (Charmaz, 1990, 2006). In doing this, theories depart from generalized universal statements to becoming contextualized statements of understandings and realities. Therefore, constructivist GTs are substantive as opposed to formal. Substantive theories are those specific to a phenomenon or population, whereas formal theories apply more widely (Glaser & Strauss, 1967).

Consistent with the constructivist approach adopted for this study, theorizing provided diffuse and comprehensive explanations of women's experiences of undergoing CABG surgery. The process of theorizing to develop substantive theory was lengthy and involved prolonged immersion in the data. This process is inherently nonlinear and involved moving back and forth between the analysis, recursive data collection through theoretical sampling, revisiting original transcripts, and on occasions, returning to the participant to seek clarification. Without adequate immersion, there is the risk that the analyses will be incomplete. This can be a risk for the inexperienced novice, as well as the established researcher who may be overburdened with other work commitments.

When moving through the analytical phases and constructing a GT, I frequently struggled to articulate relationships in a meaningful way. Mapping proved a useful technique to assist in the development and communication of this substantive theory. These useful tools can assist the researcher to articulate intricate relationships that emerge from the data and can identify gaps or inconsistencies in the emergent theoretical scheme. Strauss and Corbin (1998), in their book *The Basics of Qualitative Research*, introduce the conditional/consequential matrix. The conditional/consequential matrix is a diagrammatic coding device that displays a series of interconnected concentric circles with arrows interlinking circles toward and away from the center to represent microscopic and macroscopic factors (Strauss & Corbin, 1998). During analysis, I had attempted to develop a matrix but later decided to use more practical mapping approaches. During the construction of theory, I developed biographical maps for each participant as a means of reconnecting with the participant's illness trajectory. These helped me to progress through theory building, where I developed further maps of emerging theoretical data. I also used mapping and diagrams to articulate the research process (see Figure 9.1).

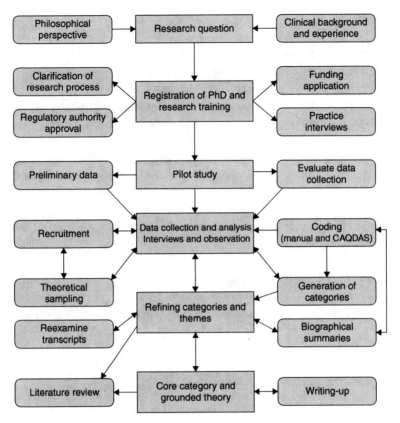

Figure 9.1 *Map of the research process.*

Grounded theory studies require deep and prolonged immersion with the data. The process of analysis can be frustrating at times, occasionally agonizing, but is filled equally with creativity and great "aha" moments. I was fortunate to have good social networks, including a highly supportive supervision team, with whom I could talk about my ideas, progress, and substantive theory. This was a crucial support as I came to start writing up the findings of this study.

DEVELOPING RIGOROUS GROUNDED THEORIES

Developing rigorous GTs requires researchers to undertake a systematic assessment of their own impact on the research process, through reflexivity and a thorough evaluation of the research process and outcomes. This section discusses reflexivity and evaluation in GT studies.

Reflexivity

Reflexivity is the way in which a researcher relates to what is being studied and seeks to provide reflection on the context, interactions, participants, self, and time. The process of reflexivity embodies a conscious and deliberate attempt to identify how our own assumptions and presuppositions influence the data and research process (Charmaz, 2006). Reflexivity has become an increasingly important concern for GT researchers. In line with the growing use of interpretivist and constructivist approaches, researchers are required to systematically examine the decisions and steps that underpin a research process, including their own positions, contexts, and structures (Charmaz, 2006; Mruck & Mey, 2010; Strauss & Corbin, 1998). Charmaz (2006) highlights that, "We *construct* our grounded theories through our past and present involvements and interactions with people, perspectives, and research practices" (p. 10).

In examining my position, I was able to situate myself within this endeavor and identified that my role as a woman, nurse, and researcher impacted on the research process. I examine my position as a nurse as an example.

Clinical and Theoretical Knowledge

As nurses, we bring with us a range of contextual and disciplinary experiences and knowledge that impact on the research process; indeed, it is typically these interests and experiences that fuel the development of a research study. This substantive knowledge is recognized in all GT models. In the classical GT, Glaser (1978) warns researchers that such preconceived ideas and assumptions can create bias and may cause a researcher to "force" rather than allow "emergence" of the data. Strauss and Corbin's (1997) later version highlights that a researcher must try to acknowledge and suspend this past knowledge. Charmaz (2006), in her constructivist approach to GT, argues that attempting to suspend such knowledge is not helpful and contends that a researcher should draw on these experiences but remain open to other explanations and interpretations (Charmaz, 2006).

The varied and dynamic nature of my clinical work within the cardiothoracic intensive care unit inevitably influenced my research journey. In addition to knowledge of the context, I had also established a good baseline knowledge of the research literature through my nursing practice and enduring interest in women's cardiac health. This was extended further during the development of the research proposal. This awareness of the literature is a significant source of contention among the different GT communities (Backman & Kyngas, 1999; McCallin, 2006; Walls, Parahoo, & Fleming, 2010). In classical models, researchers are encouraged to delay engagement with the literature to avoid contaminating the analysis process. More recent constructivist approaches see this knowledge as "orienting" and providing the researcher with sensitizing concepts, which can guide the research process (Baker, Wiest, & Stern, 1992; Carolan, 2003; Charmaz, 2006; Walls et al., 2010). In the later stages, the literature becomes an important part of evaluating the GT.

Through reflexive accounts, I was able to document, question, and tease out the ways in which these factors impacted on the research process, as well as critically examining decisions related to analysis, methodology, and theory (Rice & Ezzy, 1999). These accounts were integrated into the heart of the study, being analyzed as data where appropriate and being reported in the thesis as a means of promoting transparency in the research process. On occasions, it was these accounts that prompted me to revisit the original data, reexamine coding, and undertake a comprehensive evaluation of the research process.

Evaluating Grounded Theory Research

Critically evaluating the processes and outcomes of research is an essential mechanism through which to establish the quality and impact of a study. In the past, qualitative research studies have been evaluated using the traditional criteria rooted in the positivist or relativist approaches. Such criteria include reliability, validity, and objectivity. Over recent decades, there has been growing recognition that these are not suitable for naturalistic research (Chiovitti & Piran, 2003; Morse et al., 2001; Weinberg, 2002).

Many qualitative researchers adopt Guba and Lincoln's (1989) "naturalistic" approach to evaluation. This focuses on the establishment of trustworthiness through consideration of a study's credibility, transferability, dependability, confirmability, and authenticity. In this study, trustworthiness was demonstrated in a range of ways, including the provision of rich accounts of experiences and research processes, peer and participant checking, prolonged engagement with the data, rigorous and complete analyses, and evidence of reflexivity (Guba & Lincoln, 1989). Other evaluation criteria specific to the constructivist approach include a consideration of a study's originality, resonance, and usefulness of the emerging theory (Charmaz, 2006). This can be demonstrated through the creation of rich accounts and narratives, preservation of the participants' voice in the research, and situating the constructed theory within the contemporary literature. As part of this process, areas for further inquiry are identified, and the significance of the research at the patient, practice, and policy levels can be established (Charmaz, 2006).

SUMMARY

Researchers are faced with many considerations when embarking on a research project, including issues relating to the research problem, underlying theoretical perspectives, and the practical elements of undertaking a qualitative study. Grounded theory is a popular qualitative methodology that has evolved considerably since its advent. A number of GT approaches exist, and a researcher must have a clear grasp of these philosophical foundations and methodological principles to develop a rigorous and robust GT.

This chapter has reflected on some of my experiences when undertaking a constructivist GT study exploring women's experience of CABG surgery. It has outlined some of the practical aspects of initiating a study, collecting and analyzing data, and establishing rigor. Key messages arising from this chapter include the need for researchers to develop their research skills to collect quality data, undertake prolonged immersion with the data for complete analyses, and to critically examine their own assumptions and positions throughout the research process through reflexivity. Grounded theory studies are highly relevant to nursing and health care and lead to the development of high-quality explanatory models and substantive theories. These can enhance our understanding of complex clinical issues and can inform the development of health care services that improve patient care and outcomes.

ACKNOWLEDGMENTS

I would like to thank my supervisors from both my PhD (Drs. John Albarran, Margaret Miers, and Brenda Clark) and postdoctoral research fellowship (Drs. Martha MacLeod and Kathryn Shier) studies for their, Dr. Andrew Lukaris, and children, Sophia, Eleni, and Arabella and the encouragement of my friends, Dr. Petra Newman and Karen Shepherd for their endless hours of discussion and support. Thank you all.

REFERENCES

Annells, M. (1996). Grounded theory method: Philosophical perspectives, paradigm of inquiry, and postmodernism. *Qualitative Health Research, 6*(3), 379–393.

Ayanian J. Z., Guadagnoli E., & Cleary P. D. (1995). Physical and psychological functioning of women and men after coronary artery bypass surgery. *Journal of the American Medical Association, 274,* 1767–1770.

Backman, K., & Kyngas, H. A. (1999). Challenges of the grounded theory approach to a novice researcher. *Nursing and Health Sciences, 1*(3), 147–153.

Baker, C., Wiest, J., & Stern, P. N. (1992). Method slurring: The grounded theory/phenomenology example. *Journal of Advanced Nursing, 17*(11), 1355–1360.

Banner, D. (2007). *Women's experience of coronary artery bypass graft surgery: A grounded theory approach.* Unpublished PhD thesis. University of the West of England, Bristol, UK.

Banner, D. (2010a). Becoming a coronary artery bypass graft surgery patient: A grounded theory study of women's experiences. *Journal of Clinical Nursing, 19*(21–22), 3123–3133.

Banner, D. (2010b). Qualitative interviewing: Preparation for practice. *Canadian Journal of Nursing Research, 20*(3), 27–30.

Banner, D., & Albarran, J. (2009). Computer-assisted qualitative data analysis software: A review. *Canadian Journal of Cardiovascular Nursing, 19*(3), 24–31.

Banner, D., Miers, M., Clarke, B., & Albarran, J. (2012). Women's experiences of undergoing coronary artery bypass graft surgery. *Journal of Advanced Nursing, 68*(4), 919–930.

British Heart Foundation. (2003). *Take note of your* heart: *A review of women and heart disease in the UK 2003.* London, British Heart Foundation (2006).

Bryant, A., & Charmaz, K. (2007). Grounded theory in historical perspective: An epistemological account. In A. Bryant & K. Charmaz (2007), *The Sage handbook of grounded theory* (pp. 31–57). Thousand Oaks, CA: Sage.

Carolan, M. (2003). Reflexivity: A personal journey during data collection. *Nurse Researcher, 10*(3), 7–14.

Charmaz, K. (1990). 'Discovering' chronic illness: Using grounded theory. *Social Science and Medicine, 30*(11), 1161–1172.

Charmaz, K. (2000). Grounded theory: Objectivist and constructivist methods. In N. K. Denzin & Y. S. Lincoln (Eds.), *Handbook of qualitative research* (2nd ed.). Thousand Oaks, CA: Sage.

Charmaz, K. (2006). *Constructing grounded theory: A practical guide through qualitative analysis.* London, UK: Sage.

Chiovitti, R. F., & Piran, N. (2003). Rigour and grounded theory research. *Journal of Advanced Nursing, 44*(4), 427–435.

Coffey, A., Holbrook, B., & Atkinson, P. (1996). Qualitative data analysis: Technologies and representations. *Sociological Research Online, 1*(1). Retrieved from http://www.socresonline.org.uk/socresonline/1/1/4.html

Cupchik, G. (2001). Constructivist realism: An ontology that encompasses positivist and constructivist approaches to the sciences. *Forum: Qualitative Social Research, 2*(1). Retrieved from http://www.qualitative-research.net/index.php/fqs/article/view/968/2112

DeVon, H. A., Hogan, N., Ochs, A. L., & Shapiro, M. (2010). Time to treatment for acute coronary syndromes: The cost of indecision. *Journal of Cardiovascular Nursing, 25*(2), 106–114.

Doucherty, S., & Sandelowski, M. (1999). Focus on qualitative methods: Interviewing children. *Research in Nursing and Health Care, 22,* 177–185.

Fielding, N. (1994). Getting into computer-aided qualitative data analysis. *ESRC Data Archive Bulletin, 57,* 6–8.

Glaser, B. G. (1978). *Theoretical sensitivity: Advances in the methodology of grounded theory* (Vol. 2). Mill Valley, CA: Sociology Press.

Glaser, B. G. (2002, September). Constructivist grounded theory? In *Forum qualitative Sozialforschung/Forum: Qualitative social research* (Vol. 3, No. 3).

Glaser, B. G., & Strauss, A. L. (1967). *The discovery of grounded theory: Strategies for qualitative research.* New York, NY: Aldine.

Grace, S., Abbey, S., Bisaillon, S., Shnek, Z. M., Irvine, J., & Stewart, D. E. (2003). Presentation, delay and contraindication to thrombolytic treatment in females and males with myocardial infarction. *Women's Health Issues, 13,* 214–221.

Guba E. G., & Lincoln, Y. S. (1989). *Fourth generation evaluation.* Thousand Oaks, CA: Sage.

Hertz, R. (1997). *Reflexivity and voice.* Thousand Oaks, CA: Sage.

Hutchinson, S. A. (2001). The development of qualitative health research: Taking stock. *Qualitative Health Research, 11*(4), 505–521.

Kelle, U. (Ed.). (1995). *Computer-aided qualitative data analysis: Theory, methods and practice.* London, UK: Sage.

Kelle, U. (1997). Theory building in qualitative research and computer programs for the management of textual data. *Sociological Research Online, 2*(2). Retrieved from http://www.socresonline.org.uk/2/2/1.html

King, K. M., McFetridge-Durdle, J., LeBlanc, P., Anzarut, A., & Tsuyuki, R. (2009). A descriptive examination of the impact of sternal scar formation in women. *European Journal of Cardiovascular Nursing, 8,* 112–118.

Koch, T., & Harrington, A. (1998). Reconceptualizing rigor: The case for reflexivity. *Journal of Advanced Nursing, 28,* 882–890.

Kramer-Kile, M. (2012). Situating methodology within qualitative research. *Canadian Journal of Cardiovascular Nursing, 22*(4), 27–31.

Lee, R., & Fielding, N. (1991). *Using computers in qualitative research.* London, UK: Sage.

Lockyer, L., & Bury, M. (2002). The construction of a modern epidemic: The implications for women of the gendering of coronary heart disease. *Journal of Advanced Nursing, 39*(5), 432–440.

Marshall, C., & Rossman, G. B. (2011). *Designing qualitative research* (5th ed.). Thousand Oaks, CA: Sage.

Maynard, C., Every, N. R., Martin, J. S., Kudenchuk, P. J., & Weaver, W. D. (1997). Association of gender and survival in patients with acute myocardial infarction. *Archives of Internal Medicine, 157,* 1379–1384.

McCallin, A. M. (2006). Grappling with the literature in a grounded theory study. *The Grounded Theory Review, 5*(2/3), 11–27.

McDougall, P. (2000). In-depth interviewing: The key issues of reliability and validity. *Community Practitioner, 73,* 722–724.

McNair, R., Taft, A., & Hegarty, K. (2008). Using reflexivity to enhance in-depth interviewing skills for the clinician researcher. *BMC Medical Research Methodology*, *8*(1), 73.

Mills, J., Bonner, A., & Francis, K. (2006a). The development of constructivist grounded theory. *International Journal of Qualitative Methods*, *5*(1), 25–35.

Mills, J., Bonner, A., & Francis, K. (2006b). Adopting a constructivist approach to grounded theory: Implications for research design. *International Journal of Nursing Practice*, *12*(1), 8–13.

Morse, J. M., Swanson, J. M., & Kuzel, A. J. (Eds.). (2001). *The nature of qualitative evidence*. Thousand Oaks, CA: Sage.

Mruck, K., & Mey, G. (2010). Grounded theory and reflexivity. In A. Bryant & K. Charmaz, *The Sage handbook of grounded theory: Paperback edition* (pp. 515–538). London, UK: Sage.

Norton, L. (1999). The philosophical bases of grounded theory and their implications for research practice. *Nurse Researcher*, *7*(1), 31–43.

Powney, J., & Watts, M. (1987). *Interviewing in educational research*. London, UK: Routledge and Kegan Paul.

Redecker, N. S., Mason, D. J., Wykpisz, E., & Glica, B. (1996). Sleep patterns in women after coronary artery bypass surgery. *Applied Nursing Research*, *9*, 115–122.

Rice, P. L., & Ezzy, D. (1999). *Qualitative research methods: A health focus* (p. 291). Melbourne: Oxford University Press.

Rosenfeld, A. G., & Gilkeson J. (2000). Meaning of illness for women with coronary heart disease. *Heart & Lung*, *29*(2), 105–112.

Rubin, H. J., & Rubin, I. S. (2011). *Qualitative interviewing: The art of hearing data*. Thousand Oaks, CA: Sage.

Sandelowski, M. (1999). Time and qualitative research. *Research in Nursing & Health*, *22*(1), 79–87.

Seidel, J. (1991). Method and madness in the application of computer technology to qualitative data analysis. In R. Lee & N. Fielding (Eds.), *Using computers in qualitative research*. London, UK: Sage.

Seidel, J., & Kelle, U. (1995). Different functions of coding in the analysis of textual data. In U. Kelle (Ed.), *Computer-aided qualitative data analysis: Theory, methods and practice* (pp. 52–61). London, UK: Sage.

Stramba-Badiale, M., Fox, K. M., Priori, S. G., Collins, P., Daly, C., Graham, I., . . . Tendera, M. (2006). Cardiovascular disease in women: A statement from the policy conference of the European Society of Cardiology. *European Heart Journal*, *27*(8), 994–1005.

Strauss, A., & Corbin, J. (1998). *Basics of qualitative research: Techniques and procedures for developing grounded theory* (2nd ed.). Thousand Oaks, CA: Sage.

Strauss, A., & Corbin, J. M. (Eds.). (1997). *Grounded theory in practice*. London, Thousand Oaks: Sage.

Stroh, M. (2000). Qualitative interviewing. In Burton, D. (Ed.), *Research training for social sciences: A handbook for postgraduate researchers*. London, UK: Sage.

Strubert, H. J., & Carpenter, R. D. (2007). *Qualitative Research in nursing: Advancing the humanist imperative*. Philadelphia, PA: Lippincott Williams & Wilkins.

Vasilachis de Gialdino, I. (2009). Ontological and epistemological foundations of qualitative research. *Forum: Qualitative Social Research, 10*(2), Art. 30. Retrieved from http://www.qualitative-research.net/index.php/fqs/article/view/1299/3163

Vodopiutz, J., Poller, S., Schneider, B., Lalouschek, J., Menz, F., & Stollberger, C. (2002). Chest pain in hospitalized patients: Cause-specific and gender-specific differences. *Journal of Women's Health, 11*(8), 719–727.

Walls, P., Parahoo, K., & Fleming, P. (2010). The role and place of knowledge and literature in grounded theory. *Nurse Researcher, 17*(4), 8.

Weinberg, D. (Ed.). (2002). *Qualitative research methods.* Malden, MA: Blackwell.

Willingham, S. A., & Kilpatrick E. S. (2005). Evidence of gender bias when applying the new diagnostic criteria for myocardial infarction. *Heart, 91,* 237–238.

World Health Organization. (2013). Cardiovascular Diseases (CVDs). Retrieved from http://www.who.int/mediacentre/factsheets/fs317/en

A GROUNDED THEORY STUDY OF NURSING STUDENTS' EXPERIENCES IN THE OFF-CAMPUS CLINICAL SETTING

Brian Sengstock

*P*oor workplace relations is an issue of concern in many workplaces, and this phenomenon is not restricted to the nursing profession. Having worked in the health and education sectors for a number of years prior to the commencement of a doctoral research project investigating the experiences of nursing students in the off-campus clinical setting, the author was intrigued by the experiences of students in both the medical and nursing professions as the author's profession had not, at the time of commencing the research, transitioned to the higher education sector for entry into profession education. Although the transition had not occurred, there were clear intentions that the transition would occur. The transition to the higher education sector was effectively completed in 2011. Completing a study of nursing students' experiences of the off-campus clinical setting was insightful and allowed the author to make comparisons between his own profession and a profession that had transitioned from entry-level professional education to the higher education sector some two decades earlier.

An overview of the author's study is provided below to allow the reader to understand the context of the research study and to provide the foundation for the methodological processes that are presented. Commencing with a brief overview of the grounded theory methodology, the three "schools" of grounded theory are discussed with reference to the intricacies of each. Selection of a particular grounded theory "school" is elucidated with reference to the process adopted by the author in selecting constructivist grounded theory as the preferred school of grounded theory for the research study being undertaken. The discussion then moves on to the construction of grounded theory and the need to maintain both objectivity and sensitivity to the data. Rigor and validity are introduced and followed by a discussion on sampling for the grounded theory study. Sampling is an important aspect of any study, with two distinct approaches to purposive sampling being utilized in accordance with accepted grounded theory methods. This is subsequently followed by data collection and analysis with a description of the approaches used by the author in both aspects of the study. The intricacies of coding are presented with a sample of the data to assist the reader in comprehending the process. Finally an evaluation strategy is proposed to allow the researcher to interact with the evaluation of a grounded theory study.

BACKGROUND TO THE STUDY

It could be argued that Florence Nightingale was significant in her contribution to the reformation of the status of women through the establishment of paid training and employment in nursing in the late 1800s; her legacy is still being felt in the 21st century. Paid work for women in the nursing profession opened up employment opportunities; however, it also constrained the nursing workforce due to rules, regulations, and expectations that Nightingale enforced and which continue to be enforced (van der Peet, 1995). The rules, regulations, and expectations of the Nightingale era are still evident in nursing practice today.

As a profession, nursing is hierarchical in nature. Operating through a defined linear chain of command, individuals within the nursing profession have a particular place on that chain. A nurse is either superior to those below him or her or subordinate to those above. The hierarchy that exists within the overall profession also exists within each clinical level. Historically, hierarchical disciplinary action has been utilized by military and religious leaders to ensure that cultural norms are strictly followed and maintained. Unquestioning attitudes and obedience were rewarded, while dissidence and disobedience were met with disciplinary action and humiliation (Hadikin & O'Driscoll, 2000). Through the use of punishment, leaders ensured that group members adhered to the rules, traditions, and values that had become accepted cultural norms. Duffy (1995) argues that hierarchical systems, such as those in nursing, thrive through the use of controlling, coercive, and inflexible protocols.

Given that the central focus of nursing is caring, it is paradoxical that the literature reveals interpersonal conflict among nurses as a significant issue confronting the profession in the 21st century (Cox, 1987; Duffy, 1995; Farrell, 1997, 2001; Sengstock, Moxham, & Dwyer, 2006; Taylor, 2001). Known as "horizontal violence," interpersonal conflict is described by Duffy (1995) as hostile and aggressive behavior by individual or group members toward another member or groups of members of the larger group. Horizontal violence most commonly manifests as covert psychological harassment, which creates hostility, as opposed to overt physical aggression. This harassment involves the use of verbal abuse, threats, intimidation, humiliation, excessive criticism, innuendo, exclusion and denial of access to opportunity, disinterest, discouragement, and the withholding of relevant information (Farrell, 1997, 1999, 2001; Thomas & Droppleman, 1997). Regardless of the nomenclature that is used to describe these behaviors, they are identifiable as bullying in nature and, as such, have wide-ranging negative effects on everyone involved, either as a participant, a victim, or through exposure. For consistency in this thesis, the term "horizontal violence" is used as this is the term that nurses often use for bullying behaviors in the workplace.

The Australian model of preregistration nursing education is now university based. The previous model was more of an apprenticeship. However, in 1985 a mass movement to the tertiary sector occurred with Queensland largely making the transition in 1987. The approach to educating nursing students in the tertiary sector separated the theoretical and clinical learning environments. Now, nursing students complete a theoretical component as well as a practical skill development component in a "controlled and safe" university environment. They then complete an off-campus clinical placement where they are expected to apply their knowledge and skills in a "real" practice setting. Off-campus clinical placements allow nursing students the opportunity to integrate the skills and knowledge that they have gained at university and the time to build their confidence. Off-campus clinical placement is also a time when nursing students become socialized into the profession through their interaction with peers and the work environment, thus developing their identity both personally and professionally.

As in all professions, there are certain "norms" that are used by the members of the organization to provide stability and direction. Nursing is no exception to this cultural phenomenon. Suominen, Kovasin, and Ketola (1997) indicate that the structure of the nursing culture remains an aspect that is very much unexplored and is seldom discussed either in practice or research. The concept of culture is closely interwoven with the values espoused by a community (Robbins, Waters-Marsh, Cacioppe, and Millett, 1998) and generally sets the expected behaviors of the members of that community. In the broadest sense, culture is the deep and invisible structures of society, which are transferred from one generation to the next (Suominen et al., 1996). Nursing students are taught by nurse academics and are periodically placed in the clinical setting with preceptors and registered nurses who supervise and assess them on practicum. Both the nurse academic and the preceptor have been socialized into the cultural norms of nursing by their work environment and peers during the time that they trained and worked as a nurse.

Induction into the cultural norms of nursing is facilitated through the experiential learning that occurs in the off-campus clinical setting. Kovasin (1993, cited in Suominen, Kovasin, & Ketola, 1997) found that nurses learned the behaviors that are expected of them by working with experienced nurses and through observing what others were doing. It is through this process that they internalize the routines and rituals of the nursing profession. The "rules of work" and the work roles, tasks, and status are controlled by an elite few members of the nursing team, with the rules being enforced through ritual indoctrination that may or may not be overtly apparent (Hutchinson, Vickers, Jackson, & Wilkes, 2006).

The process of professional socialization affects the individual's self-esteem through the assimilation of professional norms. Social comparison, according to Randle (2003), plays a central role in the development and maintenance of professional self-esteem. In order to consolidate and enhance their place in the eyes of their peers, it is highly probable that student nurses will conform to the roles and standards that are expected of them (Randle, 2003). This includes behaviors associated with horizontal violence. Hutchinson and colleagues (2006) indicate that nursing staff subjected to horizontal violence either resign their positions or acquiesce to survive in the clinical environment. Indeed some perpetuate behaviors that they originally found abhorrent.

Currently there is a critical shortage of nurses worldwide (Bowen & Curtis, 2004; Delez, 2003), and although it is generally assumed that poor wages and conditions are the main contributors, recent research has begun investigating the impact of horizontal violence on recruitment and retention rates in nursing (Bowen & Curtis, 2004; Nevidjon & Erikson, 2001). An increase in the number of undergraduate nursing students who are not completing their preregistration nursing program is cited by Bowen and Curtis (2004) as a developing issue over the past decade. Jackson, Clare, and Mannix (2002) link recruitment and retention issues in the nursing profession to horizontal violence. Anecdotal evidence suggests that student nurses are subject to negative experiences during clinical placements, and this in turn may lead to an increased noncompletion rate at university. The impact that the negative behaviors experienced in the off-campus clinical setting have on the nursing students is the focus of this study.

Many of the longer serving nurses in the present nursing workforce were trained in a strictly disciplined style with a considerable amount of time allocated to the development of practical skills within the hospital environment. Nurses therefore gained extensive experience and competency in their practical skills (Davey, 2003). In contemporary preparatory programs offered through the tertiary sector, students are empowered and gain theoretical knowledge from a wide variety of health disciplines, which encourages them to ask questions and challenge. This is quite different from the hospital training and its strict adherence to hierarchy, where hospital-trained nurses did not challenge their superiors, and if they did they paid the price, often with extended demotion (Madsen, 2000).

In the majority of research studies investigating horizontal violence in the nursing profession, the focus has been on the effects of horizontal violence from an oppression theory perspective (Farrell, 2001). These studies have also exclusively focused on nurses who had graduated and were working in a nursing environment (Farrell, 1997, 2001; McKenna, Smith, Poole, & Coverdale, 2002). A study ($n = 152$) of second- and third-year undergraduate nursing students at the University of Wollongong, New South Wales, Australia, was conducted by Bowen and Curtis in 2004. This study utilized a mixed methods approach to investigate again the effects of horizontal violence. All of the studies examined (Bowen & Curtis, 2004; Delez, 2003; Farrell, 1997, 2001; McKenna et al., 2002) are unanimous in identifying horizontal violence as an ongoing issue of significant concern to the nursing profession.

GROUNDED THEORY: A METHODOLOGY

Grounded theory was conceived as a methodology by Barney Glaser, a quantitative researcher, and Anslem Strauss, a qualitative researcher, in the mid-1960s (Glaser & Strauss, 1965, 1968). In their pioneering book, *The Discovery of Grounded Theory*, Glaser and Strauss (1967) articulated the strategies that they had adopted in a collaborative research project on dying. Grounded theory was first published as "a process that articulated the discovery of theory from qualitative data" (Robrecht, 1995, p. 170), with the methodology arising out of the combined research histories of Glaser and Strauss (Charmaz, 2000a; Clarke, 2005; Dey, 1999; Stern & Covan, 2001). As a methodology, grounded theory stemmed from, and is fundamentally linked with, symbolic interactionism (Charmaz, 2000a; Clarke, 2005; Ezzy, 2002; Milliken & Schreiber, 2001; Smith & Biley, 1997). This link between the theoretical underpinnings of symbolic interactionism and the methods of conducting grounded theory research is inextricably represented by grounded theory methodology (Milliken & Schreiber, 2001).

Schools of Grounded Theory—An Empirical Challenge

Although originally described by Glaser and Strauss in the mid-1960s, a review of the literature on grounded theory reveals a divergence in the original authors' views and development of grounded theory following their classic statements on the methodology in 1967 (Glaser & Strauss, 1967) and 1978 (Glaser, 1978). Since that time, the two authors have taken grounded theory in somewhat different directions, Glaser alone, and Strauss in his treatise with his apprentice and later colleague, Juliet Corbin (Charmaz, 2000a).

The divergence of the "original" grounded theory has subsequently led to the formation of two "schools" of grounded theory: the Glaserian version based on the original work and the subsequent writings of Glaser (independently of Strauss) and the Straussian version based on refinements of the "original" methodology, which Strauss made in association with Corbin (Benoliel, 1996; Charmaz, 2006; Heath & Cowley, 2003; McCallin, 2003). This divergence in grounded theory methodology is further complicated by the emergence of a third "school" of grounded theory in which scholars have moved, and continue to move, grounded theory away from the positivism associated with both Glaser's and Strauss and Corbin's versions of grounded theory (Bryant, 2002, 2003; Charmaz, 2000a, 2005; Clarke, 2003, 2005; Seale, 1999).

McCallin (2003) suggests that the Glaserian version of grounded theory has further developed and subsequently been reframed, essentially constituting a different version of grounded theory from that developed by Glaser and Strauss in the mid-1960s. A similar issue appears to have arisen in the Straussian version in which Strauss's later works in association with Corbin have caused the roots of symbolic interactionism in the method to grow distant (Clarke, 2005). Unlike the situation with the reform of Glaserian grounded theory in which McCallin (2003) recommends that consideration should be given to a second school of thought, there is no suggestion that the evolution of Strauss's version of grounded theory should result in a second school of Straussian thought.

In designing a study, it is essential that consideration be given to methodological issues (McCallin, 2003). To assist in developing an in-depth understanding of the methodology, it is essential to undertake wide and extensive reading in the broader methodology of grounded theory. Reading widely around grounded theory methodology provides an opportunity to not only identify some of the differences between the three "schools" of grounded theory, but to also gain an understanding of the differences through engaging with each of the three "schools" of grounded theory thought. This approach allows researchers to develop their understanding of the methodological differences and the method differences, while gaining an insight into the underlying ontological and epistemological assumptions of the original authors of the different "schools" of grounded theory, which are at the center of the methodological issues.

Glaserian grounded theory is ontologically rooted in critical realism, assuming that an objective world exists independently of our knowledge and belief. As such, the researcher is considered to be independent of the research (Annells, 1996). Glaser's stance is in stark contrast to Strauss's version of grounded theory, which has its ontological roots in relativism in which it is argued that reality is interpreted. Strauss and Corbin's (1998) text encourages the researcher to be involved in the method and to interpret the reality that is being studied. Constructivist grounded theory is also ontologically rooted in relativism (Charmaz, 1990, 2000b, 2003; Charmaz & Mitchell, 2001); however, the constructivist grounded theorist takes a reflexive stance on the modes of knowing and representing studied life in that close attention is paid to the empirical realities and people's collective renderings of them and their location within these remedies (Charmaz, 2005).

Despite Glaser's divergence from Strauss's ideas in relation to the direction of the method, Glaser remained consistent in his explanation of the grounded theory method for many years. Glaser consistently defined grounded theory as a method of discovery, where the categories were emergent from the data, with the method reliant on empiricism, which Charmaz (2006) suggests was often direct and narrow in focus, analyzing a basic social process, which arose from the data. Strauss (1987) redirected the method toward a more verifiable position in his treatise with Juliet Corbin (Strauss & Corbin, 1990, 1998). Rather than focusing on the comparative methods of earlier iterations of grounded theory, Strauss and Corbin's iteration of the methodology focuses on the use of their new, technically oriented procedures. Glaser's version of grounded theory could be described as a more patient, relaxed approach, which waits for the theory to emerge from the data. Glaser's apparently patient approach is relied on by Glaser in arguing that the procedures inherent in the Straussian version of grounded theory proposed by Strauss and Corbin force the data and subsequent analysis into preconceived categories (Charmaz, 2006).

Despite adopting the traditional grounded theory guidelines posited by Glaser, and Strauss and Corbin, constructivist grounded theory does not subscribe to the positivist assumptions postulated in earlier formulations of the methodology (Charmaz, 1990, 2000b, 2003; Charmaz & Mitchell, 2001). In accordance with the apparent paradigm, constructivist grounded theorists take a reflexive stance on the modes of knowing and representing studied life; therefore, the constructivist approach to grounded theory assumes a less rigid approach. This flexibility is in part a response to Glaser and Strauss's invitation in their original statement of the grounded theory method for researchers to use the strategies flexibly and in their own way. Charmaz (2005, 2006) provides the researcher with a way of "doing" grounded theory while taking into account the theoretical and methodological developments of the past four decades.

Although often not readily apparent to novice researchers, Glaser and Strauss, in their original iteration of the method (and methodology as grounded theory is both a methodology and a method), invite the researcher to employ a strategic, flexible approach to using grounded theory, effectively encouraging the researcher to develop his or her own approach to "doing" grounded theory. The inherent flexibility in grounded theory provides the researcher with an opportunity to develop their understanding of the methodology and the methods employed in grounded theory, without compromising the researcher's ability to engage in other methodologies in later research. This is a significant positive for the use of grounded theory as the analytical skills gained through the use of grounded theory are directly transferable to other methodologies.

Decisions, Decisions—Straussian Versus Constructivist Grounded Theory

The preceding discussion on the different schools of grounded theory leads to the question of which of these schools of grounded theory is appropriate to the research project being undertaken. In respect of this research project, following the completion of an in-depth review of the literature on the various schools of grounded theory methodology, it was necessary to make a decision regarding the use of Straussian grounded theory, constructivist grounded theory, or a combination of these two "schools" of thought. Philosophically, I am more aligned to the constructivist orientations of Charmaz than I am to the interpretivist orientations of Strauss and Corbin. Charmaz (2006) emphasizes flexible guidelines as opposed to the methodological rules and requirements prescribed by Strauss and Corbin (1990, 1998). Glaser (2002) challenges the validity of Charmaz's approach to grounded theory, arguing that if constructivist data exists at all, it is only a small part of the data that grounded theory uses. Glaser's questioning of the validity of Charmaz's approach to grounded theory is countenanced by Charmaz (2006), arguing that it is possible to use the basic grounded theory guidelines, which were originally developed almost five decades ago and combine them with the methodological assumptions and approaches of the 21st century.

Immediately following the review of the literature on grounded theory methodology, it appeared as though a combination of Straussian and constructivist grounded theory may have been the most appropriate approach to the conduct of the research project. It soon became apparent that the constructivist approach to grounded theory was sufficiently flexible to allow the use of the structure from the Straussian version of grounded theory, while utilizing the additional flexibility available through the use of the constructivist approach. This decision was, ironically, supported by Strauss and Corbin's (1998) specific warning to researchers to avoid rigidly following set procedures. It was this warning about rigidity in the use of set procedures that confirmed my resolution to use constructivist grounded theory. Strauss and Corbin (1998) provided the scaffolding required to support a novice researcher in this methodology, through framing the analysis phase of the research while allowing for the maintenance of a constructivist mindset in the development of the grounded theory.

Ontological and epistemological assumptions also provide an important point of reference in determining the most suitable version of grounded theory methodology for the researcher to utilize. It is important to note that the researcher's personal preferences in respect of ontology and epistemology should be secondary to consideration of the most appropriate version of grounded theory for the research project being undertaken. Consideration of the ontological and epistemological assumptions in this research study on nursing students' experiences of the off-campus clinical setting was clearly aligned with the constructivist grounded theory methodology, leading to a confirmation that this was the most appropriate grounded theory approach to the realities of the nursing students' experiences. To discover the realities of what it meant to be a nursing student undertaking a clinical placement in the off-campus clinical setting, it was determined that it would be necessary to understand how participants constructed their own understanding of the clinical setting and their interactions with the clinical staff in a placement setting. The realities of being a nursing student were clearly appropriate to the ontological and epistemological assumptions underpinning constructivist grounded theory.

Constructing a Grounded Theory—An Approach to Construction

Despite the variations between Glaser, Strauss (and Corbin), and Charmaz in their underlying philosophical approaches to grounded theory and the actual methods employed in the development of the theory, there is consensus on the purpose of the approach. In using grounded theory, the researcher inductively develops theory from an interpretation of the data generated by a study of the phenomena that the theory represents (Glaser & Strauss, 1967); thus, the theory is "grounded" in the data. The theory that results from a grounded theory study is generally "substantive" in that it has relevance to the substantive area from which the data were collected, as opposed to a more generalizable theory, which is applicable to a wider population of participants outside the substantive area from which the participants were drawn. A substantive theory is able to be modified, whereas the more formal theories are less specific to a particular group and therefore have wider application to disciplinary concerns and problems (Strauss & Corbin, 1998). Baker, Norton, Young, and Ward (1998, p. 548) argue that the purpose of the substantive theory is to "predict, explain and interpret phenomenon." Therefore when considering the development of the substantive theory, the researcher must aim to develop a substantive theory that is relevant to the contextual boundaries of the research question that the study seeks to answer.

In constructing the substantive theory, the researcher moves between generating categories from data, which is an inductive process, and the consideration of how these categories fit with other data, which is a deductive process. The significance of induction and deduction to the development of a grounded theory is well explicated by Glaser and Strauss (1967), Glaser (1978, 1998), Strauss (1987), Strauss and Corbin (1998), and Charmaz (2006); however, the significance of the role of abduction is seldom considered by these authors despite the apparent significance of the process of abduction to the construction of a grounded theory.

A pragmatist sociologist Ezzy (2002, p. 13) discusses the work of Pierce and explains abduction as "the philosophical background to the processes that are involved in grounded theory." In contrast to induction, abduction "makes imaginative leaps . . . to general theory without having completely empirically demonstrated all the required steps" (Ezzy, 2002, p. 14). Once the researcher has made this imaginative leap, abduction relies on the process of ongoing inductive and deductive testing for confirmation. If the imaginative leap is confirmed by the ongoing process of induction and deduction, the "leaps" ultimately become the hypotheses proposed by Glaser (1978), demonstrating Glaser's strict adherence to "pure grounded theory." Strauss and Corbin (1998, p. 168) discuss *"plausible relationships proposed among concepts and sets of concepts,"* which form the vital elements of a grounded theory. Strauss and Corbin's approach to interpreting the imaginative leap has clearly deviated from Glaser's strict adherence to what many grounded theorists consider to be the "pure" form of grounded theory, which is rooted in the positivist paradigm.

The structure of the induction, deduction, and abduction processes is founded in the execution of the core elements of the grounded theory method. Glaser and Strauss, both as coauthors and separately, describe the core elements of grounded theory as coding, memoing, constant comparative method of analysis, theoretical sampling, and theoretical sensitivity (Glaser, 1978, 1992, 1998; Glaser & Strauss, 1967; Strauss, 1987; Strauss & Corbin, 1990, 1998). These core elements are discussed in detail in the data analysis below.

Maintaining Objectivity and Sensitivity—A Perspective

There can be no *tabula rasa* researchers as we all come to a research problem with some preconceived understanding of the problem that we are setting out to solve; however, prior to the commencement of a grounded theory study, researchers need to recognize their assumptions about what constitutes reality and how this "reality" impacts on their ability to perform the role of researchers in an objective manner. In a grounded theory study, there is a constant interplay between the researcher and the research act, resulting in the researcher being shaped by the data as much as the researcher shapes the data (Strauss & Corbin, 1998). The grounded theory researcher becomes immersed in the data and plays an integral role in every aspect of the research. This immersion in the data clearly raises the issue of maintaining a balance between objectivity on one hand, and sensitivity on the other, while the researcher engages with the process of shaping the data. One approach to achieving the required levels of objectivity involves elucidating how the researcher has remained open to the emergent themes in the data at the same time as using the researcher's background assumptions and disciplinary perspectives to sensitize the researcher to the data.

Although the author has never worked as a nurse, or engaged in clinical practice as an undergraduate nursing student, almost two decades of experience in a clinical care role in the out-of-hospital emergency setting and working closely with nursing staff in a variety of contexts led to background assumptions and disciplinary perspectives, which could taint the research being undertaken. As such, the author shared a level of common professional experience with the study participants, which would allow access to rich data but also potentially influence the data that were being collected. This shared understanding of the health care sector ultimately assisted, rather than hindered, the analysis of the data due to a significantly increased sensitivity to the data. A heightened sensitivity to the data was achieved through acknowledging, and being constantly cognizant of the fact, that the previous understanding was based on values, culture, experience, and training. This recognition of the underlying assumptions, which were brought to the research, was identified as a potential barrier to the objective and inductive data analysis (Strauss & Corbin, 1998) and as such, strategies had to be implemented to minimize the impact of this underlying knowledge. It is the researcher's responsibility, not the responsibility of the participants, to be reflexive about what is brought to the scene, what is seen, and how it is seen.

Strauss and Corbin (1998) propose that it is impossible for researchers to disassociate themselves from who they are, and what they know, or from their life experiences both personally and professionally. Charmaz (2006, p. 10) suggests that as researchers we "*construct* our grounded theories through both our past and our present involvements and interactions with people, perspectives and research practices." In light of this, I considered my perceptions and attitudes, as well as my experiences as a learner in the emergency out-of-hospital care setting. The analyses that were undertaken by myself, in order to develop and maintain objectivity and sensitivity, were documented in a journal entry prior to the commencement of data collection for the study. This analysis was not put aside, as suggested by Backman and Kyngas (1999), to avoid the introduction of bias; rather it was used to assist in the development of sensitivity to the concepts that were emergent in the data. It is appropriate to use this knowledge and prior experience to enhance sensitivity to the meanings in the data, while refraining from forcing explanations on the data (Strauss & Corbin, 1998). In accordance with the principles of grounded theory, it is imperative that researchers are aware of their underlying bias and that they avoid "forcing" their preconceived ideas onto the data, as the theory that emerges must be grounded in the data.

RIGOR

Ezzy (2002) makes reference to rigor in the context that rigor refers to the correct use of the research method, and as such, rigor is an important aspect of the quality control of the research processes and outcomes. Glaser (1978, 1992, 1998), Glaser and Strauss (1967), and Strauss and Corbin (1990, 1998) paid attention to enhancing rigor in grounded theory studies, and this is described in detail by the method's cofounders. Grounded theory is becoming increasingly popular as a research methodology with nursing researchers; however, there are inherent problems with how the methodology is being utilized (Benoliel, 1996; Elliott & Lazenbatt, 2005). Glaser and Strauss's (1967) criteria for the assessment of grounded theory studies included fit, workability, relevance, and modifiability. Charmaz (2005, p. 527) argues that the researcher "providing cogent explanations how the study meets high standards will advance social justice inquiry and reduce unmerited dismissals of it." The use of "interpretive sufficiency" (p. 528) was applied in the research study conducted by the author as Charmaz's approach to grounded theory formed the foundation for the study and, as such, it was deemed appropriate to adopt the criteria developed by Charmaz.

Credibility, originality, resonance, and usefulness are additional criteria proposed by Charmaz (2005) to conduct an evaluation of a grounded theory study. These criteria account for both the empirical study and the development of the theory. The criteria proposed by Strauss and Corbin (1998) for evaluating a grounded theory study included judging the "research process" used for the study and "ensuring empirical grounding" of the study. To enable the reader to evaluate the quality of the "research process," all of the research processes used in a study should be made explicit (Smith & Biley, 1997). The vital elements of a grounded theory study are the use of memo writing, constant comparative analysis, and a continuous cycle of theoretical sampling, data collection, and analysis, identification of a core category, and development of a substantive theory (Strauss & Corbin, 1998). It is these vital elements of the method which, when observed by the researcher, result in a high degree of transparency and rigor in the study.

Using a constant comparative method ensures that the validity of the emergent conceptualizations is constantly checked, effectively acting as an internal audit process, which minimizes the influence of researcher bias making its way into the ultimate theory that is produced. The in-built verification and validation in the constant comparative method alleviate the requirement for additional member verification and validation. Internal validity was enhanced through the coding process, and this is explained in more depth in the subsequent section. In the later stages of a study, the grounded theory researcher should return to the literature and undertake a comparison of the study's findings with the literature. Returning to the literature and undertaking a comparative analysis contextualizes and grounds the study in the literature as well as the data, while also providing validation of the findings. According to Backman and Kyngas (1999), the use of the participants' own words in reporting the findings will also enhance the validity of the developed theory, and this is the approach that was utilized in the research study completed by the author.

The developed substantive theory is relevant to the population from which it was developed as the theory emerges from the participants' experiences and directly attempts to offer insight, enhance understanding, and inform action (Charmaz, 2005, 2006; Strauss & Corbin, 1998). Strauss and Corbin (1998) proposed that rather than determining generalizability, it is the explanatory and predictive ability of the developed theory that is the area to be critiqued. Such an approach clearly suggests that further research is necessary to determine whether the substantive theory developed in this context is applicable in other contexts, and this remains one of the strengths of the method. A researcher could identify an area of interest from a previous grounded theory research study and undertake a further study in the area, in an attempt to further contextualize the findings.

SELECTING PARTICIPANTS

The Process of Recruitment

Although the number of participants required for a grounded theory study is small when compared to quantitative sample sizes, it is still necessary to ensure that an adequate pool of potential participants is available. In the grounded theory study undertaken by the author, all second-year nursing students enrolled in an undergraduate nursing program were identified as potential participants and invited to participate. Potential participants were identified across four separate, geographically dispersed sites, with a relatively consistent response rate of 24% across all four sites. This response rate ($n = 39$) was sufficient to provide adequate participants to achieve saturation of the data after two focus groups' and 19 semi-structured interviews. Participants were asked to consent to participation in either a focus group discussion, semi-structured interview, or both. Two focus groups ($n = 5$ each) were facilitated at two separate sites, with participants ($n = 19$) participating in an individual, semi-structured interview.

The Process of Sampling

Grounded theory uses nonprobability sampling, in which the sample numbers, or data sources, are unknown at the commencement of the study (Glaser & Strauss, 1967; Strauss & Corbin, 1990, 1998). In accordance with the prescription initiated in the original version of grounded theory proposed by Glaser and Strauss (1967) and subsequently adopted by Strauss and Corbin (1990, 1998), the sampling becomes theoretical, rather than purposive, in that the sampling is determined by the emerging theory. Purposive sampling was initially used to access undergraduate nursing students who had a diversity of educational, social, and professional backgrounds, while also having had some exposure to the off-campus clinical setting. The educational, social, and professional backgrounds of the participants were determined from a demographic questionnaire, which the respondents were asked to complete prior to being selected for a focus group or individual semi-structured interview. Purposive sampling allowed for the selection of participants for the initial focus group discussions based on the information provided in the demographic survey response (Tashakkori & Teddlie, 1998). As the analysis of the data from this initial sample of participants in the focus groups would direct future data collection, a high degree of diversity in the participants was achieved to enhance the potential for a magnanimous exploration of the issues raised in the focus group discussions.

Qualitative researchers frequently use purposive sampling as a method for extending knowledge through deliberately seeking sample participants who are known to be rich sources of data (Roberts, 1997; Tashakkori & Teddlie, 1998). Theoretical sampling is a form of purposive sampling, and it is the sampling method used in grounded theory after the initial sample is selected and the initial data collection and analysis have been undertaken.

Coyne (1997) proposed a degree of ambiguity surrounding the distinction between purposive and theoretical sampling in the literature, with Charmaz (2006) arguing that this apparent ambiguity stems from the preconceptions that researchers hold in relation to sampling. Coyne (1997) suggests that theoretical sampling is a "variation" within purposive sampling, a variation that is a complex, ongoing process, which interacts with data collection and simultaneous analysis to identify further needs, which are then met by the sampling strategy. Theoretical sampling is therefore determined by the analysis of the data, rather than being predetermined by the researcher. However, the purpose of theoretical sampling is variable and dependent on whether the initiator of the further data collection is open, axial, or selective coding (Strauss & Corbin, 1998).

Theoretical sampling seeks particular characteristics that have been identified through an analysis of the previously collected data as being potentially important for further exploration. This approach to sampling can therefore result in a sampling strategy that is not always based on all of the demographic characteristics of the individual participant. It is, however, necessary to be mindful of the broader demographics of the participant and to ensure that these are not discounted in the subsequent analysis and comparison of data with data. This approach also allows the researcher to control for potential bias, which may be present in the sampling method. Glaser (1992) proposed that the use of the constant comparative method, the requirement for saturation of the data, and also the linking of the subcategories to the core category, all reduce the potential bias associated with the sampling method, and these approaches should be utilized in all grounded theory studies to minimize bias. As a consequence of the data being so closely linked to the participants in the study and their experiences of the phenomena being studied, the findings of a grounded theory study are not generalizable to the wider population from which the participants were drawn.

In one example of theoretical sampling, participants were selected based on age demographics in an effort to develop an understanding of the experiences of a particular age demographic. Rather than sampling for prior nursing experience, education, or the number of clinical placements undertaken, the participants were theoretically sampled on age for a particular semi-structured interview in response to the categories that were emergent in the data from the focus group discussions and the preceding semi-structured interviews. Age was deemed to be a critical demographic at the particular point in the data analysis as it became apparent that the experiences of a particular age group were absent from the data.

Although it may appear essential to the novice researcher, there was no intention on the part of the researcher to imitate the broader demographic of either the nursing workforce or the undergraduate nursing student body per se. Instead, a broad range of participant demographics was sought, with this strategy ultimately enriching the data and the substantive grounded theory, which was emergent from the data. This approach is supported by Morse (2001) who argues that a well-rounded and balanced explanation of the phenomenon can only be produced when there is sufficient variation in the sample population.

DATA COLLECTION

Grounded theorists shape and reshape their data collection and, subsequently, refine their collected data (Charmaz, 2006). Methods, as proposed by Charmaz, "are merely tools" (p. 15), with some of these tools being sharper than others in a given context. Although a method may provide the researcher with a "tool" to enhance what is being seen, Charmaz also points out that the methods alone do not generate good research and astute findings, let alone provide some magical insight into the data that are collected. Through using grounded theory methods, the researcher is able to adopt a flexible approach to data collection rather than being constrained by a rigid prescription of methods. This inherent strength of the grounded theory method allows the emergent data to guide the future data collection strategies in accordance with the direction that the data are taking. Such flexibility in the use of the method has resulted in grounded theory researchers collecting data through the use of a wide range of data collection methods including, but not limited to, focus groups, semi-structured interviews, documents, and case studies. The author utilized a demographic survey, focus group discussions, and semi-structured interviews, with theoretical sampling guiding the data collection as previously indicated.

Despite Charmaz (2006) suggesting that methods are mere tools in the researcher's toolkit, methods do have consequences and these consequences do need to be considered by the researcher. When choosing methods for a study, it is essential that the appropriateness of the method is considered in respect of answering the research question that is posed. Effective methods answer the question with ingenuity and incisiveness. *How* the data are collected will also have an impact on *which* phenomena the researcher will *see; how, when,* and *where* they will be viewed; and *what* sense the researcher will make of them (Charmaz, 2006).

Cresswell (1994) discusses a variety of data collection methods that are available, including ethnographic methods. Ethnographic methods can be utilized in grounded theory research, and although the ethnographic data collection methods such as participant observation would have been possible in an on-campus clinical practice setting, due to the diversity of the off-campus clinical setting and the geographical dispersion of the participants, this method was not an option in the study undertaken by the author. This does not however rule out this approach to data collection in studies in which the tyranny of distance and dispersion of the participants is not a constraining factor. The underlying assumption of symbolic interaction allowed for a far greater integration of the participants' perceptions of the reality of their social world in the development of theory than any objective reality, which could result from participant observation. Interviews enabled the researcher to access in-depth descriptions of the continuous experiences of the participants, and this contrasted with the snapshots of data, which would have been obtained through participant observation (Morse, 2001).

DATA ANALYSIS

The grounded theorist is an instrument of the research process, and as such, data analysis is reliant on the researcher's analytical skills and creativity so that meaning and the interconnections in the data can be interpreted to develop theory (Strauss & Corbin, 1998). In analyzing the data collected in the study conducted by the author, the general procedure described by Strauss and Corbin (1998) was utilized; however, the procedural steps were not rigidly adhered to in the data analysis. Charmaz's (2006) explication of the procedures of data analysis provided valuable guidance in the data analysis. Strauss and Corbin (1998) propose the use of a conditional/consequential matrix; this concept was used in the data analysis. In addition, the Conditional Relationship Guide and Reflective Coding Matrix proposed by Scott (2004) provided a useful analytical tool, which was used to advance the conditional/consequential matrix proposed by Strauss and Corbin (1998).

Analysis of the Focus Group Discussion Data—A Special Case

Focus group data are unique in that they result in data based on the interactions of the group's participants, the dynamics and nonverbal behaviors observed. The focus group discussions were audio-recorded and transcribed verbatim resulting in transcripts that were available for analysis of individual meanings. The focus group data did, however, present some variations to the analysis as a consequence of the requirement to analyze the observational notes from the focus group discussions in conjunction with the audio-recorded data that had been transcribed. Although the group interaction that occurs during the discussion determined that the "group" should be the primary focus of the analysis, St. John (2004) argues that the data analysis should follow the approach of the underpinning methodology used in the study. Cognizance of individual and group aspects was achieved through the framework suggested by Carey and Smith (1994) and St. John (2004).

Focus group data are analyzed at the group level with the lens focused on interactional and sequential analysis. Consideration is given to censoring, conformity, and "group think." It is essential that the researcher is cognizant of these factors, as they can bias the data that is being collected as a consequence of the participants effectively censoring the discussion that is being generated, or the participants conform to the apparent group norm and provide only information that they believe is relevant or what the researcher wants to hear. At the individual participant level in the focus group, the data are analyzed without regard to the group context, and this can be achieved through analyzing each participant in the group as an individual without focusing on the group interactions. To provide a comparison, individual responses are compared against the group data as well as being contextually analyzed. To assist with this comparative process, the individual participant data from the focus group discussions were separated into a single document for each participant. This assisted in analyzing the data from an individual perspective, with the resultant findings subsequently compared against the group data.

Preliminary Procedures of Data Analysis

Prior to the commencement of intensive data analysis, focus group discussions and semi-structured interviews were transcribed verbatim by the researcher within 48 hours of the data being collected to allow the researcher to remain immersed in the data. Whereas this may make it appear as though the data analysis commences after the completion of the data collection phase, in reality and in accordance with the grounded theory method, data collection and analysis were actually simultaneous processes, which continued until saturation of the data was achieved. Each participant in the semi-structured interviews was assigned an alphabetical code, while the focus group discussion participants were assigned a random, alpha numeric code, which did not represent either the sequence in which the interviews occurred or the individual's position in the focus group discussion. All alphabetic characters between A and Z, with the exception of "I" were selected for use in the coding scheme. The rationale for excluding "I" was based on the potential for confusion in the reader, as "I" could be confused with a first person reference to the researcher in one instance, and to a participant labeled "I" in another.

To ensure the accuracy of the transcriptions, which were generated by the researcher, the audio was replayed while rereading the transcription. This approach holds two benefits for the grounded theory researcher: First, it allows for identification of any transcription errors, and second, it allows the researcher to become more fully immersed in the data.

Memo Writing—An Intermediate Step

Memo writing, Charmaz (2006) proposes, is the pivotal intermediate step between the data collection phase and the drafting of the substantive theory. Memo writing in grounded theory is a crucial method, as it prompts the researcher to analyze the data and codes early in the research process (Charmaz, 2006; Glaser, 1978; Strauss & Corbin, 1990, 1998). According to Strauss and Corbin (1998, p. 217), memos contain "products of analysis or directions for the analyst." Writing memos should begin at the commencement of the study and continue until after the completion of the write-up of the study's findings. The author used memos to analyze the internal bias present in the researcher as a consequence of having spent a number of years working in the health sector and having observed the behaviors that were emergent in the data. The use of memos in this sense allowed the researcher to articulate this internal bias and to subsequently use this as a tool in identifying and relating to the experiences of the participants. Memos are essentially kept as a series of notes to one's self and provide an efficient means of documenting thoughts related to the codes, the emergent categories, and the interaction of the categories as the study progresses. These notes should be recorded when they occur and can take the form of handwritten or typed notes, dependent on when the ideas surface. Memos have a further significant use in that they allow the researcher to identify leads to follow through the process of theoretical sampling (Charmaz, 2006; Glaser, 1978; Glaser & Strauss, 1967; Strauss & Corbin, 1990, 1998). They are also a useful tool for research students to demonstrate their understanding and analysis of concepts to their research supervisor.

Strauss and Corbin (1998) expanded the original notion of grounded theory memoing through identifying a variety of memo types, which the researcher can use. Code notes, theoretical notes, operational notes, and logical and interactive diagrams were all proposed in Strauss and Corbin's expansion, with an expectation that these memos would be at the conceptual level, corresponding to the coding stage to which they relate. Charmaz (2006) suggests that memos may be free and flowing, with the researcher encouraged to write freely in relation to the analysis that is being undertaken. The author adopted the approach recommended by Charmaz, as the approach described by Strauss and Corbin (1998) was too procedural and somewhat restrictive to the author's flow when conducting the data analysis.

Clustering

To assist with writing memos, a process of clustering is recommended by Charmaz (2006). Clustering provides a nonlinear, visual, and flexible technique, which allows the researcher to identify how the phenomenon "fits" together. This approach also allows the researcher to visually identify how the categories are interrelated, and this is a particularly powerful tool in the later stages of theory development as the researcher grapples with formulating the core category. Clustering shares similarities with conceptual, or situational, mapping in grounded theory (Clarke, 2003, 2005). Diagramming is simply an extension of the clustering approach and again is a useful tool for the "visual" researcher. One advantage of diagrams is that they provide a visual representation of the categories and their relationships.

Constant Comparative Analysis

Strauss and Corbin (1998) identify comparative analysis as an essential feature of the grounded theory methodology. Throughout the analytic process, the constant comparative method is used to compare incident with incident and to identify the similarities and differences to facilitate the development of concepts (Ezzy, 2002; Strauss & Corbin, 1998). Constant comparative analysis assists in grouping the identified concepts under higher order categories (Strauss & Corbin, 1998).

In grounded theory studies, data earn their way into the developing theory when the data analysis process reveals repeated patterns in the data (Chiovitti & Piran, 2003). This approach allows for a comparison of data against itself, against other data, and also against conceptualizations (Duchscher & Morgan, 2004). Abduction is one of the processes utilized in constant comparative analysis, as abduction allows for the sudden understanding of the fit between a particular event and its context (Ezzy, 2002). It is important to realize that while the inductive strategies predominate, deductive processes are also at play as the grounded theory approach simultaneously validates theory through the constant comparative method (Strauss & Corbin, 1998).

The Process of Coding—Open, Axial, and Selective Coding

Open coding is the process through which labels are assigned to the data for the purpose of identifying categories, their properties, and dimensions. Initial coding remains close to the data (Charmaz, 2006) and, where possible, in vivo codes are used. Open coding occurred while the transcripts were reread while listening to the audio recording during the process of transcript checking. Through fracturing the data into sections for closer scrutiny and subsequently the assignment of a label, open coding could be considered the first "real" stage in data analysis in a grounded theory study. Labeling of data is synonymous with the creation of a code, with the label consisting of a participant's actual words (in vivo code), for example, *snide comments, covert approach,* or other words that reflect the understanding of the data. In the initial coding, the labels are generally descriptive.

Throughout the process of open coding, cognizance is placed on the relationship between grounded theory and symbolic interactionism. Meaning given to a particular situation or event, by the nursing student participants, needed to be reflected in the code labels that were assigned to the data. *Segregation* in the off-campus clinical setting was reported by participants in two different ways with the common theme being the *attitude of the staff* toward nursing students. When the segregation was obvious, through verbal or nonverbal communication, indicating that a staff member did not want a nursing student, the nursing students reported active avoidance of that particular staff member, thus using deliberate self-segregation or isolation as a protective strategy. This contrasted with the other form of segregation in which staff were reported to delegate menial tasks to the nursing students or to send a nursing student on a break. Upon returning from completing the menial task or imposed break, the nursing student would find that a task that was clinically relevant to their achievement of the learning outcomes for a placement had been completed in his or her absence. Through the use of theoretical sampling and probing questions in subsequent interviews, it was possible to determine the meaning that the nursing students attributed to these behaviors and to assign code labels during open coding.

Keeping the research question in mind is important during the open coding process, while making as many interpretations of the data as possible (Charmaz, 2005, 2006; Glaser, 1978; Strauss, 1987; Strauss & Corbin, 1990, 1998). Initially this is done by asking, *What does this mean?* or *What is going on here?* At times, this meant that a section of text was assigned more than one code in the open coding process; as an example, when a participant reported avoiding one particular staff member, the text was labeled *avoidance* and *individual attitude* to encompass the fact that the participant avoided this staff member based predominantly on the staff member's attitude toward students. Questioning the data can occur at both the macro- and micro-level in open coding; at times questions are asked of a participant's entire response to questioning in the interview, while at other times the focus may be restricted to a couple of words or a phrase. Impressions and questions about the codes can be documented in the memos, and this assists in the subsequent coding processes.

Line-by-line analysis of the transcripts allows for careful comparison of new data with data that have already been coded (Glaser, 1978). Strauss and Corbin (1998) suggest assigning code labels to incidents, events, actions, or objects in the data that were understood as indicators of a particular phenomenon. These concepts are then analyzed for common themes, grouped together according to these themes, and subsequently assigned to a higher order label (Corbin & Strauss, 1990). Grouping concepts together under a higher order label marks the commencement of category development (Strauss & Corbin, 1998). Participants reported *tailing the RN, shown our place,* and *dressed,* each of these codes becoming part of a higher order category labeled *segregation*. This category was later elevated even further to a category labeled *interpersonal relations*.

Comparison of the code labels allows for the identification of properties and their dimensions. Properties are "attributes of a category" and dimensions "represent the location of a property along a continuum" (Strauss & Corbin, 1998, p. 117).

An Addition to the Open Coding Arsenal

Charmaz (2006) introduces the concept of focused coding, proposing that this is the second major phase in the coding process, falling between the traditional open coding and axial coding regimes prescribed by Glaser and Strauss (1967) and Strauss and Corbin (1990, 1998). Focused codes are more directed, selective, and conceptual than the initial word-by-word, and line-by-line coding proposed by Glaser (1978). Focused coding is used to capture, synthesize, and understand the main themes in a participant's statement. The code *avoiding disclosure* was selected to capture, synthesize, and understand the theme in the following excerpt from a participant's interview.

> I actually make out that I have no nursing experience because I find sometimes, like you know, if you say to them I am like an AIN or an EN it's sort of like, "Oh well you know what you are doing, you don't need us [RNs]" sort of thing, so I tend to play a little bit dumb sometimes.

The assigned codes from focused coding, like the traditional approach to open coding, remain active and close to the data allowing movement across interviews to effect comparison of the experiences, actions, and interpretations of the participants.

Coding, in accordance with the framework of grounded theory, is an emergent process with the development of the code *avoiding disclosure* subsequently illuminating other codes. This illumination allowed the author to "see" the interactions between the participants who identified as having nursing experience and the staff, in a different light. The experiences of the participants who had "disclosed," were subsequently compared with the experiences of the participants who had not "disclosed."

Axial Coding—Data Reassembly

Axial coding, the process of "reassembling data that were fractured [and labelled] during open coding" (Strauss & Corbin, 1998, p. 124) was performed alternatively with open coding (Glaser, 1978; Strauss & Corbin, 1990, 1998) and not in isolation as a separate approach to coding following the completion of axial coding. Axial coding commenced following the identification of a number of potential categories, which emerged from the open coding of the first focus group discussion data. Identification of potential categories through the open coding process is imperative to the commencement of the axial coding process, because the development of categories and relational statements revolves "around the axis of a category" (Strauss & Corbin, 1998, p. 125). In the study conducted by the author, Strauss and Corbin's approach to axial coding was supplemented by the use of Scott's (2004) Conditional Relationship Guide, which was used to assist in the development of subcategories that answered Strauss and Corbin's (1998, p. 125) "when, where, why, who, how and with what consequences" questions about a category. An example of axial coding in action is presented below with reference to *segregation*.

A participant indicated that participants could be segregated in various ways, with various consequences:

> I think they just used us as we were extra workers not students, they weren't helpful in showing us anything, in teaching us, helping us with anything, um, and yea if you asked the RN anything such as a question they would fob you off as if they didn't have time for you so yea, I didn't feel that we learnt a lot out of it at all.

This excerpt provides evidence of "how" the nursing students perceived they were segregated in the off-campus clinical setting and also provides evidence of the consequences of the segregation on the nursing students in the study. At the other end of the continuum were the experiences related by a different participant, in a different clinical setting:

> Yes, it was good, the hospital was good, like you could go to the nurse and they'd just answer your questions and help, all very helpful and if something was going on, they'd come and find you and show us. Yeah, no it was really good . . ..

Although both participants reported very different experiences in relation to *segregation*, the experiences of both participants are particularly insightful for the researcher in respect of answering the "how" and "with what consequences" questions.

An important point in relation to using axial coding stems from the version of grounded theory that the researcher is using, as there is a major point of departure between Glaser, and Strauss and Corbin in their understanding of axial coding and the exact nature of this coding process. Glaser (1978) calls this process "theoretical coding," and like Strauss and Corbin (1990, 1998), recommends that this activity be undertaken alternatively with open coding. Glaser (1992) argues that theoretical codes preclude the need for axial coding because the theoretical codes "weave the fractured story back together" (Glaser, 1978, p. 72). As such, Glaser does not agree with the coding paradigm proposed by Strauss and Corbin (1990, 1998). Strauss and Corbin's (1990, 1998) coding paradigm is essentially a guiding framework, which allows processes, as well as structures, to be considered in relation to the context of the social phenomenon being studied. Identifying structures and processes in turn allows for an exploration of why certain events happen and how they happen (Strauss & Corbin, 1998).

Strauss and Corbin (1998) argue against using their proposed axial coding matrix as a prescription for the conditions and consequences to be identified. The Conditional Relationship Guide developed by Scott (2004) was utilized as an aid in locating the scope of the study; although this approach is supported by Strauss and Corbin, Glaser is vehemently opposed to such an approach, arguing that using a coding paradigm amounts to preconception. Glaser (1992) is of the opinion that any preconceptions in relation to the data, such as locating the scope of the study within the existing research, is paramount to "forcing" the data, as opposed to allowing the themes to emerge from the data. For this reason, the researcher needs to remain cognizant of the version of grounded theory that he or she is using and remain true to the method.

Axial coding, according to Charmaz (2006), provides a framework for the researcher to apply with a recognition that the framework may extend, or limit, the researcher's vision. The axial coding framework used by the author illuminated the clarity of the links between the categories and their subcategories. Using *segregation* as an example, *segregation: divided and dividing work practices between students and allied nursing staff* was a contextual condition impacting on the nursing students' efforts to determine their position within the hierarchy, both within the clinical setting in which they were placed and in the broader profession. At the same time, *role ambiguity* influenced the way in which nursing students responded to *segregation: divided and dividing work practices between students and allied nursing staff.* Strauss and Corbin's approach to axial coding also allowed for an exploration of particular actions or strategies that were used by the participants when they experienced *segregation,* such as *focusing on getting through.*

Role ambiguity was elaborated on by a participant who suggested strategies that could be employed to minimize conflict:

> . . . where we're on one level thinking that we need to do our tasks, they're on another level thinking we're extra AINs to work with them . . . that probably adds to the conflict. So if there was a more even keel, and say well this is what the student is here for, and say to us students this is what you're here to do, but you've got to do this as well . . .

Axial coding located the properties and dimensions on a continuum, and through this process it became apparent that the participants were using strategies to focus on getting through placement.

> They [AINs] don't have the level of education that you know if you see a wound it may need further investigation and dressing . . . you have to, just sort of try to accept that and try not to be confrontational to them and um yea I sort of put that into practice the best I could . . .

Another participant adopted a different strategy to assist in getting through placements when staff demonstrated a negative attitude toward nursing students:

> I don't let that [negative attitude] bother me so I just got on, I always had a smile on my face and thought oh well if they're going to be like that, that's them but I am not going to do the same thing because I wanted to enjoy my time. So if they wanted to be like that, well I hope they get something out of it because I am not going to let it come into it.

As understanding of the relationships between the categories developed, these were portrayed in diagrams, a strategy supported by Strauss (1987) and Strauss and Corbin (1990, 1998). When, how, and why nursing students were segregated in the off-campus clinical setting are some of the other aspects that were coded during the data analysis.

Selective Coding—The Final Stage of Coding

Strauss and Corbin identify selective coding as the "process of integrating and refining the theory." This stage of the coding process was the most challenging and involved the identification of the "core" category, or major theme of the research from which the theory emerged (Strauss & Corbin, 1998). The core category that emerges is central, with all other categories subsequently becoming subcategories, which frequently appear in the data. Selective coding identified *anxiety* as the core category in the study completed by the author, with *tradition bearing, staff performance, student performance, expectations,* and *fit* constituting the subcategories that were directly related to, and integral to, the core category. The core category appeared in all of the interviews to some extent, and this allowed for a logical and consistent explanation of what was occurring in the off-campus clinical setting through relating the subcategories to the core category. Using this constant comparative analysis and going back and forward between open (focused), axial, and selective coding allowed the basic theoretical theme to emerge from the data without forcing the themes.

Once the basic theoretical scheme was identified, the theory was continually refined through further theoretical sampling and data analysis until data saturation occurred (Strauss & Corbin, 1998). Two additional semi-structured interviews were conducted following determination of saturation to ensure that the data were in fact saturated and that no new themes were emergent in the data. Selective coding also acts as a validity check, allowing the researcher to account for variations both within, and between, the identified categories.

EVALUATING THE GROUNDED THEORY

Grounded theory research is a journey that the researcher takes with the participants, as the researcher is immersed in the data, with Charmaz (2006) arguing that the end point of the research makes sense to the researcher due to the extent of his or her immersion in the data and the process; however, for the reader, the lines between process and product can become blurred. Other scholars are liable to judge the grounded theory process as an integral part of the final product, and as such, Charmaz (2006) proposes that the researcher needs to consider his or her audience. Whether the audience is nurses, nurse educators, or academic colleagues, ultimately it will be the audience that judges the usefulness of the methods employed through the quality of the final product. In an effort to ensure that the criteria for grounded theory have been met, a review of the credibility, originality, resonance, and usefulness of the study should be considered.

Credibility

Credibility in the study completed by the author was demonstrated by the fact that the researcher achieved intimate familiarity with the research topic through immersion in the data. Despite the fact that the source of the data was essentially a single institution's school of nursing, the data collection occurred across a number of geographically dispersed locations and included participants with diverse education and professional backgrounds from previous employment within and outside the health sector. This facilitated credibility, as the participants with experience in other professions and employment provided an opportunity to make systematic comparisons between their experiences and the experiences of the participants with previous nursing experience. These comparisons ultimately formed an important component of data analysis in the study.

Making links between the data and the final theory that is developed and articulating this link in the write-up or dissemination of the findings significantly increases the credibility of the research. Integrating the development of the categories provides an insight into the data, giving the reader an opportunity to come to his or her own conclusions in relation to the data and the emergent categories. This strategy allows the reader the opportunity to develop an independent assessment of the study.

Originality

The categories must be original and offer new insights into the topic; in the case of the author's study, the categories provided an original and insightful understanding of how nursing students experience the off-campus clinical setting from the perspective of the participants in this study. Prior to the completion of this study, there was a dearth of knowledge in relation to the experiences of nursing students in the off-campus clinical setting, despite a vast wealth of literature on the negative workplace behaviors of qualified nurses. The analysis of the data provided a conceptual rendering of the nursing students' experiences and explained the realities associated with the development of a cultural identity and being a nursing student in a regional Australian setting. This study was original in a second context in that it, for the first time, investigated the experiences of nursing students in a regional Australian setting, whereas other studies tended to be centered on metropolitan centers. Originality was further enhanced, as there were limited studies investigating the development of a professional identity in nursing students.

Grounded theory studies have both social and theoretical implications. The author's study highlighted, for the first time, the societal and professional implications of negative workplace relations directed toward nursing students and the cost to the nursing students in developing their professional identity. The theoretical implications arise from the fact that for the first time there is a substantive theory of the effects of negative workplace relations on nursing students in the off-campus clinical setting. This provides an original explanation of some of the experiences of the nursing students. Through achieving a greater awareness of workplace conflict, and the impact that this has on the development of a professional identity in nursing students, it is possible to address the issues that may be contributing to both nursing student attrition rates and the nursing workforce turnover rates.

Resonance

Resonance was demonstrated in the author's study through the categories of *tradition bearing, staff expectations,* and *student performance,* along with the concepts associated with these categories portraying the fullness of the experience of negative workplace behaviors by nursing students in the off-campus clinical setting. Experiences that have traditionally been taken for granted have been exposed through the grounded theory analysis of the nursing students' experiences of these processes. Further enhancement of the resonance of the study was achieved through the drawing of links between the larger collectivities such as registered nurses, enrolled nurses, and auxiliary nursing staff associated with the nursing profession, highlighting that although the profession is on the one hand the largest collective of health professionals in the medical and allied health arena, on the other hand it is a profession that is divided.

The substantive theory that was developed provides the reader with a deeper understanding of the circumstances that the nursing students are faced with in the management of their experiences of negative workplace behaviors while in the off-campus clinical setting. This insight is achieved through the theory explicating the concepts that impact on this development.

Usefulness

The substantive grounded theory in the author's study offers interpretations of the nursing students' experiences of off-campus clinical placement, which can be used by the nursing profession and academia in an effort to improve the experiences of nursing students. The interpretation allows for the integration of theory into practice, both within the nursing profession and the educational institutions providing entry-level nurse education. Analytic categories that were developed in the study proposed generic processes were operating across all of the facilities in which the participants were placed. It became apparent that there were individual facilities that set expectations for "fitting in" with the facility and within the professional hierarchy as a whole. A number of tacit implications inherent in the generic processes were identified, and these were examined in the analysis of the data and subsequently reported in the findings and the discussion.

The study contributes insight into the issues associated with the seemingly entrenched traditions of the nursing profession, recommending that the hierarchical culture of the profession must change if the profession is to fully embrace the new generation of nurses in their development of a professional identity.

SUMMARY

Grounded theory provides the researcher with a range of tools, which can be used to provide a useful social and theoretical insight into the phenomena being considered by the researcher. Given that there are essentially three "schools" of grounded theory, the researcher should consider the advantages and disadvantages of each "school" of thought and determine which of the various "schools" is optimally aligned to the research question that the researcher seeks to address as well as to the researcher's own epistemological and ontological perspectives. This approach to determining the best fit between method, research question, and researcher results in a valid and reliable grounded theory that can be defended. Like other qualitative research methods, the findings from a grounded theory study are not generalizable to the broader population in the study area. However, the substantive theory that emerges is well grounded in the data and generates a useful social and theoretical insight into the phenomenon under investigation. Grounded theory methods are directly transferable to other research methodologies, and it is not unusual for researchers using other methodologies to dip into grounded theory methods to use the tools that grounded theory provides to the researcher.

REFERENCES

Annells, M. (1996). Grounded theory method: Philosophical perspectives, paradigm of inquiry and postmodernism. *Qualitative Health Research, 6*(3), 379–393.

Backman, K., & Kyngas, H. A. (1999). Challenges of the grounded theory approach to a novice researcher. *Nursing & Health Sciences, 1*(3), 147–153.

Baker, C., Norton, S., Young, P., & Ward, S. (1998). An exploration of methodological pluralism in nursing research. *Research in Nursing and Health, 21*(6), 545–555.

Benoliel, J. Q. (1996). Grounded theory and nursing knowledge. *Qualitative Health Research, 3*(6), 406–428.

Bowen, I., & Curtis, J. (2004, July). Horizontal violence: Students' clinical experience. *RCNA National Conference, 38th Patricia Chomley Oration, Nursing Leadership Policy and Politics*, July 14–16, Alice Springs.

Bryant, A. (2002). Regrounding grounded theory. *The Journal of Information Technology Theory and Application, 4*(1), 25–42.

Bryant, A. (2003). A constructive/ist response to Glaser. *Forum Qualitative Sozialforschung/Forum: Qualitative Social Research,* viewed November 22, 2005, http://www.qualitative-research.net/index.php/fqs/article/view/757/1642

Carey, M., & Smith, M. (1994). Capturing the group effect in focus groups: A special concern in analysis. *Qualitative Health Research, 4*(1), 123–127.

Charmaz, K., (1990). Discovering chronic illness: Using grounded theory. *Social Science and Medicine, 30*(11), 1161–1172.

Charmaz, K. (2000a). Grounded theory: Objectivist and constructivist methods. In N. K. Denzin & Y. S. Lincoln (Eds.), *Handbook of qualitative research* (2nd ed.). Thousand Oaks, CA: Sage.

Charmaz, K. (2000b). Looking backward, moving forward: Expanding sociological horizons in the twenty-first century. *Sociological Perspectives, 43*(4), 527–549.

Charmaz, K. (2003). Grounded theory. In J. A. Smith (Ed.), *Qualitative psychology: A practical guide to research methods.* London, UK: Sage.

Charmaz, K. (2005). Advancing social justice research. In N. K. Denzin & Y. S. Lincoln (Eds.), *Handbook of qualitative research* (3rd ed.). Thousand Oaks, CA: Sage.

Charmaz, K. (2006). *Constructing grounded theory: A practical approach through qualitative analysis.* Thousand Oaks, CA: Sage.

Charmaz, K., & Mitchell, R. G. (2001). Grounded theory in ethnography. In P. Atkinson, A. Coffey, S. Delamont, J. Lofland, & L. H. Lofland (Eds.), *Handbook of Ethnography,* London, UK: Sage.

Chiovitti, R., & Piran, N. (2003). Rigour and grounded theory research. *Journal of Advanced Nursing, 44*(4), 427–435.

Clarke, A. E. (2003). Situational analyses: Grounded theory mapping after the postmodern turn. *Symbolic Interaction, 26*(4), 553–576.

Clarke, A. E. (2005). *Situational analysis: Grounded theory after the postmodern turn.* Thousand Oaks, CA: Sage.

Corbin, J., & Strauss, A. L. (1990). Grounded theory research: Procedures, canons and evaluative criteria. *Qualitative Sociology, 13*(1), 13–21.

Cox, H. (1987). Verbal abuse in nursing: Report of a study. *Nursing Management, 18*(11), 47–50.

Coyne, I. T. (1997). Sampling in qualitative research. Purposeful and theoretical sampling: Merging or clear boundaries? *Journal of Advanced Nursing, 26*(3), 623–630.

Cresswell, J. W. (1994). *Research design: Qualitative and quantitative approaches.* London, UK: Sage.

Davey, L. (2003). Nurses eating nurses: The caring profession which fails to nurture its own! *Contemporary Nurse, 13*(2–3), 192–197.

Delez, J. (2003). *Student experiences of horizontal violence in the clinical setting: Nurses eating their young.* (MS Thesis). Florida Atlantic University, Florida.

Dey, I. (1999). *Grounding grounded theory: Guidelines for qualitative inquiry.* San Diego, CA: Academic Press.

Duchscher, J. E. B., & Morgan, D. (2004). Grounded theory: Reflections on the emergence vs. forcing debate. *Journal of Advanced Nursing, 48*(6), 605–612.

Duffy, E. (1995). Horizontal violence: A conundrum for nursing. *Collegian, 2*(2), 5–17.

Elliot, N., & Lazenbatt, A. (2005). How to recognise a 'quality' grounded theory research study. *Australian Journal of Advanced Nursing, 31*(3), 623–630.

Ezzy, D. (2002). *Qualitative analysis: Practice and innovation.* Sydney, Australia: Allen & Unwin.

Farrell, G. A. (1997). Aggression in clinical settings: Nurses' views. *Journal of Advanced Nursing, 25*(3), 501–508.

Farrell, G. A. (1999). Aggression in clinical settings: Nurses' views: A follow-up study. *Journal of Advanced Nursing, 29*(3), 532–541.

Farrell, G. A. (2001). From tall poppies to squashed weeds: Why don't nurses pull together more? *Journal of Advanced Nursing, 35*(1), 26–33.

Glaser, B. G. (1978). *Theoretical sensitivity.* Mill Valley, CA: Sociology Press.

Glaser, B. G. (1992). *Basics of grounded theory analysis.* Mill Valley, CA: Sociology Press.

Glaser, B. G. (1998). *Doing grounded theory: Issues and discussions.* Mill Valley, CA: Sociology Press.

Glaser, B. G. (2002). Constructivist grounded theory? *Forum Qualitative Sozialforschung/ Forum: Qualitative Social Research.* Retrieved November 22, 2005, http://www .qualitative-research.net/fqs-texte/3-02/3-02glaser-e.pdf

Glaser, B. G., & Strauss, A. L. (1965). *Awareness of dying.* Chicago, IL: Aldine.

Glaser, B. G., & Strauss, A. L. (1967). *The discovery of grounded theory: Strategies for qualitative research.* Chicago, IL: Aldine.

Glaser, B. G., & Strauss, A. L. (1968). *Time for dying.* Chicago, IL: Aldine.

Hadkin, R., & O'Driscoll, M. (2000). *The bullying culture.* Oxford, UK: Heinemann.

Heath, H., & Cowley, S. (2003). Developing a grounded theory approach: A comparison of Glaser and Strauss. *International Journal of Nursing Studies, 41*(2), 141–150.

Hutchinson, M., Vickers, M. H., Jackson, D., & Wilkes, L. (2006). They stand you in a corner; you are not to speak: Nurses tell of abusive indoctrination in work teams dominated by bullies. *Contemporary Nurse, 21*(2), 228–238.

Jackson, D., Clare, J., & Mannix, J. (2002). Who would want to be a nurse?— Violence in the workplace a factor in recruitment and retention. *Journal of Nursing Management, 10*(1), 13–20.

Madsen, W. (2000). Learning to be a nurse: The culture of training in a regional Queensland hospital 1930–1950. *Transformations, 1*, 1–9.

McCallin, A. (2003). Designing a grounded theory study: Some practicalities. *Nursing in Critical Care, 8*(5), 203–208.

McKenna, B. G., Smith, N. A., Poole, S. J., & Coverdale, J. H. (2002). Horizontal violence: Experiences of registered nurses in their first year of practice. *Journal of Advanced Nursing, 42*(1), 90–96.

Milliken, P. J., & Schreiber, R. S. (2001). Can you "do" grounded theory without Symbolic Interactionism. In R. S. Schreiber & P. N. Stern (Eds.), *Using grounded theory in nursing.* New York, NY: Springer.

Morse, J. M. (2001). Situating grounded theory within qualitative inquiry. In R. S. Schreiber & P. N. Stern (eds), *Using grounded theory in nursing.* New York, NY: Springer.

Nevidjon, B., & Erikson, J. I. (2001). The nursing shortage: Solutions for the short term and the long term. *Online Journal of Issues in Nursing, 6*(1).

Randle, J. (2003). Bullying in the nursing profession. *Journal of Advanced Nursing, 31,* 452–460.

Robbins, S. P., Waters-Marsh, T., Cacioppe, R., & Millett, B. (1998). *Organisational behaviour: Concepts, controversies and applications.* Sydney, Australia: Prentice Hall.

Roberts, P. (1997). Planning and running a focus group. *Nurse Researcher, 4*(4), 78–82.

Robrecht, L. C. (1995). Grounded theory: Evolving methods. *Qualitative Health Research, 5*(2), 169–177.

Scott, K. W. (2004). Relating categories in grounded theory analysis: Using a conditional relationship guide and reflective coding matrix. *The Qualitative Report, 9*(1), 113–126.

Seale, C. (1999). *The quality of qualitative research.* London, UK: Sage.

Sengstock, B., Moxham, L., & Dwyer, T. (2006, July). University and workplace culture: Lifelong learning in nursing students. In D. Orr, F. Nouwens, C. MacPherson, R. E. Harreveld, & P. A. Danaher (Eds.), *Lifelong learning: Partners, pathways and pedagogies. Keynote and referred papers from the 4th International Lifelong Learning Conference.* Rockhampton, Australia: Central Queensland University Press.

Smith, K., & Biley, F. (1997). Understanding grounded theory: Principles and evaluation. *Nurse Researcher, 4,* 17–30.

St. John, W. (2004). Focus group interviews. In V. Minichielo, G. Sullivan, K. Greenwood, & R. Axford (Eds.), *Handbook of research methods for nursing and health science* (2nd ed.). Frenchs Forest, Australia: Pearson Education Australia.

Stern, P. N., & Covan, E. K. (2001). Early grounded theory: Its processes and products. In R. S. Schreiber & P. N. Stern (Eds.), *Using grounded theory in nursing.* New York, NY: Springer.

Strauss, A. L. (1987). *Qualitative analysis for social scientists.* New York, NY: Cambridge.

Strauss, A. L., & Corbin, J. (1990). *Basics of qualitative research: Techniques and procedures for developing grounded theory.* Newbury Park, CA: Sage.

Strauss, A. L., & Corbin, J. (1998). *Basics of qualitative research: Techniques and procedures for developing grounded theory* (2nd ed.). Thousand Oaks, CA: Sage.

Suominen, M., Kovasin, M., & Ketola, O. (1997). Nursing culture—Some viewpoints. *Journal of Advanced Nursing, 25*(1), 186–190.

Tashakkori, A., & Teddlie, C. (1998). *Mixed methodology: Combining qualitative and quantitative approaches.* Thousand Oaks, CA: Sage.

Taylor, B. (2001). Identifying and transforming dysfunctional nurse-nurse relationships through reflective practice and action research. *International Journal of Nursing Practice, 7*(6), 406–413.

Thomas, S. P., & Droppleman, P. (1997). Channeling nurses' anger into positive interventions. *Nursing Forum, 32*(2), 13–21.

van der Peet, R. (1995). *The Nightingale model of nursing.* Edinburgh, Scotland: Campionan Press.

CHAPTER ELEVEN

DISCOVERING THE THEORY OF MORAL RECKONING

Alvita Nathaniel

Writing a dissertation is an academic feat accomplished on an emotional roller coaster. With so much riding on the outcome, the first decisions are the most important and difficult—choosing a research topic and method.

CHOOSING A RESEARCH TOPIC

Soon after I began my doctoral education, the PhD faculty started asking about areas of interest. "What phenomenon do you want to study?" they would ask. Or they would say, "Find something that will still interest you after 4 or 5 years of study." Oh, the anxiety this evoked. I was not ready. I was on faculty in a school of nursing and also practiced as a primary care provider in a free clinic. Should I choose a health problem from the indigent population, a social problem that influenced the health of Appalachian indigent people, a facet of nursing education? I was interested in all of these, but nothing had emotional grab. As I thought about studying diabetes, obesity, or the effects of poverty on health, my heart was heavy. I did not want to be yoked to a topic that did not excite me.

One day, I began rereading a section of an ethics textbook that a friend and I had written before I began my doctoral education (Burkhardt & Nathaniel, 1998). I had written a section on moral problems. As I read over my own work, I became absorbed thinking about Andrew Jameton's description of moral distress in nursing. He had discovered a new category of moral problem in which nurses were distressed because they had participated in actions they believed were morally wrong. I found myself looking for more information about moral distress—searching for journal articles—just because I was interested. When moral distress occurred, Jameton asserted, nurses involved believed they knew the morally correct solution, yet they were forced to follow through with someone else's decision, violating their own moral standards. This fascinated me. At some point, the idea swept over me like a wave in the ocean: Moral distress was the topic I had to study! I wanted to know more about what was going on when nurses experienced moral distress. But, what method would be appropriate and how could I decide?

CHOOSING A RESEARCH METHOD

I was drawn to qualitative inquiry, perhaps because of my long-standing interests in ethics, social behavior, and philosophy. I liked the idea of discovery. So, as I read about the different qualitative methods, it became clear to me that grounded theory was appropriate to study moral distress because (it seemed to me) the problem was best understood as a process—and only understood from the participants' perspective.

I wanted to know about the process that nurses experienced when they encountered a morally troubling situation. Grounded theory was perfect for this investigation. In grounded theory, a concept is the name for a social pattern that has emerged from the data. It denotes a pattern that is meticulously discovered through the process of constantly comparing data, word by word, incident by incident, and so forth. Glaser calls this "a form of latent structure analysis, which reveals the fundamental patterns . . ." (Glaser, 2002, p. 4). This type of data-based conceptualization sometimes brings into focus previously unnamed latent patterns. The grounded theory method corrects for error or bias through constant comparison and abstraction, which further clarifies the underlying latent patterns (Glaser, 2002, rev. 2007). Therefore, all grounded theories depict discovered latent social patterns—just what I wanted to study.

I needed to hear the stories from the nurses to understand what was going on with them. Grounded theory was perfect for this because it seeks to understand the main concern and its resolution from participants' perspectives. Glaser calls this a "perspective-based" methodology by which the researcher tries to objectively figure out "what's going on" and then to conceptualize it (Glaser, 2002, rev. 2007). As soon as I read about grounded theory, I knew that it was the research method best suited to my research study.

DEVELOPMENT OF THE THEORY OF MORAL RECKONING

As mentioned above, I had read a nursing ethics text written by Andrew Jameton, a philosopher and ethicist, who first described moral distress in nursing. When he asked nurses to talk about moral dilemmas, Jameton noticed that their stories failed to meet the definition of dilemma (Jameton, 1984). Relating their personal stories, nurses consistently talked about situations in which they believed they knew the morally right actions to take, yet felt constrained from following their convictions (Jameton, 1993). Jameton concluded that nurses were compelled to tell these stories because of their profound suffering and their belief about the importance of the situations. Mentioning this concept only briefly, Jameton proposed that "moral distress arises when one knows the right thing to do, but institutional constraints make it nearly impossible to pursue the right course of action" (Jameton, 1984, p. 6). Jameton also stipulated that nurses who participate in an action that they have judged to be morally wrong experience moral distress (Jameton, 1993).

As I searched the literature, I found that even though the early literature offered a few emotionally charged descriptions of nurses' moral distress, the knowledge was limited in four essential ways. First, there were few studies, with few informants, so even though several nurses had written about moral distress, we really knew very little about it. Second, only a handful of published studies identified moral distress in their purpose statements. In addition, most published studies were rudimentary and exploratory in nature. Third, theoretical foundations did not adequately explain moral distress. Fourth, there were gaps in the literature in terms of the impact of moral distress on nursing care and patients' health outcomes (Nathaniel, 2014). Awareness of these four limitations compelled me to try to learn more about the process.

I began conducting interviews with nurses who reported that they had experienced morally troubling patient care situations. My purpose was to address gaps in knowledge by seeking answers to one basic research question: What transpires in morally laden situations in which nurses experience distress? I was surprised to find that when I asked nurses to tell me about troubling patient care situations, each participant was eager to talk. I needed to do very little coaxing because I had stumbled on a phenomenon that was important to these nurses. Using the inductive approach of classical grounded theory (Glaser, 1965, 1978, 1998; Glaser & Strauss, 1967), I soon recognized that more was going on in these situations than could be explained adequately by the concept of moral distress. Distinct patterns and processes emerged from the data, making it clear that nurses' experiences followed a relatively predictable pattern as each nurse made important choices before, during, and after becoming entangled in a morally significant situational bind (Nathaniel, 2014).

As required by the classical grounded theory method, I made a conscious effort to lay aside preconceived notions, logical elaborations, and ideas gleaned from the extant literature. New concepts, processes, and tentative hypotheses began to emerge from the empirical data through careful investigation, inductive reasoning, and analysis. Early in the data-gathering phase, I noticed that nurses vividly recalled important junctures in their professional lives that included morally troubling patient care situations, yet seemed to be part of a much bigger process. Extant research focusing on moral distress remained pertinent and was subsequently interwoven into the larger, more explanatory and predictive process of moral reckoning, adding depth and complexity to the resultant theory (Nathaniel, 2014).

The theory of moral reckoning emerged through the inductive process of the classical grounded theory method. I recorded the interviews as field notes immediately after each interview. Analysis began with the first episode of data gathering and was simultaneous with other steps of the process. Using constant comparison as suggested by Glaser (1965), data were analyzed sentence by sentence as they were coded. Data were organized into concepts and further into categories. I composed conceptual-level memos as concepts became evident. As the research continued, social psychological processes began to surface (Nathaniel, 2014). Moral reckoning emerged as the main concept to which all other concepts related. It described the way that these nurses continually resolved the moral problems they encountered. Identification of moral reckoning enabled subsequent selective theoretical sampling, coding, and memoing. Theoretical sampling began when concepts seemed to require more refinement or areas needed more depth. For example, the theory was starting to take shape, but I realized that I had no information about nurses before they encountered a situational bind. So, I extended my interviews to include a question about their memories of nursing before they experienced moral problems in the workplace. I wrote memos, which consisted of the emerging concepts and categories (highly abstract concepts). When it became clear that the indicators were saturated, I began sorting and organizing the memos.

As I sorted the memos and the theory began to take shape, I found that the larger process of moral reckoning overlaps moral distress as described in the extant literature. Both moral reckoning and moral distress include a situational bind (unnamed in moral distress literature) and short- and long-term consequences for nurses. Because it explicates choices and actions and includes precursor conditions and long-term consequences, the substantive and more comprehensive and explanatory theory of moral reckoning effectively synthesizes, organizes, and transcends what was previously known about moral distress (Nathaniel, 2014).

But, I have gotten a bit ahead of myself. I discovered the pattern—the basic social process, but it did not have a name. I searched dictionaries and a thesaurus, reading words and meanings, trying to find the best word to represent the process. I found it when I came across the term *reckon*. To reckon is to enumerate serially or separately; to name or mention one after another in due order; to go over or through (a series) in this manner; to recount, relate, narrate, tell; to mention; to allege; to calculate, work out, decide the nature or value of; to consider, judge, or estimate by, or as the result of calculation; to consider, think, suppose, be of opinion; to speak or discourse of something; to render or give an account (of one's conduct, etc.); and to regard in a certain light (Simpson & Weiner, 1989, pp. 335–336). Reckoning is "the action of rendering to another an account of one's self or one's conduct; an account, statement of something" (Simpson & Weiner, 1989, p. 336). In other words, nurses were recounting, relating, telling, and accounting for their actions. I had a theory and it had a name.

THE THEORY OF MORAL RECKONING

Moral reckoning consists of a three-stage process and critical juncture as nurses reflect on motivations, choices, actions, and consequences of a morally troubling patient care situation (Nathaniel, 2004, 2006). The relationship among the stages is depicted in the model (Nathaniel, 2006). In the middle range theory of moral reckoning, the stage of ease is disrupted by a situational bind and then followed by the processes of resolution and reflection (Nathaniel, 2014).

The Stage of Ease

I talked to nurses about their first experiences in nursing. After the initial novice phase, nurses experience a stage of ease in which they enjoy a sense of satisfaction and at-homeness in the workplace. They feel comfortable with their knowledge and skills. Properties central to the stage of ease include becoming, professionalizing, institutionalizing, and working. There is a fragile balance among the properties during the stage of ease such that each property is related to the other, creating a feeling of comfort.

Becoming

As Strauss once wrote, "The human experience of time is one of process: the present is always a becoming" (Strauss, 1959, p. 31). Through the process of becoming, every person evolves a set of core beliefs and values, which are a product of lifelong learning about what is important and how to behave in society. Core beliefs evolve through experience, from the testimony of authority, and from the modeling of parents, teachers, ministers, peers, and others. Integration and consistency of core values produce moral integrity (Beauchamp & Childress, 2008). Through the lifelong process of becoming, nurses develop core beliefs and values.

Professionalizing

When I talked to nurses, I found that the process of becoming a nurse includes inculcation of certain cultural norms learned in nursing school and early practice (Nathaniel, 2014). Professional norms are conceptual ideals that contribute to the nurse's idea of what a good nurse should be or do. Explicitly, nurses learn that they have unique relationships with patients and are responsible to keep promises, which are sometimes implicit in the relationship. Penticuff identified moral goals that are part of nursing's common perspective, such as "the protection and enhancement of human dignity, the alleviation of vulnerability, the promotion of growth and health, and the enhancement of coping and comfort in the face of hardship" (Penticuff, 1997b, p. 51). Likewise, nurses honor the common professional norms of knowing patients as persons, listening to their needs and preferences, supporting their everyday choices through advocacy, and maintaining their dignity (Doutrich, Wros, & Izumi, 2001).

Professionalizing is supported by the theoretical work of Strauss (1959) and Glaser (1998). Strauss suggested that to become a member of a group, a person must invest in the goals of the group. Investment in a group occurs through the transmission of ideas and signifies shared meanings. Insofar as the person thinks of himself or herself as an integral part of the group, he or she embraces its goals. The person, then, has dual commitment to the group and to self. Strauss also suggested that a person may be so heavily identified with the group that "he is no longer quite himself" (Strauss, 1959, p. 37). Validation by the group is so important that the person reinterprets activity and meaning. Thus, as can be seen in moral reckoning, the person's core values may be either supported or challenged by the values of the group as the person becomes professionalized. Similarly, Glaser (1998) proposed that personal identities may merge with properties of a profession so that members find it difficult to break through the boundaries (Glaser, 1998). In this situation, the unit identity becomes the person's self-image. Professional norms sometimes lead nurses to act according to role-set behavior, governed by blind adherence to professional norms and by their perception of the expectations of others.

Institutionalizing

The third property rests on the premise that the nurse works in an institutional setting with both implicit and explicit institutional norms. This is corroborated by the studies of Liaschenko (1995) and Ehrenreich and Ehrenreich (1990), who propose that institutionalized medicine is a complex interconnected tangle of practice patterns, cultural beliefs, and values in which the practice of nursing takes place. Institutional health care delivery norms constitute basic social structural processes within which the practice of nursing takes place. Explicit institutional norms include completing a job according to institutional standards and respecting lines of authority. Implicit institutional norms include such concepts as ensuring that the business makes a profit, following orders, and handling crises without making waves.

Working

The work of nursing is varied, challenging, and rewarding. Nurses attend to the most personal and private needs and learn much about patients' hopes, fears, and desires (Penticuff, 1997a). They get to know patients who stay on their unit for extended periods or return many times. Doing the work of nursing includes knowing patients intimately, witnessing their suffering, accepting the responsibility to care, desiring to do the work well, and knowing what to do.

Situational Binds

Sometimes, troubling events occur that challenge the integration of core beliefs, professional norms, and institutional norms. When this happens, nurses find themselves in *situational binds* that force them into a critical juncture in their professional lives (Nathaniel, 2004, 2006).

A situational bind terminates the stage of ease and throws the nurse into turmoil when core beliefs and other claims conflict. Three types of situational binds include conflicts between core values and professional or institutional norms, moral disagreement among decision makers in the face of power imbalance, and workplace deficiencies that cause real or potential harm to patients (Nathaniel, 2004, 2006). These binds produce dramatic consequences for nurses when they must choose one value or belief over another—forcing a turning point in their professional lives.

Situational binds in nursing involve an intricate interweaving of many factors including professional relationships, divergent values, workplace demands, and other implications with moral overtones. Situational binds vary in their complexity, context, and particulars but are similar in terms of their immediate and long-term effects. When situational binds occur, nurses must make critical decisions—choosing one value or belief over another. Specific types of binds include conflict between the nurse's core beliefs and professional or institutional norms, power imbalance complicated by differences in beliefs and values, conflicting loyalty, and serious workplace deficiencies (Nathaniel, 2004, 2006). Types of cases most frequently mentioned in the extant literature included causing needless suffering by prolonging the life of dying patients or performing unnecessary tests and treatments, especially on terminal patients; lying to patients; incompetent or inadequate treatment by a physician; and coercing consent from poorly informed patients (Cavaliere, Daly, Dowling, & Montgomery, 2010; Corley, 1995; Cummings, 2011; Deady & McCarthy, 2010; Dewitte, Piers, Steeman, & Nele, 2010; Dunwoody, 2011; Gaeta & Price, 2010; Hall, Brinchmann, & Aagaard, 2012; Halpern, 2011; Huffman & Rittenmeyer, 2012; McArthur, 2010; Mueller, Ottenberg, Hayes, & Koenig, 2011; Piers et al., 2011, 2012; Rodney, 1988).

The disruption of ease that nurses experience during situational binds results from a number of dynamic internal and external tensions (Nathaniel, 2004, 2006). For example, the ability to act on moral decisions may be constrained by socialization to follow orders, self-doubt, lack of courage, and conflicting loyalty. Penticuff (1997b) also found that nurses struggle with conflicting loyalties to patients, nursing peers, physicians, and institutions. Asymmetrical power relationships and powerlessness often lead to situational binds. Nurses may have insight into the problem at hand, yet believe they cannot participate in the decision-making process. They sense a moral responsibility, want the best outcome for patients, know what is needed, and yet believe they are powerless to get it done. In some instances, nurses experience distress when they know the professional and institutional norms, are aware of their own core beliefs, and yet are unable to uphold them because of workplace deficiencies. Workplace deficiencies include such factors as chronic staff shortage, unreasonable institutional expectations, and equipment inadequacy (Nathaniel, 2004, 2006). Situational binds force nurses to make difficult decisions in the midst of crises characterized by intolerable internal conflict. Something must be done to rectify the situation; one must make a choice.

In the midst of the situational bind or soon after, nurses experience consequences such as profound emotions, reactive behaviors, and physical manifestations. Nurses may experience feelings of guilt, anger, powerlessness, conflict, depression, outrage, betrayal, and devastation. Physical manifestations such as light-headedness, crying, sleeplessness, and vomiting may also occur.

During the time of or after situational binds, nursing care is affected—sometimes negatively and sometimes positively. Some nurses are unable to care for the patient or to even return to the unit after a troubling incident. Some nurses make up for what they consider to be wrongdoing by giving more compassionate care—even to the point of sacrificing personal time. For others, care improves in the long term because of lessons learned in the process.

The Stage of Resolution

Situational binds constitute crises of intolerable internal conflict. The nurse seeks to resolve the problem and set things right. This signifies the beginning of the stage of resolution. This stage often alters professional trajectory. There are two properties of the stage of resolution: making a stand and giving up. These properties are not mutually exclusive. In fact, a nurse might give up, reconsider, and make a stand.

Making a Stand

In the midst of a situational bind, some nurses choose to make a stand. Making a stand takes a variety of forms—all of which include professional risk. Nurses may even make a stand by stepping beyond the usual boundaries of the profession to do what, to them, seems to be the morally correct action. Nurses may make a stand by refusing to follow physicians' orders, initiating negotiations, breaking the rules, whistle blowing, and so forth. Making a stand is rarely successful in the short term. Not a single informant in Liaschenko's (1995) study reported an instance in which treatment was stopped on his or her testimony. Nevertheless, making a stand may occasionally improve the overall situation in the long term.

Giving Up

Sometimes nurses resolve a morally troubling situation by giving up. Giving up may overlap with making a stand in some instances. Nurses often give up because they recognize the futility of making an overt stand. They are simply not willing to sacrifice for no purpose. They may give up to protect themselves or to seek a way or find a place where they can better integrate core beliefs, professional norms, and institutional norms. Giving up includes participating (with regret) in an activity they consider to be morally wrong or leaving the unit, the institution, or the profession altogether. Sometimes nurses seem to give up in the short term but move toward more advanced or autonomous roles or toward leadership positions—all of which prepare them to make a stand in the future.

The Stage of Reflection

The stage of reflection is the last stage in the process of moral reckoning. Nurses whom I interviewed were all progressing through this stage, so I could observe the stage as well as hear about it from the nurses. During the stage of reflection the nurse thoughtfully examines beliefs, values, and actions. Properties of the stage of reflection include remembering, telling the story, examining conflicts, and living with the consequences. During this stage, which may last a lifetime, nurses reflect on the moral problem and their response. Nurses recall vivid mental pictures and evoked emotions such as feelings of guilt and self-blame, lingering sadness, anger, and anxiety. Moral reckoning continues over time as nurses remember, tell the story, examine conflicts, and live with the consequences.

Remembering

One of the more intriguing properties of moral reckoning is the manner in which nurses remember critical events. After particularly troubling situations, nurses retain vivid mental pictures, which tend to evoke emotions many years later. Nurses remember sensory particulars of the incident—the sights, sounds, and smells. Even after many years, the images are seared into their minds. Remembering evokes emotions including feelings of guilt and self-blame, lingering sadness, anger, and anxiety. Lingering emotional effects may be profound for many.

Strauss (1959) proposed that a remembered act is never finished. As a person recalls the act, he or she selectively reconstructs it, remembering certain aspects and dropping others. The person reassesses acts many times, seeking new perspectives or new facts. Thus, learning leads to revision of concepts that, in turn, leads to reorganization of behavior. Strauss further proposed that the process of continual learning and revision results in a new identity. This sort of ambiguity raises challenges and the discovery of new values through which transformation takes place.

Telling the Story

Nurses want to tell the story to sympathetic others. After I asked a simple question, they spilled their stories to me. Even now, when I discuss the theory, many nurses cannot wait to tell me their stories of moral reckoning. I found that they may tell a friend or family member immediately after an incident occurs or meet with other nurses to discuss the event. Nurses rely on others to hear the story and to understand it from their perspective. A listening, nonjudgmental person allows the nurse to tell the story as he or she attempts to seek meaning and to reckon belief and action. Nurses continue the process over time—telling and retelling the story as they try to make sense of it. Smith and Liehr (2014) write that engaging in dialogue about unique human experience catalyzes the beginning of a process of personal change. Through following the story path as recollected, one begins a process of discovery, self-revelation, and reckoning. As the story unfolds, the person attempts to understand the meaning of experiences and gain new perspectives and wisdom. The person goes into the depths of the story to find unique meanings and reconstruct a story that has a beginning, middle, and end. Consistent with the theory of moral reckoning, Smith and Liehr propose that, as the person tells the story, he or she gains a full-dimensional, reflective awareness of bodily experiences, thoughts, feelings, emotions, and values. Patterns are discerned, made explicit, and named. Telling the story relieves pain and creates possibilities for human development.

Examining Conflicts

As nurses tell their stories, they begin to examine conflicts in the troubling situation. They examine their values and ask themselves questions about what actually happened, who was to blame, and how they can avoid similar situations in the future. As they thoughtfully examine the conflicts, some intellectualize their participation, some set limits, and some gain strength to make a stand and accept the consequences in future situations.

Nurses continue to struggle with conflicts between personal values and professional ideals. They want to be able to identify themselves as good nurses. Similarly, Kelly (1998) reported that some nurses have a painful awareness of the discrepancy between who they aspired to be and what they have become. These nurses suffered the loss of their own professional self-concept, their vision of the kind of nurses they wanted to be, and their image of nursing as they believed it was.

As nurses think about their roles in what they consider past moral wrongdoing, some set limits or make pronouncements about their future actions. Some identify a point beyond which they will not again be willing to go. Others vow to step outside their boundaries to help a patient in the future, fully aware and willing to accept the consequences of their future actions. Thus, the nurse's ethical practice evolves through the iterative process of experience and reflection.

Living With the Consequences

Nurses live with the consequences of morally troubling situations for a prolonged period of time. Consequences other than those already mentioned include fracturing professional relationships and changing one's life trajectory. Following a situational bind in which the nurse believes another person committed moral wrongdoing, he or she may be unable to work collaboratively with that person or others who were unsupportive. They lose faith in the persons' integrity or lose respect for them as practitioners. Since they are no longer comfortable in the original workplace and have fractured professional relationships, many nurses change their work setting and often their life trajectory following a situational bind. They may change employers or specialties, and they are likely to seek further education, many times intending to correct the type of moral wrongs they experienced in the past.

This middle range theory of moral reckoning encompasses moral distress, yet reaches further—identifying a life event experienced through disruption of ease as one confronts a situational bind demanding resolution and reflection. The concepts of the theory—ease, situational bind, resolution, and reflection—name the stages of the basic social process of moral reckoning. The theory has been developed in the context of the discipline of nursing, but its use in other contexts promises meaningful guidance and ongoing development.

SUMMARY

Gathering the stories of nurses, analyzing the data, and discovering the theory of moral reckoning was one of the worst and best experiences of my life. Writing a dissertation is a solitary endeavor, filled with emotional ups and downs. I listened to nurses weep as they told their stories, and sometimes I wept with them. I read and coded my field notes over and over, looking for patterns, thinking none would ever emerge. Before I knew it, the theory emerged from the data, fully formed. I sometimes think I had little to do with it—the theory was just waiting to be uncovered. Now, the fourth edition of the ethics text that I authored includes a section devoted to moral reckoning (Burkhardt & Nathaniel, 2013), and master's and doctoral students from around the globe contact me to ask about the theory. It has passed the test of time.

REFERENCES

Beauchamp, T. L., & Childress, J. F. (2008). *Principles of biomedical ethics* (6th ed.). New York, NY: Oxford University Press.

Burkhardt, M. A., & Nathaniel, A. K. (1998). *Ethics & issues in contemporary nursing.* New York, NY: Delmar.

Burkhardt, M. A., & Nathaniel, A. K. (2013). *Ethics & issues in contemporary nursing* (4th ed.). New York, NY: Delmar.

Cavaliere, T. A., Daly, B., Dowling, D., & Montgomery, K. (2010). Moral distress in neonatal intensive care unit RNs. *Advances in Neonatal Care, 10*(3), 145–156. doi:10.1097/ANC.0b013e3181dd6c48

Corley, M. C. (1995). Moral distress of critical care nurses. *American Journal of Critical Care, 4*(4), 280–285.

Cummings, C. L. (2011). What factors affect nursing retention in the acute care setting? *Journal of Research in Nursing, 16*(6), 489–500. doi:10.1177/1744987111407594

Deady, R., & McCarthy, J. (2010). A study of the situations, features, and coping mechanisms experienced by Irish psychiatric nurses experiencing moral distress. *Perspectives in Psychiatric Care, 46*(3), 209–220. doi:10.1111/j.1744-6163.2010.00260.x

Dewitte, M., Piers, R., Steeman, E., & Van Den Noortgate, N. (2010). Moral distress and burn-out in nurses on acute geriatric wards. Fourth European Nursing Congress. *Journal of Clinical Nursing, 19*, 19–20. doi:10.1111/j.1365-2702.2010.03439.x

Doutrich, D., Wros, P., & Izumi, S. (2001). Relief of suffering and regard for personhood: Nurses' ethical concerns in Japan and the USA. *Nursing Ethics, 8*(5), 448–458.

Dunwoody, D. (2011). Nurses' level of moral distress and perception of futile care in the critical care environment. *Dynamics, 22*(2), 22–24.

Ehrenreich, B., & Ehrenreich, J. (1990). The system behind the chaos. In N. F. McKenzie (Ed.), *The crisis in health care: Ethical issues* (pp. 50–69). New York, NY: Meridian.

Gaeta, S., & Price, K. J. (2010). End-of-life issues in critically ill cancer patients. *Critical Care Clinics, 26*(1), 219–227.

Glaser, B. G. (1965). The constant comparative method of qualitative analysis. *Social Problems, 12,* 10.

Glaser, B. G. (1978). *Theoretical sensitivity: Advances in the methodology of grounded theory.* Mill Valley, CA: Sociology Press.

Glaser, B. G. (1998). *Doing grounded theory: Issues and discussion.* Mill Valley, CA: Sociology Press.

Glaser, B. G. (2002). Conceptualization: On theory and theorizing using grounded theory. *International Journal of Qualitative Methods, 1*(2), 1–31.

Glaser, B. G. (2002, rev. 2007). Constructivist grounded theory. *Forum: Qualitative Social Research, 3*(3).

Glaser, B. G., & Strauss, A. L. (1967). *The discovery of grounded theory: Strategies for qualitative research.* Chicago, IL: Aldine.

Hall, E. O. C., Brinchmann, B. S., & Aagaard, H. (2012). The challenge of integrating justice and care in neonatal nursing. *Nursing Ethics, 19*(1), 80–90. doi:10.1177/0969733011412101

Halpern, S. D. (2011). Perceived inappropriateness of care in the ICU: What to make of the clinician's perspective? *JAMA: Journal of the American Medical Association, 306*(24), 2725–2726. doi:10.1001/jama.2011.1897

Huffman, D. M., & Rittenmeyer, L. (2012). How professional nurses working in hospital environments experience moral distress: A systematic review. *Critical Care Nursing Clinics of North America, 24*(1), 91–100.

Jameton, A. (1984). *Nursing practice: The ethical issues.* Englewood Cliffs, NJ: Prentice-Hall.

Jameton, A. (1993). Dilemmas of moral distress: Moral responsibility and nursing practice. *Clinical Issues in Perinatal and Women's Health Nursing, 4*(4), 542–551.

Kelly, B. (1998). Preserving moral integrity: A follow-up study with new graduate nurses. *Journal of Advanced Nursing, 28*(5), 1134–1145.

Liaschenko, J. (1995). Artificial personhood: Nursing ethics in a medical world. *Nursing Ethics, 2*(3), 185–196.

McArthur, A. (2010). How professional nurses working in hospital environments experience moral distress: A systematic review. *Journal of Advanced Nursing, 66*(5), 962–963. doi:10.1111/j.1365-2648.2010.05310.x

Mueller, P. S., Ottenberg, A. L., Hayes, D. L., & Koenig, B. A. (2011). "I felt like the angel of death": Role conflicts and moral distress among allied professionals employed by the US cardiovascular implantable electronic device industry. *Journal of Interventional Cardiac Electrophysiology: An International Journal of Arrhythmias and Pacing, 32*(3), 253–261.

Nathaniel, A. K. (2004). A grounded theory of moral reckoning in nursing. *Grounded Theory Review, 4*(1), 43–58.

Nathaniel, A. K. (2006). Moral reckoning in nursing. *Western Journal of Nursing Research, 28*(4), 419–438; discussion 439–448.

Nathaniel, A. K. (2014). Theory of moral reckoning. In M. J. Smith & P. Liehr (Eds.), *Middle range theory for nursing* (pp. 329–346). New York, NY: Springer.

Penticuff, J. H. (1997a). Neonatal nursing ethics: Toward a consensus. *Neonatal Network, 5*(6), 7–16.

Penticuff, J. H. (1997b). Nursing perspectives in bioethics. In K. Hoshino (Ed.), *Japanese and Western bioethics* (pp. 49–60). The Dordrecht: Kluwer Academic.

Piers, R. D., Azoulay, E., Ricou, B., Dekeyser Ganz, F., Decruyenaere, J., Max, A., . . . Benoit, D. D. (2011). Perceptions of appropriateness of care among European and Israeli intensive care unit nurses and physicians. *JAMA: The Journal of the American Medical Association, 306*(24), 2694–2703.

Piers, R. D., Magali Van den Eynde, Steeman, E., Vlerick, P., Benoit, D. D., & Nele, J, N. (2012). End-of-life care of the geriatric patient and nurses' moral distress. *Journal of the American Medical Directors Association, 13*(1), 80.e7–80.e13. doi:10.1016/j.jamda.2010.12.014

Rodney, P. (1988). Moral distress in critical care nursing. *Canadian Critical Care Nursing Journal, 5*(2), 9–11.

Simpson, J. A., & Weiner, E. S. C. (1989). *The Oxford English dictionary, Vol. XIII* (2nd ed.). New York, NY: Oxford University Press.

Smith, M. J., & Liehr, P. (2014). Story theory. In M. J. Smith & P. Liehr (Eds.), *Middle range theory for nursing* (pp. 225–252). New York, NY: Springer.

Strauss, A. L. (1959). *Mirrors and masks: The search for identity.* Glencoe, IL: Free Press.

Chapter Twelve

Moderated Guiding: The Process of Generating a Grounded Theory of End-of-Life Care

Antoinette M. McCallin

This study began with an interest in extending my skills as a grounded theory researcher. I had used classical grounded theory (Glaser, 1978; Glaser & Strauss, 1967) for my doctoral research (McCallin, 1999, 2004). As a doctoral student I had learned grounded theory from textbooks, minus mentoring (Glaser, 1998; McCallin, Nathaniel, & Andrews, 2011). At the time the seminal texts on grounded theory were available (Glaser, 1978; Glaser & Strauss, 1967), and the debate about the different approaches to grounded theory (Glaser, 1992) had begun. The series of grounded theory methodological books that were to become key texts for classical grounded theory researchers in the future (Glaser, 1998, 2001, 2003, 2005, 2009) was not available though.

However, in 2004 Dr. Barney Glaser invited me to present my theory of pluralistic dialoguing (McCallin, 1999) at a grounded theory workshop at Mill Valley in California. The workshop was significant for my development as a researcher. Listening to Dr. Glaser discuss methodology had a major impact on my understanding of key methodological issues that influenced the quality of a grounded theory study (McCallin, 2003, 2006a, 2006b). Although Dr. Glaser had examined my theory of pluralistic dialoguing and spoke about it warmly, I realized I still had much to learn. The emphasis on conceptualization made me question the level of my theory development. Several years later, I was interested to read that, "in the early days of grounded theory studies, researchers primarily used the descriptive or gerund mode to describe the situation of interest" (Artinian, 2009, p. 77). The descriptive mode is a description of what is happening in an area; it describes the types of behaviors and is not integrated under a theoretical code, while the gerund mode describes stages of a basic social process. Looking back I realize that the Mill Valley seminars were important for my development as a grounded theory researcher. I became aware that learning about methodology is an ongoing process that is learned best by doing. Indeed, Glaser (2009) argues that "it takes time and research experience to really understand the meaning [of grounded theory] . . . to develop a level of expertise" (p. 3). Although I went on to become involved with teaching and mentoring international grounded theory students at Mill Valley and in the United Kingdom, I wanted to improve my research skills so that I could supervise students better. The end-of-life care study was designed with this in mind.

The topic was chosen because I had taught some postgraduate students who worked at the local hospice. I was curious about nursing practice in the specialty. What concerns did nurses have in end-of-life care, and how did they manage these? It was an area in which I could enter the field without being influenced by the professional interests that are more common when health professionals become researchers. I had nursed people at the end of their lives but had not worked specifically in the area. I believed that I was well positioned to focus on participants' problems and find out how they resolved them. In this chapter, I will briefly summarize the theory of moderated guiding and discuss the methodological decisions that influenced the research process, highlighting significant issues. The chapter concludes with a summary of key points a researcher may wish to consider when designing a study.

DESCRIPTION OF THE STUDY

Summary of the Study

In this chapter, some of the processes that influenced the development of the theory of moderated guiding are discussed. As will be shown, the main concern of nurses in end-of-life care was different expectations. This was managed using the process of moderated guiding, which included the subprocesses of checking out, which referred to informational understanding and potential alternatives; involving that comprised conversational maneuvering and negotiating choices; and supporting, which included deliberating and safeguarding (McCallin, 2011). The theory was developed according to a highly organized, systematic process.

Conceptual Issues

The process began with the identification of baseline information about the topic. A definition of the central concept was required. End-of-life care was defined as the palliative and hospice care needed to provide support and promote quality of life for the patient and family during the end-of-life period (Kuebler, Berry, & Heidrich, 2002). Scanning library books established that end-of-life care was a broad term, which covered terminal, hospice, and palliative care. I found that end-of-life care referred to the transition phase between living and dying (Kuebler, Heidrich, & Esper, 2002; Nolan & Mock, 2004), encompassed short-term or long-term care, and included the supportive and comfort care provided for patients at the end of their lives (Clarke, Flanagan, & Kendrick, 2002; Kinghorn & Gamlin, 2001).

As I familiarized myself with some general literature, I read for evidence of complexity in nursing practice. I searched for situations that were potentially problematic. As the researcher, I looked for a complex context where there were many issues. It quickly became clear that nursing practice in end-of-life care was not straightforward (Redpath, 1995). One issue was that nurses worked with patients who had either a malignant or nonmalignant disease that was incurable, recurrent, increasingly unresponsive to treatment, or in a stage of relapse. Redpath argued that end-of-life care nursing practice was blurred once symptom relief replaced curative care. As a result, nurses managed situations with distressed patients and families who had contradictory treatment goals for an irreversible disease. Another issue involved managing communication in patient–family decision making (Weissman, 2004). At the end of life some patients were especially vulnerable, passive recipients of care who were more likely to misinterpret the seriousness of their condition. Not surprisingly, outcome misunderstandings occurred. Nurses managed these, even though health professionals had problems with time prognostication predictions and with diagnosing dying (Connolly, 2001). Clearly, there were issues with information sharing that affected patient–family treatment expectations and nursing practice.

Additionally, nurses managed professional challenges, such as maintaining their competency and keeping up to date with new approaches to practice. Flanagan, Clarke, Kendrick, and Lane (2002) reported on the importance of up-skilling and multi-skilling, as nurses learned how to integrate disease management with supportive care and symptom management. Interestingly, a number of nurses welcomed caring for patients in the final stages of their lives (Brykczynska, 2002), but Henderson (2003) noted that partnership working with patients and families was not necessarily straightforward.

Similarly, Sepulveda, Marlin, Yoshida, and Ullrich (2002) observed that there were a number of problems with collaborative practice, which did not typically include patients and family. Overall, nursing practice seemed challenging, and practice-based knowledge was sparse.

As a grounded theory researcher, the intricacies of the issues caught my attention. Definitional imprecision was evident. Yet the problems of practice were difficult to define. This was ideal for a grounded theory study in which participants define the research problem and discuss how they resolve that. The focus is on "participant explanations of the how, why, when and where or what they and others are doing or experiencing" (Stern & Porr, 2011, p. 42).

Although these ideas helped me think through the significance of the project, it was more difficult to predict the precise benefits that a theoretical explanation might have on knowledge development. Fortunately I had noticed that end-of-life care research was relatively new, and scientific knowledge was required (George, 2002). Grounded theory was useful when little was known about a topic. Therefore, I argued that developing knowledge about the patterns of behavior in end-of-life care had the potential to influence nursing practice and potentially improve quality, efficiency, and effectiveness of service delivery for patients, families, the profession, educators, and the wider community. At the time, the rationale for the study was not linked to policy development. A retrospective perusal of the New Zealand Palliative Care Strategy (Ministry of Health, 2001) indicates that the research could have been justified according to policy development that emphasized "developing quality requirements for palliative care services" (p. 18), and improving "a palliative care workforce and training requirements" (p. 19). This omission meant that the project significance was more simplistic than what would be acceptable in research circles today. The aim of the study was clearly stated as using grounded theory to discover the main concern of nurses working in end-of-life care and to explain how they resolved practice problems in the area.

As has been seen, general literature was scanned initially. I understood Glaser's view (1998) that researchers should not review literature in advance of collecting data, as the researcher may be influenced by the received view of the world (McCallin, 2006a, 2006b). As a research supervisor I had noticed that familiarity with the professional literature tended to emphasize professional problems in practice and block the researcher's sensitivity to the participant's definitions of problems. Glaser does however support the notion of general reading around the area of interest (Glaser & Strauss, 1967). Because this was not a doctoral project, I followed this Glaserian directive (Cone & Artinian, 2009).

It needs to be noted though that few researchers are free to begin research without a full literature review. A doctoral student must critically review literature to show that he or she has the capability to analyze existing knowledge and clarify a rationale for research. The knowledge gap and the potential for original knowledge development need to be identified. Providentially, end-of-life care was a new area of research. There were few articles on the databases and a limited number of books on the topic. Most literature focused on palliative care nursing.

Nonetheless, I rechecked available textbooks about end-of-life care to make sure that knowledge was actually as sparse as it seemed. I found that most authors of end-of-life care followed a medical model approach emphasizing physical and functional needs, with perhaps a brief mention of spiritual and psychosocial issues (Kuebler, Berry, & Heidrich, 2002; Kuebler, Heidrich, & Esper, 2002). I also checked the contents pages of some palliative care books for chapters on end-of-life care (Aranda & O'Connor, 1999; Clarke et al. 2002; Kinghorm & Gamlin, 2001; Parker & Aranda, 1995). The search confirmed that there was little written in the area. This was ideal for beginning a grounded theory study.

Consistent with classical grounded theory, a theoretical framework did not inform study design. In some grounded theory projects, symbolic interactionism or pragmatism may be used to guide data collection and analysis (Strauss & Corbin, 1998). However, Glaser (2001) reminds researchers that imposing a theoretical framework on the data in advance interferes with the researcher's openness to the participant's problems. A predefined theoretical framework preconceives the direction of the study and may reinforce the researcher's professional interests (Kwok, McCallin, & Dickson, 2012), allowing the researcher to push a study in a certain direction, which may be important for the researcher, not the participants. The classical grounded theory emphasis, however, is on participants identifying the problem that will be researched, not the researcher.

METHODOLOGY

Design

As stated, I wanted to consolidate my learning about Glaserian grounded theory. I had read various versions of grounded theory and wanted to improve my research skills. Since then, I have supervised students using different forms of grounded theory. A decade later, I believe that methodology should be decided according to the state of knowledge in the topic area, the research question, and the prospective audience for the new knowledge. For example, clinicians working in practice may welcome an open, emergent approach to identifying practice problems. In contrast, a professional body is more likely interested in finding out about causal conditions, key contextual issues, strategies for action, and outcomes of action (Strauss & Corbin, 1998) in the research area. These decisions are also affected by the students' philosophy and value system and their willingness to recognize their strengths and to learn.

Several other points stand out in relation to researcher design and researcher choices. First, some researchers, nurses in particular, value descriptions about practice, and may be less interested in conceptualization and explanations about practice. Second, other researchers prefer to work with a research methodology that has a clear philosophical framework. Charmaz's version of grounded theory (2000), or the Strauss and Corbin (1998) model, probably has more appeal there than Glaser's grounded theory, which is not philosophical (Glaser, 1998). Third, grounded theory requires that the researcher be flexible and open to emergence. The researcher needs to be capable of dealing with simultaneous inductive–deductive thinking. The ability to work through incongruence and mental confusion in data analysis, and at the same time be able to remain organized and focused for constant comparative analysis, is challenging, especially for concrete thinkers. I had used grounded theory on several occasions, understood the challenges, and wanted to extend my research skills.

Sample

In the theory of moderated guiding, participants were chosen because they could talk about nursing practice in end-of-life care. The initial sample was purposive in that participants were approached because they worked in end-of-life care situations. The full nature of the sample was unknown at the beginning of the study, although I knew that I would need to control the sample direction as I developed the theory. Once categories and the core process were identified (after interview 15), sampling became specific, moving to theoretical sampling. From that point, participants were chosen because I wanted to discuss specific concepts. Glaser's (1978, 1998) advice to follow concepts, not people, helped me make decisions about who to talk to next.

The sample size was 30 nurses. My predicted sample size in the ethics application was 25 to 35 nurses. I named a larger sample than was required so that I would not have to return to the ethics committee for permission to talk to more participants. That would have delayed data collection by another 4 weeks. The sample numbers were also chosen to ensure the sample size would be viewed favorably by the high impact factor nursing journals. I intended to publish the findings in an international journal and wanted the theory to have analytical depth. Although I was to learn later in supervisions that a grounded theory can be completed with approximately 20 to 25 interviews, it is worth considering sample size in relation to publication issues during study design. Nowadays, some journals state that they will not publish small-sized sample studies. Although that view can be critiqued as a quantitative directive, which has little application in a qualitative study, the critical point underpinning my sample size decisions was the need to collect sufficient, meaningful data to generate a theory.

Another point related to sampling was that numbers of participants do not necessarily equate with good, usable data. A researcher, for instance, may have 15 participants, who all have something to say. The quality of the data, however, is unknown. Participants may talk about superficial issues they think the researcher is interested in (Glaser, 1978). The real story about what is happening, the hidden patterns of behavior, may not be discussed at all. Or, participants may focus on discussing professional interests popular in the professional literature, providing the well-known received view of the world. Or else, they may become vague and speak about very little that is relevant to the research. Fortunately, there are occasions when expert people, who have an in-depth knowledge and experience of their area, share willingly and openly, talking about the problems of practice and their solutions. In this project, sample size was significant. Data collected in the earlier interviews were very general. It was not until the fifteenth interview that I really began to have a clearer idea of the theory of guiding and its categories. Having to wait so long to clarify the main concern and its resolution slowed the process of theory generation. It is worth pointing out here that the breadth and generality of the data did not mean information shared was not relevant. The problem was that early in the study I did not recognize the importance of particular data in my initial analysis.

Earlier data may have been broad, but interestingly, enough participants had over 20 years of nursing experience and had worked in wide-ranging specialties such as community, general medicine, intensive care, and emergency department. On paper they were a highly experienced group of nurses. I assumed they would be well able to talk about end-of-life care. That assumption was underpinned by Glaser's advice (Glaser, 1978, 1998) to seek several experts in an area early in the sampling, so that data collection and analysis is off to a robust start. In this instance, that did not quite work out as I hoped. Participants were not especially articulate in talking about the specifics of practice. Few had engaged in postgraduate study. They were not used to discussing the complexity of their work. At the same time, my personal insistence on remaining open and not making assumptions about what was happening interfered with refining the research focus. It was hardly surprising that the research got off to a slow start. It made it more difficult for me to identify the main concern and the resolution process. Luckily, interview 15 was significant. The participant, a nurse specialist who had engaged in postgraduate study, had a deep understanding of end-of-life care. Her communication skills were well developed. Her analysis and reflections about practice were clear and opened up my thinking about what was happening. Her interpretations gave me a new insight and understanding, providing me with a lens to reanalyze the earlier interviews. Once I had a better understanding of what was happening in practice I could look back on previous interviews and compare and contrast her views with previously gathered data.

Ethical Issues

Managing ethical issues in a study tends to depend on the ethics committee that grants permission for the researcher to proceed. Several points were addressed during design. Paying attention to time frames, ethical guidelines, probable methodological questions, and access issues went some way to ensuring that ethical proposal development was rigorous. First, I allowed several weeks for the preparation and submission process. As a research supervisor, I realized that the whole process would take about 3 months. This time was used to prepare the application and engage in consultation. I consulted with colleagues who would act as intermediaries and the faculty ethics representative who was asked to review the application before it was submitted for formal review. This last step ensured that the application was as polished as possible and potential problems were picked up in advance. It did not ensure the application would be approved but minimized errors and reduced the time taken for a full ethical clearance.

The second ethical issue I paid attention to was following the guidelines. Being familiar with research protocols, using the correct latest version of the forms, actually answering the questions on the forms, and submitting the application to the correct committee went some way to having a successful experience with the committee. Included in this stage was reading through the guidelines, examples, and book chapters on ethics to refresh my memory about the key ethical principles.

As I had worked on the university ethics committee, I knew that members usually asked methodological questions when qualitative projects were reviewed. Invariably, the committee requested a list of questions for a grounded theory study. Although this was completely at odds with grounded theory methodology, it was quite clear that the research would not be signed off without it. Therefore, I presented specifics. For example, the first four to six participants would be asked to describe and explain their practice in end-of-life care. The beginning question was, "I want to understand more about nursing practice in end-of-life care and would value talking with you about your experiences with patients and families. Perhaps we could begin with you telling me a little about the work you do . . . ." The question provided a beginning focus for the interview. I supplied a list of open-ended questions that could be used in the interview. A few examples include, "that's interesting; perhaps you would tell me more about that . . ."; "how did that happen . . ."; "is that so . . ."; and "what did you have in mind when . . ." I noted that toward the end of the interview all participants would be asked what their main concern working in end-of-life care situations was, and how did they manage that. In addition, I mentioned that questions would vary, depending on the time the nurse joined the study and the concepts that needed to be followed through in the constant comparative analysis.

The other ethical issue that was addressed was planning access to participants. I invited colleagues who had professional contacts in the community to identify nurses who were knowledgeable about end-of-life care. These colleagues acted as intermediaries, telling a potential participant about the study and tentatively checking interest in having an interview. I coached the intermediaries about the ethical principles, emphasizing the importance of not being overpersuasive in their approaches. If a nurse was interested in the research, the intermediaries obtained an e-mail address, and I took the responsibility for contact from there. E-mail was an ideal contact. I introduced myself, asked the person whether they were interested in talking with me, and attached a participant information sheet, which explained the research. That way a potential participant had the option to reply or not. On the information sheet I stated that I would follow a person up 1 week after the initial e-mail to check their interest. This was useful, as some people had not made contact because they were busy, due on leave, sick, or had some other commitment, which interfered with communication. Overall, the details satisfied the committee that ethical principles would be upheld.

Setting

The research began with interviewing nurses in hospices, aged care facilities, and hospitals. Participants chose their interview venue. The ethics committee did not allow researchers to interview participants in their own home. I suggested possible places such as the local library, a coffee shop in a shopping mall, the participant's workplace office, or my office at the university. Most participants chose the coffee shop location. That place was informal and supported casual conversation. In reality, the venue was full of background noise of clattering dishes and people talking. I was concerned about the interview being overheard. Participants waived that aside however. Three participants were interviewed in their offices. They were very comfortable in their own space, talking easily about practice issues. Those meetings worked well, as interruptions were rare. I was more relaxed and could focus on the questions and the constant comparative analysis that underpinned my questioning. Another participant was interviewed in a large main foyer of a hospital. I was hesitant at first. Nonetheless, that place worked very well. We had comfortable sofas to sit on and a coffee table for my recorder and interview book. Although there were plenty of people coming and going, the area was carpeted, so extraneous sound was not disturbing. In contrast, another participant chose an empty staff cafeteria, which seemed a good choice at first glance. However, it was very noisy, resonating with the sounds of the kitchen staff banging pots and pans in the back kitchen. Loud background noise distracted me, interfering with my concentration on the new data that was coming out and thinking about the implications it had in relation to the constant comparative analysis. Several participants decided to come to my office at the university. That worked well, as all I had to do was organize a car park and a central meeting place.

In retrospect, interview settings affected the interview. It was easier to establish a relaxed atmosphere in a person's office. Public spaces were readily accessible, but distracting. Participants were more relaxed in a public area, suggesting that an open venue gave them space for involvement or otherwise, when meeting and talking to someone new. The interview location was also significant in terms of travel time and parking. I scheduled at least 2 hours to find the place, locate a car park, and move into interview mode, whereby I sat quietly and thought about previous interviews, data analysis, and the interview to come.

Interviews and Rigor

The first interviews were open-ended, beginning with the research question. I followed through with ideas participants raised, asking open-ended questions about what was going on. I reminded myself periodically that I was looking for *group* interaction and behaviors. I wrote field notes about the key concepts covered in the interview immediately afterwards. I then had a list of codes to follow through at the next interview. I jotted down any questions that stood out and wrote memos about what seemed to be happening in the data.

Early interviews required me to balance openness and flexibility with control depending on the constant comparative analysis. I concentrated on using open-ended questions, so I would not force the data. I constantly monitored myself not to make assumptions, to clarify the participant's meaning, to ensure I was as open as possible to hearing the participant's interpretation. The emphasis was on listening.

Another strategy that helped was my interview book. Prior to the interview, I listed the main concepts from earlier interviews. The list was not exclusive. It included concepts that recurred in the discussions. I aimed to check out whether participants understood a concept in the same way, or whether they had different views about what was happening, and how, or why did behavior and interactions change. I wrote down very short, open-ended questions around a concept, so that I had some immediate trigger questions available. At the beginning of the interview, I put my book down on the table and pointed to the questions. I told the participant I would probably refer to it during the interview. That short explanation eased the way to the interview. The questions were invaluable if I needed to change the direction of the interview. Sometimes, interviewees talked very fast and covered numerous concepts very quickly. It was difficult to know which idea to follow up. As an interviewer I needed some space and thinking time to work through what had been said. When that happened, I let the participant know that I needed to think more about what he or she had said outside the interview. I then deliberately put my hand on the book of questions, slowed my speech down to gain some space, and asked whether they would mind if I moved in a different direction according to my questions. I let them know too that the ideas I wanted to check out had come from previous participants. I wanted to know how things worked, or did not work, for them in their situation. That approach relaxed us both, and the interview proceeded.

Although I had a list of concepts to compare at interview, I learned quickly that participants would only talk about what interested them. If a point was not relevant for them, they wandered onto another topic. They simply did not answer the question. Their strategy was more noticeable when I later transcribed the interviews and was looking to see whether I had forced the data in a particular direction. Once I saw the participant response in writing, I was more careful to slow the pace of the interview if I could and not to dwell on topics a participant was not interested in. At the back of my mind sat Glaser's (1998) advice that if something is important participants will talk about it. And they did. I was always disconcerted how participants in totally different situations would use exactly the same words as previous participants.

As I interviewed, I was conscious that rigor was important in relation to the results. I had the concepts of rigor, fit, workability, relevance, and modifiability (Glaser & Strauss, 1967) at the back of my mind, and kept reminding myself, is this relevant? Has this issue or problem been mentioned by others? Is the issue isolated, or is it a category that keeps coming up in the data? That constant internal monitoring of the theoretical concepts of the emerging theory helped me to focus on participants' issues. As I raised ideas that had been discussed by previous participants I would say, "some nurses have talked about maneuvering conversations when they work with patients and their families. Is that something you have experienced . . . perhaps you could tell me a little more about that . . . ." That way the question was open for a response if the participant wanted to follow the lead. If the question was not important for a participant, he or she usually spoke about something else, or maybe said, "I don't know what you are talking about." These types of responses gave me confidence that participants would talk about what was relevant to them; my job was to listen and make sure I compared and contrasted their experiences with those of others.

The fit of the theory of moderated guiding was judged and will continue to be evaluated by others. Fit is about whether the theory matches up with nurses' experience in end-of-life care. I presented the theory to several groups of nurses (about 40 in total) and had very positive responses about my interpretation. One nurse asked me whether I had been an end-of life care nurse, as the theory explained exactly what she did in practice and could not find the words for. Although such positive responses were encouraging, I received very negative feedback from a journal reviewer who insisted nurses were much more controlling in guiding than I suggested. This will be discussed in more detail in the section on data analysis.

Data Collection Procedures

As stated already, data were collected from interviews. I taped all interviews but did not transcribe them at first. I relied on field notes, memos, and listening to the recordings. After 10 interviews, I was thoroughly frustrated with this way of managing data. It may have been correct for Barney Glaser, but it certainly did not work for me. I am a visual learner and concentrating on auditory data for analysis was irritating. I wanted to see the full printed word. I needed a hard copy, to reread several times, so that I could think about what had been said and compare it with other interviews. Eventually, I had all the interviews typed up and resorted to working with hard copies of the interviews. That suited my style of analysis better and gave me the freedom to write notes in the margins, code, and move around between the interviews, comparing and contrasting responses as I wished.

Timeline

The original timeline for the first study was 15 months. I completed data collection and analysis in 11 months. Extra time was required to write up the findings and deal with revisions. The major issue factored into data collection was allowing time for constant comparative analysis. I usually had one interview a week. There were times however in academia when it was too difficult to get out to the field or to find large chunks of time such as several days to focus on data analysis. Also, participants were not readily available. They sounded willing to talk but had other commitments. Sometimes I had to book an interview several weeks in advance, or I had to reschedule a meeting because of other priorities.

Data Analysis and Dissemination

In this study, data analysis was an ongoing challenge. In the early stages of the research, the process proceeded well. The main concern was diversity containment, which was resolved using a humanistic guiding relationship. I identified the practice problem as diversity containment, because everyone involved had a very different understanding of what would happen and what might happen in end-of-life care. My data analysis suggested that families lacked knowledge about probabilities and possibilities in the dying process. Those involved had different cultural beliefs and philosophies about care, not to mention wide-ranging expectations. At the same time, nurses worked with colleagues from different professions that had various worldviews. As a result, someone had to manage the differences, and that role was passed on to nurses who were required to manage one and all to ensure the dying process proceeded smoothly. The properties of humanistic guiding were professional ethos (categories = locus of control and power differentials); shuttle diplomacy (categories = conversational maneuvers and intentional negotiations); and complexity management (categories = situational moderation and human-to-human involvement). The humanistic part of the theory was clear across the data in that participants said that when there was nothing left to do for a dying patient, all that was left was the human-to-human response.

Participants talked about the empathy, listening, and therapeutic relationship that underpinned guiding. I believed this interpretation fit the data, and it was the one that was taken back to participant groups and received positive feedback.

However, data analysis fell apart when the paper was submitted to a journal. One reviewer was complimentary about my theory of humanistic guiding; the other was highly critical. Extensive changes were requested. I had stated that humanistic guiding was both a controlled and uncontrolled process. The reviewer refused to accept my interpretation, arguing that end-of-life care was controlled. I was asked to review my analysis again. I argued that the interpretation was possibly due to different cultural value systems that underpinned different ways of practicing. In New Zealand, we have a Treaty of Waitangi, and professionals are expected to honor the principles of partnership, participation, and protection when working with patients and their families. These principles are an inherent value system that pervades New Zealand society and I believe influences how professionals practice. The reviewer did not accept this at all and continued to demand that control be recognized in the theory.

Not surprisingly, I was not impressed and refused to make the changes. A summer break improved my frame of mind, however, and helped me to remember my professional obligation to produce research outputs. I could not afford to let a year's worth of research go. I returned to the data, reminding myself that everything is data. Even if a different view is introduced late in analysis, as a researcher I was obliged to consider it as part of constant comparative analysis. I had not factored into my timeline the need to review rigor and modify the theory so soon. However, I took another 3 months to review the data. I began again with clean transcripts and worked through the analysis, looking for evidence of control. The final result was the theory of moderated guiding. I presented it as a process that was both controlling and noncontrolling. The analytical challenges illustrate that often there are alternative interpretations to data, and it is up to the analyst to decide which way to go for the final theory (Glaser, 1978). Further details of the analysis are available in the published paper (McCallin, 2011).

SUMMARY

In this chapter, I have discussed the process of generating the theory of moderated guiding. I have presented various examples that influenced the study design and impacted on how the methodology was applied. The process of researching is very different from the neat and tidy examples presented in chapters of a qualitative research textbook. Differences occur because context influences what happens when a researcher is in the field, as does the personality and experience of the researcher. Problems are likely inevitable. The critical issue is the researcher's willingness to learn from experience and his or her commitment to produce a scholarly piece of work. Grounded theory, like any other qualitative methodology, has its challenges. It takes time and patience to become an effective grounded theorist. The rewards lie in making a significant contribution to disciplinary knowledge development and above all generating knowledge that has potential to improve the care and outcomes for patients and their families.

REFERENCES

Aranda, S., & O'Connor, M. (1999). *Palliative care nursing: A guide to practice.* Melbourne, Australia: Ausmed.

Artinian, B. M. (2009). Studies using early modes of grounded theory. In B. M. Artinian, T. Giske, T., & P. H. Cone (Eds.), *Glaserian grounded theory in nursing research* (pp. 77–78). New York, NY: Springer.

Brykczynska, G. G. (2002). The critical essence of advanced practice. In D. Clarke, J. Flanagan, & K. Kendrick (Eds.), *Advancing nursing practice in cancer and palliative care* (pp. 20–42). Basingstoke, UK: Palgrave Macmillan.

Charmaz, K. (2000). Grounded theory: Objectivist and constructivist methods. In N. Denzin, & Y. Lincoln (Eds.), *Handbook of qualitative research* (2nd ed., pp. 506–535). Thousand Oaks, CA: Sage.

Clarke, D., Flanagan, J., & Kendrick, K. (2002). *Advancing nursing practice in cancer and palliative care.* Basingstoke, UK: Palgrave Macmillan.

Cone, P. H., & Artinian, B. M. (2009). Bending the directives of Glaserian grounded theory in nursing research. In B. M. Artinian, T. Giske, & P. H. Cone (Eds.), *Glaserian grounded theory in nursing research* (pp. 35–48). New York, NY: Springer.

Connolly, M. J. (2001). The disadvantaged dying—Care of people with non-malignant conditions. In S. Kinghorn & R. Gamlin (Eds.), *Palliative nursing: Bringing new hope and comfort* (pp. 231–244). London, UK: Balliere Tindall.

Flanagan, J., Clarke, D., Kendrick, K., & Lane, C. (2002). The advancing role of nurses in cancer care. In D. Clarke, J. Flanagan, & K. Kendrick (Eds.), *Advancing nursing practice in cancer and palliative care* (pp. 3–19). Basingstoke, UK: Palgrave Macmillan.

George, L. K. (2002). Research design in end-of-life care research: State of science. *The Gerontologist, 42*(3), 86–98.

Glaser, B. G. (1978). *Theoretical sensitivity: Advances in the methodology of grounded theory.* Mill Valley, CA: Sociology Press.

Glaser, B. G. (1992). *Basics of grounded theory analysis. Emergence vs. forcing.* Mill Valley, CA: Sociology Press.

Glaser, B. G. (1998). *Doing grounded theory: Issues and discussions.* Mill Valley, CA: Sociology Press.

Glaser, B. G. (2001). *The grounded theory perspective: Conceptualization contrasted with description.* Mill Valley, CA: Sociology Press.

Glaser, B. G. (2003). *The grounded theory perspective II: Description's remodeling of grounded theory.* Mill Valley, CA: Sociology Press.

Glaser, B. G. (2005). *The grounded theory perspective III: Theoretical coding.* Mill Valley, CA: Sociology Press.

Glaser, B. G. (2009). *Using the grounded theory vocabulary.* Mill Valley, CA: Sociology Press.

Glaser, B. G., & Strauss, A. L. (1967). *The discovery of grounded theory: Strategies for qualitative research.* Chicago, IL: Aldine.

Henderson, S. (2003). Power imbalance between nurses and patients: A potential inhibitor of partnership in care. *Journal of Clinical Nursing, 12*(4), 501–512.

Kinghorn, S., & Gamlin, R. (2001). *Palliative nursing: Bringing new hope and comfort.* London, UK: Balliere Tindall.

Kuebler, K. K., Berry, P. H., & Heidrich, D. E. (2002). *End-of-life care: Clinical practice guidelines.* Philadelphia, PA: Saunders.

Kuebler, K. K., Heidrich, D. E., & Esper, P. (2002). *Palliative and end-of-life care: Clinical practice guidelines* (2nd ed.). Philadelphia, PA: Saunders.

Kwok, K., McCallin, A. M., & Dickson, G. (2012). Working through preconception: Moving from forcing to emergence. *Grounded Theory Review, 11*(2), 1–10.

McCallin A. M. (1999). *Pluralistic dialogue: A grounded theory of interdisciplinary practice.* Unpublished doctoral dissertation. Palmerston North, New Zealand: Massey University.

McCallin, A. M. (2003). Designing a grounded theory study: Some practicalities. *Nursing in Critical Care, 8*(5), 203–208.

McCallin, A. M. (2004). Pluralistic dialoguing: A theory of interdisciplinary teamworking. *The Grounded Theory Review: An International Journal, 4*(1), 25–42.

McCallin, A. M. (2006a). Grappling with the literature in a grounded theory study. *The Grounded Theory Review: An International Journal, 5*(2/3), 11–27.

McCallin, A. M. (2006b). Methodological issues: Have we forgotten the place of thinking here? *The Grounded Theory Review: An International Journal, 5*(2/3), 51–57.

McCallin, A. M. (2011). Moderated guiding: A grounded theory of nursing practice in end-of-life care. *Journal of Clinical Nursing, 20,* 2325–2333.

McCallin, A. M., Nathaniel, A. & Andrews, T. (2011). Learning methodology minus mentorship. In V. B. Martin & A. Gynnild (Eds.), *Grounded theory: The philosophy, method and work of Barney Glaser* (pp. 69–84). Boca Raton, FA: BrownWalker.

Ministry of Health. (2001). *The New Zealand palliative care strategy.* Wellington, New Zealand: Government Printer.

Nolan, M. T., & Mock, V. (2004). A conceptual framework for end-of-life care: A reconsideration of factors influencing the integrity of the human person. *Journal of Professional Nursing, 20*(6), 351–360.

Parker, J., & Aranda, S. (1995). *Palliative care: Explorations and challenges.* Sydney, Australia: McLennan and Petty.

Redpath, R. (1995). Negotiating new goals and care options in the presence of irreversible disease. In J. Parker & S. Aranda (Eds.), *Palliative care: Explorations and challenges* (pp. 123–133). Sydney, Australia: McLennan and Petty.

Sepulveda, C., Marlin, A., Yoshida, T., & Ullrich, A. (2002). Palliative care: The World Health Organization's global perspective. *Journal of Pain and Symptom Management, 24*(2), 91–96.

Stern, P. N., & Porr, C. J. (2011). *Essentials of accessible grounded theory.* Walnut Creek, CA: Left Coast Press.

Strauss, A. L., & Corbin, J. (1998). *Basics of qualitative research: Techniques and procedures for developing grounded theory* (2nd ed.). Thousand Oaks, CA: Sage.

Weissman, D. E. (2004). Decision making at a time of crisis near the end of life. *Journal of the American Medical Association, 292*(14), 1738–1743.

LIST OF JOURNALS THAT PUBLISH QUALITATIVE RESEARCH

Mary de Chesnay

Conducting excellent research and not publishing the results negates the study and prohibits anyone from learning from the work. Therefore, it is critical that qualitative researchers disseminate their work widely, and the best way to do so is through publication in refereed journals. The peer review process, although seemingly brutal at times, is designed to improve knowledge by enhancing the quality of literature in a discipline. Fortunately, the publishing climate has evolved to the point where qualitative research is valued by editors and readers alike, and many journals now seek out, or even specialize in publishing, qualitative research.

The following table was compiled partially from the synopsis of previous work identifying qualitative journals by the St. Louis University Qualitative Research Committee (2013), with a multidisciplinary faculty, who are proponents of qualitative research. Many of these journals would be considered multidisciplinary, though marketed to nurses. All are peer reviewed. Other journals were identified by the author of this series and by McKibbon and Gadd (2004) in their quantitative analysis of qualitative research. It is not meant to be exhaustive, and we would welcome any suggestions for inclusion.

An additional resource is the nursing literature mapping project conducted by Sherwill-Navarro and Allen (Allen, Jacobs, & Levy, 2006). The 217 journals were listed as a resource for libraries to accrue relevant journals, and many of them publish qualitative research. Readers are encouraged to view the websites for specific journals that might be interested in publishing their studies. Readers are also encouraged to look outside the traditional nursing journals, especially if their topics more closely match the journal mission of related disciplines.

NURSING JOURNALS

Journal	Website
Advances in Nursing Science	www.journals.lww.com/advancesinnursingscience/pages/default.aspx
Africa Journal of Nursing and Midwifery	www.journals.co.za/ej/ejour_ajnm.html
Annual Review of Nursing Research	www.springerpub.com/product/07396686#.UeaXbjvvv6U
British Journal of Nursing	www.britishjournalofnursing.com
Canadian Journal of Nursing Research	www.cjnr.mcgill.ca
Hispanic Health Care International	www.springerpub.com/product/15404153#.UeaX7jvvv6U
Holistic Nursing Practice	www.journals.lww.com/hnpjournal/pages/default.aspx
International Journal of Mental Health Nursing	www.onlinelibrary.wiley.com/journal/10.1111/(ISSN)1447-0349
International Journal of Nursing Practice	www.onlinelibrary.wiley.com/journal/10.1111/(ISSN)1440-172X
International Journal of Nursing Studies	www.journals.elsevier.com/international-journal-of-nursing-studies
Journal of Advanced Nursing	www.onlinelibrary.wiley.com/journal/10.1111/(ISSN)1365-2648
Journal of Clinical Nursing	www.onlinelibrary.wiley.com/journal/10.1111/(ISSN)1365-2702
Journal of Family Nursing	www.jfn.sagepub.com
Journal of Nursing Education	www.healio.com/journals/JNE
Journal of Nursing Scholarship	www.onlinelibrary.wiley.com/journal/10.1111/(ISSN)1547-5069
Nurse Researcher	www.nurseresearcher.rcnpublishing.co.uk
Nursing History Review	www.aahn.org/nhr.html
Nursing Inquiry	www.onlinelibrary.wiley.com/journal/10.1111/(ISSN)1440-1800
Nursing Research	www.ninr.nih.gov
Nursing Science Quarterly	www.nsq.sagepub.com
Online Brazilian Journal of Nursing	www.objnursing.uff.br/index.php/nursing

(continued)

Journal	Website
The Online Journal of Cultural Competence in Nursing and Healthcare	www.ojccnh.org
Public Health Nursing	www.onlinelibrary.wiley.com/journal/10.1111/(ISSN)1525-1446
Qualitative Health Research	www.qhr.sagepub.com
Qualitative Research in Nursing and Healthcare	www.wiley.com/WileyCDA/WileyTitle/product Cd-1405161221.html
Research and Theory for Nursing Practice	www.springerpub.com/product/15416577#.Ueab lTvvv6U
Scandinavian Journal of Caring Sciences	www.onlinelibrary.wiley.com/journal/10.1111/(ISSN)1471-6712
Western Journal of Nursing Research	http://wjn.sagepub.com

REFERENCES

Allen, M., Jacobs, S. K., & Levy, J. R. (2006). Mapping the literature of nursing: 1996–2000. *Journal of the Medical Library Association, 94*(2), 206–220. Retrieved from http://nahrs.mlanet.org/home/images/activity/nahrs2012selectedlist nursing.pdf

McKibbon, K., & Gadd, C. (2004). A quantitative analysis of qualitative studies in clinical journals for the publishing year 2000. *BMC Med Inform Decision Making, 4*, 11. Retrieved from http://www.ncbi.nlm.nih.gov/pmc/articles/PMC503397

St. Louis University Qualitative Research Committee. Retrieved July 14, 2013, from http://www.slu.edu/organizations/qrc/QRjournals.html

ESSENTIAL ELEMENTS FOR A QUALITATIVE PROPOSAL

Tommie Nelms

1. Introduction: Aim of the study
   a. Phenomenon of interest, and focus of inquiry
   b. Justification for studying the phenomenon (how big an issue/problem?)
   c. Phenomenon discussed within a specific context (lived experience, culture, human response)
   d. Theoretical framework(s)
   e. Assumptions, biases, experiences, intuitions, and perceptions related to the belief that inquiry into a phenomenon is important (researcher's relationship to the topic)
   f. Qualitative methodology chosen, with rationale
   g. Significance to nursing (How will the new knowledge gained benefit patients, nursing practice, nurses, society, etc.?)
   Note: The focus of interest/inquiry and statement of purpose of the study should appear at the top of page 3 of the proposal
2. Literature review: What is known about the topic? How has it been studied in the past?
   Include background of the theoretical framework and how it has been used in the past.
3. Methodology
   a. Introduction of methodology (philosophical underpinnings of the method)
   b. Rationale for choosing the methodology
   c. Background of methodology
   d. Outcome of methodology
   e. Methods: general sources, and steps and procedures
   f. Translation of concepts and terms

4. Methods
   a. Aim
   b. Participants
   c. Setting
   d. Gaining access, and recruitment of participants
   e. General steps in conduct of study (data gathering tool(s), procedures, etc.)
   f. Human subjects' considerations
   g. Expected timetable
   h. Framework for rigor, and specific strategies to ensure rigor
   i. Plans and procedures for data analysis

WRITING QUALITATIVE RESEARCH PROPOSALS

Joan L. Bottorff

PURPOSE OF A RESEARCH PROPOSAL

- Communicates research plan to others (e.g., funding agencies)
- Serves as a detailed plan of action
- Serves as a contract between investigator and funding bodies when proposal is approved

QUALITATIVE RESEARCH: BASIC ASSUMPTIONS

- Reality is complex, constructed, and, ultimately, subjective.
- Research is an interpretative process.
- Knowledge is best achieved by conducting research in the natural setting.

QUALITATIVE RESEARCH

- Qualitative research is unstructured.
- Qualitative designs are "emergent" rather than fixed.
- The results of qualitative research are unpredictable. (Morse, 1994)

KINDS OF QUALITATIVE RESEARCH

- Grounded theory
- Ethnography (critical ethnography, institutional ethnography, ethnomethodology, ethnoscience, etc.)
- Phenomenology
- Narrative inquiry
- Others

CHALLENGES FOR QUALITATIVE RESEARCHERS

- Developing a solid, convincing argument that the study contributes to theory, research, practice, and/or policy (the "so what?" question)
- Planning a study that is systematic, manageable, and flexible (to reassure skeptics):
  - Justification of the selected qualitative method
  - Explicit details about design and methods, without limiting the project's evolution
  - Attention to criteria for the overall soundness or rigor of the project

QUESTIONS A PROPOSAL MUST ANSWER

- Why should anyone be interested in my research?
- Is the research design credible, achievable, and carefully explained?
- Is the researcher capable of conducting the research? (Marshall & Rossman, 1999)

TIPS TO ANSWER THESE QUESTIONS

- Be practical (practical problems cannot be easily brushed off)
- Be persuasive ("sell" your proposal)
- Make broad links (hint at the wider context)
- Aim for crystal clarity (avoid jargon, assume nothing, explain everything) (Silverman, 2000)

SECTIONS OF A TYPICAL QUALITATIVE PROPOSAL

- Introduction
  - Introduction of topic and its significance
  - Statement of purpose, research questions/objectives
- Review of literature
  - Related literature and theoretical traditions
- Design and methods
  - Overall approach and rationale
  - Sampling, data gathering methods, data analysis
  - Trustworthiness (soundness of the research)
  - Ethical considerations
- Dissemination and knowledge translation
  - Timeline
  - Budget
  - Appendices

INTRODUCING THE STUDY—FIRST PARA

- Goal: Capture interest in the study
  - Focus on the importance of the study (Why bother with the question?)
  - Be clear and concise (details will follow)
  - Provide a synopsis of the primary target of the study
  - Present persuasive logic backed up with factual evidence

THE PROBLEM/RESEARCH QUESTION

- The problem can be broad, but it must be specific enough to convince others that it is worth focusing on.
- Research questions must be clearly delineated.
- The research questions must sometimes be delineated with sub-questions.
- The scope of the research question(s) needs to be manageable within the time frame and context of the study.

PURPOSE OF THE QUALITATIVE STUDY

- Discovery?
- Description?
- Conceptualization (theory building)?
- Sensitization?
- Emancipation?
- Other?

LITERATURE REVIEW

- The literature review should be selective and persuasive, building a case for what is known or believed, what is missing, and how the study fits in.
- The literature is used to demonstrate openness to the complexity of the phenomenon, rather than funneling toward an a priori conceptualization.

METHODS—CHALLENGES HERE

- Quantitative designs are often more familiar to reviewers.
- Qualitative researchers have a different language.

METHODS SECTION

- Orientation to the Method:
  - Description of the particular method that will be used and its creators/interpreters
  - Rationale for qualitative research generally and for the specific method to be used.

QUALITATIVE STUDIES ARE VALUABLE FOR RESEARCH

- It delves deeply into complexities and processes.
- It focuses on little-known phenomena or innovative systems.

- It explores informal and unstructured processes in organizations.
- It seeks to explore where and why policy and local knowledge and practice are at odds.
- It is based on real, as opposed to stated, organizational goals.
- It cannot be done experimentally for practical or ethical reasons.
- It requires identification of relevant variables. (Marshall & Rossman, 1999)

SAMPLE

- Purposive or theoretical sampling
  - The purpose of the sampling
  - Characteristics of potential types of persons, events, or processes to be sampled
  - Methods of making decisions about sampling
- Sample size
  - Estimates provided based on previous experience, pilot work, etc.
- Access and recruitment

DATA COLLECTION AND ANALYSIS

- Types: Individual interviews, participant observation, focus groups, personal and public documents, Internet-based data, videos, and so on, all of which vary with different traditions.
- Analysis methods vary depending on the qualitative approach.
- Add DETAILS and MORE DETAILS about how data will be gathered and processed (procedures should be made public).

QUESTIONS FOR DATA MANAGEMENT AND ANALYSIS

- How will data be kept organized and retrievable?
- How will data be "broken up" to see something new?
- How will the researchers engage in reflexivity (e.g., be self-analytical)?
- How will the reader be convinced that the researcher is sufficiently knowledgeable about qualitative analysis and has the necessary skills?

TRUSTWORTHINESS (SOUNDNESS OF THE RESEARCH)

- Should be reflected throughout the proposal
- Should be addressed specifically, with the relevant criteria for the qualitative approach used
- Should provide examples of the strategies used:
  - Triangulation
  - Prolonged contact with informants, including continuous validation of data
  - Continuous checking for representativeness of data and fit between coding categories and data
  - Use of expert consultants

EXAMPLES OF STRATEGIES FOR LIMITING BIAS IN INTERPRETATIONS

- Planning to search for negative cases
- Describing how analysis will include a purposeful examination of alternative explanations
- Using members of the research team to critically question the analysis
- Planning to conduct an audit of data collection and analytic strategies

OTHER COMPONENTS

- Ethical considerations
  - Consent forms
  - Dealing with sensitive issues
- Dissemination and knowledge translation
- Timeline
- Budget justification

LAST BITS OF ADVICE

- Seek assistance and pre-review from others with experience in grant writing. (plan time for rewriting)
- Highlight match between your proposal and purpose of competition.
- Follow the rules of the competition.
- Write for a multidisciplinary audience.

REFERENCES

Marshall, C., & Rossman, G. B. (1999). *Designing qualitative research.* Thousand Oaks, CA: Sage.

Morse, J. M. (1994). Designing funded qualitative research. In N. Denzin & Y. Lincoln (Eds.), *Handbook of qualitative research* (pp. 220–235). Thousand Oaks, CA: Sage.

Silverman, D. (2000). *Doing qualitative research.* Thousand Oaks, CA: Sage.

OUTLINE FOR A RESEARCH PROPOSAL

Mary de Chesnay

The following guidelines are meant as a general set of suggestions that supplement the instructions for the student's program. In all cases where there is conflicting advice, the student should be guided by the dissertation chair's instructions. The outlined plan includes five chapters: the first three constitute the proposal and the remaining two the results and conclusions, but the number may vary depending on the nature of the topic or the style of the committee chair (e.g., I do not favor repeating the research questions at the beginning of every chapter, but some faculty do. I like to use this outline but some faculty prefer a different order. Some studies lend themselves to four instead of five chapters.).

Chapter I: Overview of the Study (or Preview of Coming Attractions) is a few pages that tell the reader:

- What he or she is going to investigate (purpose or statement of the problem and research questions or hypotheses)
- What theoretical support the idea has (conceptual framework or theoretical support). In qualitative research, this section may include only a rationale for conducting the study, with the conceptual framework or typology emerging from the data.
- What assumptions underlie the problem
- What definitions of terms are important to state (typically, these definitions in quantitative research are called *operational definitions* because they describe how one will know the item when one sees it. An operational definition usually starts with the phrase: "a score of ... or above on the [name of instrument]"). One may also want to include a conceptual definition, which is the usual meaning of the concept of interest or a definition according to a specific author. In contrast, qualitative research usually does not include measurements, so operational definitions are not appropriate, but conceptual definitions may be important to state.

- What limitations to the design are expected (not delimitations, which are intentional decisions about how to narrow the scope of one's population or focus)
- What the importance of the study (significance) is to the discipline

Chapter II: The Review of Research Literature (or Why You Are Not Reinventing the Wheel)

For Quantitative Research:
Organize this chapter according to the concepts in the conceptual framework in Chapter I and describe the literature review thoroughly first, followed by the state of the art of the literature and how the study fills the gaps in the existing literature. Do not include non-research literature in this section—place it in Chapter I as introductory material if the citation is necessary to the description.

- Concept 1: a brief description of each study reviewed that supports concept 1 with appropriate transitional statements between paragraphs
- Concept 2: a brief description of each study reviewed that supports concept 2 with appropriate transitional statements between paragraphs
- Concept 3: a brief description of each study reviewed that supports concept 3 with appropriate transitional statements between paragraphs
- And so on for as many concepts as there are in the conceptual framework (I advise limiting the number of concepts for a master's degree thesis owing to time and cost constraints)
- Areas of agreement in the literature—a paragraph, or two, that summarizes the main points on which authors agree
- Areas of disagreement—where the main issues on which authors disagree are summarized
- State of the art on the topic—a few paragraphs in which the areas where the literature is strong and where the gaps are, are clearly articulated
- A brief statement of how the study fills the gaps or why the study needs to be conducted to replicate what someone else has done

For Qualitative Research:
The literature review is usually conducted after the results are analyzed and the emergent concepts are known. The literature may then be placed in Chapter II of the proposal as shown earlier or incorporated into the results and discussion.

Chapter III: Methodology (or Exactly What You Are Going to Do Anyway)

- Design (name the design—e.g., ethnographic, experimental, survey, cross-sectional, phenomenological, grounded theory, etc.)
- Sample—describe the number of people who will serve as the sample and the sampling method: Where and how will the sample be recruited? Provide the rationale for sample selection and methods. Include the institutional review board (IRB) statement and say how the rights of subjects (Ss) will be protected, including how informed consent will be obtained and the data coded and stored.
- Setting—where will data collection take place? In quantitative research, this might be a laboratory or, if a questionnaire, a home. If qualitative, there are special considerations of privacy and comfortable surroundings for the interviews.
- Instruments and data analysis—how will the variables of interest be measured and how will sense be made of the data, if quantitative, and if qualitative, how will the data be coded and interpreted—that is, for both, this involves how the data will be analyzed.
- Validity and reliability—how will it be known if the data are good (in qualitative research, these terms are "accuracy" and "replicability").
- Procedures for data collection and analysis: a 1-2-3 step-by-step plan for what will be done
- Timeline—a chart that lists the plan month by month—use Month 1, 2, 3 instead of January, February, March.

The above three-chapter plan constitutes an acceptable proposal for a research project. The following is an outline for the final two chapters.

Chapter IV: Results (What I Discovered)

- Some researchers like to describe the sample in this section as a way to lead off talking about the findings.
- In the order of each hypothesis or research question, describe the data that addressed that question. Use raw data only; do not conclude anything about the data and make no interpretations.

Chapter V: Discussion (or How I Can Make Sense of All This)

- Conclusions—a concise statement of the answer to each research question or hypothesis. Some people like to interpret here—that is, to say how confident they can be about each conclusion.

- Implications—how each conclusion can be used to help address the needs of vulnerable populations or nursing practice, education, or administration.
- Recommendations for further research—that is, what will be done for an encore?

INDEX

grounded theory (*cont.*)
    recruitment strategies, 77–78
    results and findings, 80–83
    rewards, 83–87
    rigor, 79–80
    sample population, 77
    saturation, 85–87
    vs. Straussian grounded theory,
        176–177
    definition, 1
    description of method, 5–6
    history of, 2
    literature review
        areas of emphasis, 9–14
        search method, 9
    misconceptions, 6
    ongoing development, 4–5
    theoretical framework
        Berkeley school of symbolic
            interactionism, 4
        Chicago school of symbolic
            interactionism, 2–3
        Iowa school of symbolic
            interactionism, 2–3

HCP. *See* health care provider
health care provider (HCP), 64–65
human inquiry method, CABG surgery,
    152–153

implicit institutional norms, 209
incident coding, 84
in-depth interviewing, 155–156
infertility case study, generating theory
    formal fertility work, 24–25
    formal theory, 25–26
    identity as infertile, 24
    identity of self as infertile, 25
    informal fertility work, 24
    substantive theory, 25–26
    theoretical elaboration, 25
initial coding, 78–79, 84, 189
institutionalized medicine, 209
International Obesity Task Force
    (IOTF), 29

interviews
    Chinese women with breast cancer,
        106–107
    end-of-life care, 228–230
IOTF. *See* International Obesity Task
    Force
Iowa school of symbolic
    interactionism, 3

literature review
    areas of emphasis, 9–14
        clinically relevant studies, 12
        descriptive studies, 11
        ethical dilemmas, 12
        mental health studies, 12–13
        middle range theories, 14
        nursing education, 13
        as research method, 10
        theory of "finding home," 10–11
    obese child, parents health promotion,
        33–34
    search method, 9
    writing qualitative research
        proposal, 246
long-term care decision making, rural
    African American families
    conceptual issues, 137
    methodology
        data analysis, 145–146
        data collection procedures, 144
        design, 139–140
        dissemination, 146
        ethical considerations, 142–143
        instruments, 143–144
        rigor, 143–144
        sample, 140–141
        setting, 141–142
        timeline, 144–145
    purpose of study, 136–137
    theoretical framework, 137–139

memo writing, 187–188
microscopic data analysis, 157–158
mixed-method research design,
    122–123